Above All Thy Name

THOU HAST MAGNIFIED THY WORD

Above All Thy Name

עַלכָּלשִׁמְ

Martin Klein

Published by Savannah Pictures.

Second edition.
Second printing.

ISBN: 978-0-9975897-5-7 (2nd edition paperback)
978-0-9975897-0-2 (1st edition paperback)
978-0-9975897-1-9 (1st edition e-book)
978-0-9975897-2-6 (1st edition abridged)
Religion: Christian Theology: Apologetics

New in the second edition:
The second edition contains 36 pages of new material, including an additional chapter titled *Messages from Outer Space*, on the Biblical gift of prophecy. The foreword now includes two brief but inspiring stories: the first of God's dramatic answer to William Tyndale's dying prayer, and the second of nineteen-year old William Hunter's ultimate sacrifice for the true word of God.
Five pages of additional evidence appears near the end of the chapter *Fingerprints of the Antichrist*. Additional biographical information on the translators of the King James Bible are included in the chapter *The Glorious King James Version*.
Four highly significant statements from the Spirit of Prophecy relating to the subject of bible versions, were just released for the first time in 2015. These four statements have been woven into the text of the second edition of *Above All Thy Name*, occurring on pages 27, 60-61, 216, and 251.
The second edition also includes an index.
Finally, the back-cover text has been revised to more clearly define the scope of the book.

www.savannahpictures.com

Dedicated to all who love and long for the precious, preserved Words of Truth: "ye shall know the truth, and the truth shall make you free."

Table of Contents

Forward

On one of the first days of October, 1536 William Tyndale was sentenced to death for his work of translating the Scriptures into English.[1] Tyndale had fulfilled his promise to a learned Catholic doctor: "if God spare my life, ere many years I will cause a boy who driveth the plow to know more of the Scriptures than you do." "By virtue of the emperor's decree, fulfilling the bloody will of revengeful Rome, he was condemned to suffer death. At the town of Filsord [Netherlands], he was tied to the stake, and there strangled by the hangman, fervently and loudly exclaiming, with his last gasp, 'Lord, open the king of England's eyes!' He was then consumed with fire."[2]

Less than seventy years later, on January 16, 1604, God answered the prayer of this faithful martyr. King James I of England, ordered the translation of the world's most famous Bible, the King James Version of the Holy Scriptures.

A few months before Tyndale's death, a baby was born in England, named William Hunter, whose love for the pure Word of God would outshine his love for this world. On March 27, 1555, nineteen-year-old William Hunter was led to the stake to be burned. The previous nine months he had spent under irons until he was sentenced to death by the bloody Edmund Bonner, Bishop of London, for reading the Bible. Kneeling for his final prayer he read Psalm 51. As he read verse 17, "The sacrifices of God are a broken spirit: a broken and contrite heart, O God, thou wilt not despise," he was interrupted by one of the papal executioners, "who told him the translation was wrong, the words being 'an humble spirit' [referring to the Catholic Latin Vulgate wording]. William replied that his translation said 'contrite heart,'"[3] to which the executioner replied that heretics [protestants] translated books as they please. William was offered a pardon from Queen Mary if he would retract his beliefs, which he refused. As the flames ignited about him, William threw his prayer

---

[1] The 1611 King James Version of the Bible was partially based on Tyndale's work, by order of James I, King of England. See chapter 10, *The Glorious King James Version.*

[2] Charlotte Elizabeth, *The English Martyrology Abridged from Fox*, (Philadelphia: Presbyterian Board of Publication, 1843), p. 92-93.

[3] John Fox, A. M., *Fox's Book of Martyrs*, (Philadelphia: Key, Mielke & Biddle, 1832), Vol. 1, Book XI, Section IV.

book to his brother Robert, who encouraged him to remember the sufferings of his saviour, to which William replied, "I fear neither torture nor death; Lord Jesus receive my departing spirit."

Can you say with the same confidence that your faith is based on the infallible word of God? Were the Scriptures compiled by a messy group of councils and revised by a multitude of scribes? Is it true that there are errors and contradictions in the Bible and its manuscripts? Are there corrupted copies of Scripture? Do you know with the certainty of young Hunter that the version of Scripture you read is a copy of God's pure Word? The facts and history of the preservation of Scripture are the foundation of our faith upon which depends our eternal destiny. Without God's Word, the human race would have no knowledge of God. We must have full assurance that we are indeed reading the true and pure word of Truth.

The Bible's power, feared by its enemies, precious to those who love its precepts, is the power to transform those who submit to its claims. The written words of Scripture have had a greater influence on this world than any other literary work the planet has ever seen. They have changed the course of nations, and altered history in ways that will only be comprehended in eternity. The Bible is the revelation of God's love for the human race. It contains the treasures of eternal riches. "In His Word, God has committed to men the knowledge necessary for salvation. The Holy Scriptures are to be accepted as an authoritative, infallible revelation of His will. They are the standard of character, the revealer of doctrines, and the test of experience."[4] Though every power of hell and demons has been arrayed against this book, "in a most wonderful manner it was preserved uncorrupted through all the ages of darkness. It [bears] not the stamp of man, but the impress of God."[5] "The Bible, and the Bible alone, is to be our creed... all who bow to this Holy Word will be in harmony. Our own views and ideas must not control our efforts. Man is fallible, but God's Word is infallible. Instead of wrangling with one another, let men exalt the Lord. Let us meet all opposition as did our Master, saying, 'It is written.' Let us lift up the banner on which is inscribed, The Bible our rule of faith and discipline."[6]

---

[4] E. G. White, *The Faith I Live By* (1958), p. 13.2.

[5] E. G. White, *The Great Controversy* (1911), p. 69.2.

[6] E. G. White, "A Missionary Appeal," *Review and Herald,* December 15, 1885, p. 770.

Introduction[1]

We may be told that which is absolutely true, the essential truth of God; yet if we doubt it, and as long as we doubt it, we never can know it. Therefore, doubt is only the open door to ignorance.

Further, we may be told that which is completely false, an outright lie; yet though we believe it, however implicitly, we never can know it. This is for the simple reason that it is not true. It is impossible to know what is not true.

Therefore, there are just two things which are essential to knowledge—truth and faith.

Truth and faith are the two essentials to knowledge: and the first of these in order is truth. This is because however implicitly we may believe that which is not true, we never can know it. Therefore, since that which is believed must be true in order to be known, it follows that truth is the first essential to knowledge. And since even the sincerest truth, when told, cannot be known without our believing it, it follows that the second essential to knowledge is faith. Truth and faith, therefore, working together—the truth believed—is the way to knowledge.

This can be illustrated by an experience familiar to almost all. It is the truth that A is A. We believed this truth, and thus, and thus only, we know that A is A. If we had not believed that truth when we were told it, we would not now know that A, B, C, D, etc., are what they are; and had we never believed this, we never could have known it. If we had asked for proof as a basis for belief, we never could have had it, and so never could have believed, and so never could have known this fundamental thing in all literary knowledge. We could have had no proof, apart from itself, that A or any other letter of the alphabet is what it is.

There is proof of this, but the proof is in the letter itself; and by believing it, by receiving it for what it is we obtain the knowledge; and in this knowledge and by experience we obtain the proof. For in each

---

[1] Adapted from A. T. Jones, *The Place of the Bible in Education*, Ch. III, "The Essentials to Knowledge" (Oakland, CA: Pacific Press, 1903), p. 17-22.

of the letters of the alphabet there is a value which responded to our belief: a value which has never failed and which never will fail us. We know that each of the letters is what it is: and all the philologists, philosophers, and scientists in all the world could not convince us that any letter of the alphabet is other than it simply is. And yet the means by which we know this is simple belief of a simple, and simply-told, truth.

This illustration does not stop here. The first two letters of the Greek alphabet are Alpha and Beta. Dropping the "a" from Beta, these two Greek letters give us our word Alpha-bet. This word "Alphabet" signifies all the letters of the English language. How is this, when the word itself is derived from only the first two letters of the Greek language? It comes in a very simple way. When we in our language wish to ask whether a person knows, or we wish to say that a person does not know, the alphabet, we most commonly do not ask: "Does he know the alphabet?" nor, "Does he know the A B C D E F G H I J K L M N, and so on through to "Z?" but we ask, "Does he know the A B C's?" or we say, "He does not know his A B C's." The Greeks did the same: When they wished to express the same thought, they did not say, "Does he know the Alpha, Beta, Gamma, Delta, Epsilon," and so on to "Omega?" but simply, "Does he know the Alpha Beta?" or, "He does not know the Alpha Beta." And this Greek abbreviation of the whole list of the letters of that language into only "Alpha Beta" comes down to us with the dropping of the "a" from Beta; and so, becomes our word "Alphabet," the abbreviation of the whole list of the letters of our language.

In common English there is a concise way of saying that a person knows little or nothing of a subject, in the expression, "He does not know the A B C of it." The Greeks had the same, "He does not know the Alpha Beta of it." On the other hand, there is a concise way of saying that a person is thoroughly informed, or knows all of a subject, in the expression, "He knows that subject from A to Z." The Greeks had the same, "He knows that subject from Alpha to Omega"—he knows all there is to be known of it. And this is the basis and the thought in the expression of Christ in the book of Revelation several times, "I am Alpha and Omega, the beginning and the end, the first and the last."

Jesus is the Alphabet of God. As the expression "Alpha and Omega" signifies the whole alphabet, and embraces all there is in the Greek language; and "A to Z" signifies the whole alphabet, and all that there is in the English language; so, Jesus Christ, the Alphabet of God, embraces all that there is of the language or knowledge of God. As in the twenty-four letters of the Greek Alphabet from Alpha to Omega there are hid all the treasures of wisdom and knowledge in the world of that language; and as in the twenty-six letters of the English alphabet there are hid all the treasures of wisdom and knowledge that there are in the world of the English language; so in Jesus Christ, the Alphabet of God, there are "hid all the treasures of wisdom and knowledge"[2] that there are in the universe of the language of God.

And this Alphabet of God is learned in precisely the same way and with precisely the same faculty as is the alphabet of Greek, or English, or any other language. The Alphabet of God is the truth. We believe that truth and this is how we know that he is what he is. There is proof of this, but the proof is in himself. By believing this Alphabet, by receiving him for what he is, we obtain the knowledge; and in this knowledge and by experience of it we have the constant living proof. For in this Alphabet of God, in each letter, yea, in each jot and tittle, there is a value that responds to our faith: a value that never has failed, that never will fail, and that never can fail, to respond to any man's belief of that Alphabet. And to him who thus knows the Alphabet of God, all the philosophers and all the scientists and all the unbelievers in all the world cannot prove to him that any part of this Alphabet is not what he is. Indeed, anyone attempting to prove any such thing only thereby reveals the fact that he does not yet know the true Alphabet: he does not yet know his A B C's.

It is only as a little child that we learn—anyone can learn—the alphabet of the English language. Though a man were a thousand years old, and fully possessed of all his faculties, and yet did not know the A B C's—the alphabet of English—he would have to become as a little child in order to learn it, in order to receive the knowledge that A is A: he would simply have to believe it as does the little child, and by believing that each letter is what it is, when he is told, he would know. And if he should refuse to believe this, by this

---

[2] Colossians 2:3

very refusal—by his unbelief itself—he would condemn himself, to the everlasting loss of all the treasures of wisdom and knowledge that are hid in the world of English.

So also, it is with the Alphabet of the language and knowledge of God. It is only by believing this Alphabet that any person can ever know him. If anyone refuses to believe, he cannot know. And whoever does not believe is by this very unbelief condemned to the everlasting loss of all the treasures of wisdom and knowledge of God: all of which lie hidden in the Alphabet of God. For as it is by various combinations of the contents of the alphabet that words are formed, and words express thought; so, the manifold combinations of the contents of the Alphabet of God form the word of God, and the word of God expresses the thought of God.

Therefore, Jesus Christ announced the eternal principle of true learning when he declared, "Whosoever shall not receive the kingdom of God as a little child shall in nowise enter therein."[3] The little child receives the kingdom of God by simply believing the simple statement of the Word of the kingdom. This is how everyone receives, and how everyone must receive, the kingdom of English or of any other language. It is how everyone must receive the kingdom of God. To receive the kingdom of God, and to know the Alphabet of God, is as easy as to know the A B C's. Therefore, to learn, not as a philosopher, but as a little child, is the true way to knowledge. The truth and faith, working together—the truth believed—is forever the true way to knowledge.

---

[3] Luke 18:17

1 A Conspiracy of Silence

The Bible makes the claim to absolute truthfulness and infallibility.[1] It then provides the internal evidence to verify that claim. Complete harmony through sixty-six books, by about forty different writers, spanning one and a half millennia, would be impossible if the author were not the Holy Spirit. Thus, the Bible is a miraculous combination of the human and the divine, just as "God was manifest in the flesh."[2]

Scripture says: "For the prophecy came not in old time by the will of man: but holy men of God spake as they were moved by the Holy Ghost."[3] "Thy word is true from the beginning..."[4] "Every word of God is pure: he is a shield unto them that put their trust in him."[5] "Sanctify them through thy truth: thy word is truth."[6]

In order for Scripture to make the claim of truthfulness, it must also contain the promise of preservation. For food to be safe and nourishing, it must be preserved from spoilage and contamination. It would not be enough for the food manufacturer to claim that the food was uncontaminated when it left the factory without making provision for its preservation by canning or refrigeration, all the way to the point of purchase by the customer. It is not enough for God to originate a truthful presentation of Scripture, thousands of years ago, without his ability to protect and preserve that Scripture from corruption, destruction, or contamination. If there were a pure Scripture at one time, it really does not matter unless we have the ability to access that Scripture in its pure, true, and uncorrupted form, in a language that we can understand, without it having been lost, destroyed, or tampered with; and having full assurance that we are indeed reading the true and pure word of God.

---

[1] 1 Kings 8:56

[2] 1 Timothy 3:16

[3] 2 Peter 1:21

[4] Psalm 119:160

[5] Proverbs 30:5

[6] John 17:17

Scripture says that it endures forever and is even preserved in heaven: "But the word of the Lord endureth for ever…"[7] "For ever, O LORD, thy word is settled in heaven."[8]

The one name exalted above every name is the name of Jesus: "Wherefore God also hath highly exalted him, and given him a name which is above every name: That at the name of Jesus every knee should bow, of things in heaven, and things in earth, and things under the earth; And that every tongue should confess that Jesus Christ is Lord, to the glory of God the Father."[9]

In all the universe, only God's Word is exalted above the name of Jesus: "for thou hast magnified thy word above all thy name."[10] How much reverence should we have for a Word that is exalted above the name of God? The very truthfulness of God himself is staked on the truthfulness of his Word. "But to this man will I look, even to him that is poor and of a contrite spirit, and trembleth at my word."[11]

Not only has God promised that his Word is true, but also that he would preserve it from the time it was written, through all eternity. "The words of the LORD are pure words: as silver tried in a furnace of earth, purified seven times. Thou shalt keep them, O LORD, thou shalt preserve them from this generation for ever."[12]

So serious is God about the preservation of his Word, that he gives severe warnings against attempts to tamper with Scripture. "For I testify unto every man that heareth the words of the prophecy of this book, If any man shall add unto these things, God shall add unto him the plagues that are written in this book: And if any man shall take away from the words of the book of this prophecy, God shall take away his part out of the book of life, and out of the holy city, and from

---

[7] 1 Peter 1:25

[8] Psalm 119:89

[9] Philippians 2:9-11

[10] Psalm 138:2

[11] Isaiah 66:2

[12] Psalm 12:6-7

the things which are written in this book."[13] "Ye shall not add unto the word which I command you, neither shall ye diminish ought from it, that ye may keep the commandments of the LORD your God which I command you."[14] "What thing soever I command you, observe to do it: thou shalt not add thereto, nor diminish from it."[15] "Every word of God is pure: he is a shield unto them that put their trust in him. Add thou not unto his words, lest he reprove thee, and thou be found a liar."[16]

Though God promised to preserve his Word, the stern facts of history and the unyielding testimony of Scripture prove that attempts have been made to pervert God's Word. "What hath the LORD answered? and, What hath the LORD spoken? **Ye have perverted the words of the living God**, of the LORD of hosts our God."[17]

Thus, to fulfill the promise of preservation, the Scripture must contain a way to distinguish between the genuine and the counterfeit. With demonstrable and rather serious differences in so many current versions of the Bible, how can we be certain what is God's true and preserved Word? To this question we now turn.

Comparing the *King James Version* in Job 19:26 with the *American Standard Version*[18] illustrates the problem of someone perverting the Word of the living God.

KJV Job 19:26 "yet **in my flesh** shall I see God:"

ASV Job 19:26 "then **without my flesh** shall I see God;"[19]

Simple logic demands that two opposite statements cannot both be true. One of these two statements cannot be true. Therefore, one must be false. The one that is false cannot be God's pure, true,

---

[13] Revelation 22:18-19

[14] Deuteronomy 4:2

[15] Deuteronomy 12:32

[16] Proverbs 30:5-6

[17] Jeremiah 23:35-36

[18] Also, BBE, CJB, ERV, JPS.

[19] *American Standard Version* (New York: Thomas Nelson & Sons, 1901), p. 452.

unperverted Word. To begin the process of discovering clues to reveal the genuine and unmask the counterfeit, let us consider Luke 4:4. In meeting the temptations of Satan in the wilderness, Jesus here quotes from the Old Testament passage Deuteronomy 8:3.

KJV Luke 4:4 "And Jesus answered him, saying, It is written, That man shall not live by bread alone, **but by every word of God**."

Here the Bible testifies that every word is not only important but also necessary to our life. However, the bold words are missing in the NASB, NIV, ASV, CEV, ERV, ESV, GNB, GS, MSG, Moff, RV, RSV, NWT, TNIV, etc.[20]

Jesus' statement really would not make any sense without the phrase "**but by every word of God**." Is he making some ridiculously obvious statement that man has to have water and air and fruit and vegetables in order to live—not just bread? Or is he making a spiritual application, comparing the necessity of physical bread to the necessity of eating the Bread of Life? The entire statement must be included in order for the declaration not to seem ridiculous.

Both the Old and New Testaments testify to the fact that there are those who intentionally corrupt the word of God. We have already read Jeremiah's testimony; let us read what Paul says:

KJV 2 Corinthians 2:17 "For we are not as many, **which corrupt the word of God**: but as of sincerity, but as of God, in the sight of God speak we in Christ."

Scripture clearly declares that many were corrupting the word of God, even in Paul's day. We also have extra-biblical evidence that these changes were occurring by the second century: Irenaeus states, "Wherefore also Marcion and his followers have betaken themselves to mutilating the Scriptures, not acknowledging some books at all; and, curtailing the Gospel according to Luke and the

---

[20] For the full names of each version, see Appendix: Abbreviations.

Epistles of Paul, they assert that these are alone authentic, which they have themselves thus shortened."[21]

If there were individuals and/or organizations that were intentionally corrupting the word of God,[22] they would most certainly not want it widely known that this is what they were doing, for surely people who value God's Word would no longer trust or tolerate their activities. Therefore, they would probably try to hide the fact that the Bible predicted their exploits by modifying this verse. Indeed, this appears to be the case:

NKJV[23] 2 Corinthians 2:17 "For we are not, as so many, **peddling the word of God**; but as of sincerity, but as from God, we speak in the sight of God in Christ."[24]

Now peddling and corrupting God's Word are most certainly not the same thing. Is it wrong to sell Bibles? If it is, then the modern bibles are self-condemned, because it is only the modern bibles which are copyrighted. A copyright means that no one is legally allowed to duplicate or reprint significant portions without obtaining permission and paying appropriate royalties. Copyrights also mean that the copyright owner owns the words—they are his intellectual property. Does any human being have the right to lay claim to ownership of the Words of God? Should people be restricted from making copies of Scripture and distributing it freely? Historically, in U.S. patent law, patents were not allowed to be taken on life, because life is not

---

[21] Philip Schaff, D.D., *Ante-Nicene Fathers*, Vol. 1 (New York: Charles Scribner's Sons, 1905), p. 434, 435.

[22] Later it will be more fully demonstrated that there are such individuals and organizations that explicitly tell us in their own published writings that they are intentionally changing God's Word, and why.

[23] Also, NIV, NASB, CEV, ERV, ESV, GNB, NWT, RSV, etc.

[24] *New King James Version,* Red Letter ed. (Nashville: Thomas Nelson Publishers, 1983), p. 1177.

manmade.[25] If a human copyrights the words of Scripture, then by definition, they are not the Words of God.[26]

Under inspiration of the Holy Spirit, the prophet Amos predicted that, one day, there would be "a famine in the land, not a famine of bread, nor a thirst for water, but of hearing the words of the LORD."[27] Since "faith cometh by hearing, and hearing by the word of God,"[28] could it be that in this day of the proliferation of bibles that people are no longer hearing the Words of God? Souls are starving for the bread of life in the midst of plenty.

Some readers may find it difficult to accept that there have been intentional attempts to change God's Word. In an age when the media has indoctrinated our society with the idea that it would be lunacy to believe in a conspiracy, some might be tempted to think that such an assertion might be dangerously close to the "c" word. Yet, the Bible tells us otherwise: "There is a **conspiracy** of her prophets in the midst thereof, like a roaring lion ravening the prey; they have devoured souls; they have taken the treasure and precious things; they have made her many widows in the midst thereof."[29]

Conspiracy theories will not here be introduced—only documented first hand evidence of a "conspiracy of silence." "In June [Hort] joined the mysterious company of the 'Apostles'.... He remained always a grateful and loyal member of the secret Club, which has now become famous for the number of distinguished men who have belonged to it. In his time the Club was in a manner reinvigorated,

---

[25] This began to change in 1980 in Diamond v. Chakrabarty with the first patent of a genetically modified organism—and the implications are rather serious, but, that is for another story.

[26] The words of the King James Bible are not copyrighted. Anyone may copy, duplicate, and distribute freely the King James Version. While some publishers do place a copyright notice on their King James Bibles, this copyright is only on the format, footnotes, and supplemental materials, not on the Words of God.

[27] Amos 8:11

[28] Romans 10:17

[29] Ezekiel 22:25

and **he was mainly responsible for the wording of the oath which binds the members to a conspiracy of silence.**"[30]

Here we are told, by his son, that the famous bible translator, Fenton John Anthony Hort, belonged to a secret club whose members were bound by an oath to a conspiracy of silence—an oath Hort himself was responsible for writing. Is it any wonder that another famous Biblical textual scholar of the day said, "all this... I frankly avow, to me, looks very much indeed like what, in the language of lawyers, is called 'Conspiracy.'"[31]

So, here at the outset, are provided a couple of examples demonstrating that, if nothing else, Satan is conspiring against God's Word.

KJV Psalm 22:16 "For dogs have compassed me: the assembly of the wicked have enclosed me: they pierced my hands and my feet."

In a most amazing way, Scripture prophesies specific details of the way in which Jesus would die, and the subsequent verses even describe the soldiers casting lots for his vesture.

"In the sufferings of Christ upon the cross prophecy was fulfilled. Centuries before the crucifixion, the Saviour had foretold the treatment He was to receive. He said, 'Dogs have compassed Me: the assembly of the wicked have enclosed Me: they pierced My hands and My feet. I may tell all My bones: they look and stare upon Me. They part My garments among them, and cast lots upon My vesture.' Psalm 22:16-18."[32]

Yet, the *Good News Bible* removes the prophecy of his crucifixion by saying: "they tear at my hands and feet."[33] *The New English Bible*

---

[30] A. F. Hort, *Life and Letters of Fenton John Anthony Hort*, Vol. 1 (London: MacMillan and Co.,1896), p. 170, 171.

[31] John William Burgon, B.D., *The Revision Revised* (London: William Clowes and Sons, 1883), p. 398.

[32] E. G. White, *The Desire of Ages* (Nampa, ID: Pacific Press,1898), p. 746.1.

[33] *Good News Bible* (New York: American Bible Society, 1976), p. 607.

says, "they hacked off my hands and feet,"[34] which directly contradicts another prophecy that not a bone of his body would be broken.[35]

In **KJV Zechariah 13:6** the Bible prophesies that he would be killed by his own people or friends,[36] and predicts his manner of death by crucifixion. "And one shall say unto him, What are these wounds in thine hands? Then he shall answer, Those with which I was wounded in the house of my friends."

But the *Good News Bible*, again, brazenly removes the prophecy about Christ's crucifixion by putting the wounds in the chest, instead of the hands: "Then if someone asks him, 'What are those wounds on your chest?' he will answer, 'I got them at a friend's house.'"[37]

The Living Bible takes the brazen to the preposterous: "What are these scars on your chest? 'These are the scars I received when I was in a brawl with my friend.'"[38]

The Moffat translation goes from preposterous to blasphemous, by putting the scars back on the hands, but claiming they came from a prostitute: "When he is asked, 'Then what are these scars on your hands?' He will answer 'I got these in my harlot's house.'"[39]

The Message changes the blasphemous into clumsy comedy: "And if someone says, 'And so where did you get that black eye?' they'll say, 'I ran into a door at a friend's house.'"[40]

---

[34] *The New English Bible* (New York: Oxford University Press, 1970), p. 626.

[35] Psalm 34:20; John 19:36

[36] "Even the manner of His death had been shadowed forth. As the brazen serpent had been uplifted in the wilderness, so was the coming Redeemer to be lifted up, 'that whosoever believeth in Him should not perish, but have everlasting life.' John 3:16. 'One shall say unto Him, What are these wounds in Thine hands? Then He shall answer, Those with which I was wounded in the house of My friends.' Zechariah 13:6."
E. G. White, *The Acts of the Apostles* (Nampa, ID: Pacific Press, 1911), p. 226.3-4.

[37] *Good News Bible* (1976), p. 1036.

[38] *The Living Bible* (Wheaton, IL: Tyndale House Publishers, 1978), p. 728.

[39] James Moffatt, D.D., D.Litt., M.A. (Oxon.), *The Bible: A New Translation* (New York: Harper & Brothers Publishers, 1935), p. 1035.

[40] Eugene H. Peterson, M.A., *The Message: The Bible in Contemporary Language,* Version 2.0 (Colorado Springs, CO: NavPress Publishing Group, 2002), p. 1729.

This is not Bible translation. This is first degree adulteration—high treason against the government of God. Surely Satan laughs at such mockery of our Savior and mutilation of his Word. Simple logic demands that these widely varying versions cannot all be true. Therefore, some must be false. The ones that are false cannot be God's pure, true, and unperverted Word.

Because God promised to preserve the truth and purity of his Word, and yet told us that many would "corrupt the word of God," it becomes imperative to understand how to recognize the genuine from the counterfeit. In order to do that we need to know the pattern of the problem, the extent of the problem, the history of the problem, those causing the problem, and their connections. Once we know who is changing God's Word, the intention becomes clear as well as the pattern the changes will follow. In this manner the mystery can be unraveled, the truth discovered, and the conspiracy of silence broken. Satan's deceptions will be unmasked.

"It is the duty of every faithful servant of God, to firmly and decidedly withstand these perverters of the faith, and to fearlessly expose their errors by the word of truth."[41]

[41] E. G. White, *Sketches from the Life of Paul* (Nampa, ID: Pacific Press, 1883), p. 192.2.

2 The Ripped-Up Bible

Imagine that you arrive at church one day, perhaps a little late, and just as you ease into the pew and open your Bible, the minister, who has already started his sermon, turns to a passage in his Bible and asks the congregation to turn to the same passage. You look up the passage just in time to hear him say, "Beloved, this chapter does not belong in your Bibles, please tear out these two pages." With wide eyes, your head jerks up in time to see him rip those pages from his Bible. Would this disturb you?

Let us change the story slightly: rather than telling you to tear out two pages, what if the deacons were handing out little cardboard cutting boards and x-acto knives, and the pastor asked you to cut certain verses from your Bible? Or, perhaps he simply says, "Please turn to Mark 7:16 and take your pen and cross out that verse, because it does not belong in your Bible." Would you feel uncomfortable with this request?

What if some scholar did this for you ahead of time, and printed it that way, so your preacher did not have to resort to such drama in church?

Sadly, many people have accepted just these changes. Many Christians are aware that Jehovah's Witnesses have their own bible version—the *New World Translation*. This version has certain changes that are compatible with Witness theology, particularly changing verses that demonstrate the divinity of Christ, since they do not accept that Jesus was divine. Certainly, most Christians would not accept the *New World Translation* as the true and uncorrupted word of God. Surely you would agree that this bible should not be our main study Bible, or the Bible from which the pastor preaches. However, Jehovah's Witnesses have not always used the *New World Translation*.[1] They used to use the King James Version. At one point their Watch Tower Bible and Tract Society actually printed a KJV Bible that had a page in the front which said: "The following words, found in our Common Version, are not found in the oldest MSS [manuscripts], and are evidently no part of the Divine Word. Let

---

[1] Edmond C. Gruss, *Apostles of Denial* (Newhall, CA: Presbyterian and Reformed Publishing Co., 1970), p. 191-193.

each Berean go through his Bible, pencil in hand, and mark out these words: then read the passage affected and note the improvement. This list comprises all the important interpolations discovered to date. The compiler has condensed this list time and again until what remains represents about all there is of value to us in the Tischendorf work. From the compiler's point of view there exists very good reasons why everything in this list should be crossed out of our Bibles."[2]

Following this statement was a list of some one hundred and twenty passages that should have all or portions crossed out. This was a start, but eventually the Jehovah's Witnesses felt it necessary to create their own bible to support their unique doctrines. Is this how Christians are to arrive at truth—by creating a bible that supports their preconceived opinions?

An example of a change that supports their doctrine is found in John 1:1, perhaps the most famous statement of the divinity of Christ, which Jehovah's Witnesses deny: "In the beginning was the Word, and the Word was with God, and the Word **was God**."[3]

In order to support their theology, the *New World Translation* changes this verse into: "In the beginning the Word was, and the Word was with God, and the Word was **a god**."[4]

"The Jehovah's Witnesses teach that Jesus was a created god, rather than having eternally existed with the Father and Holy Ghost. However, God's word states that the Lord Jesus Christ was not created, but was instead the Creator of all things."[5]

They added only one little, simple, single letter word—a. But the meaning and the theology are entirely changed.

---

[2] Les Garrett, *Which Bible can we Trust?* (Australia: Christian Centre Press, 1982), p. 219.

[3] Verse 14 shows conclusively that "the Word" is Jesus, because the Word became flesh and dwelt among us.

[4] *New World Translation of the Holy Scriptures* (New York: Watchtower Bible and Tract Society of New York, Inc., 1984), p. 1327.

[5] Douglas Stauffer, Ph.D., *One Book Stands Alone* (Millbrook, AL: McCowen Mills Publishers, 2013), Kindle ed., Kindle Locations 645-646.

The problem is that many readers who are rightly disturbed by this are reading from bibles that have even more words removed than the Jehovah's Witness translation—many of them from the exact same passages. It is not only the *New World Translation* that undermines the deity of Christ, but almost all modern versions do the same. This will be demonstrated in more detail later. For now, two examples should suffice:

KJV John 9:38 "And he said, Lord, I believe. And he worshipped him."

The *American Standard Version*, published in 1901, is the father of all modern bibles in America. It, along with the *Revised Version* of 1881, initiated most of the changes we see in modern bibles today. Interestingly, John 9:38 in the ASV is identical to how the verse reads in the KJV. However, the translators added a footnote, which shows their theology—perhaps even better than could a change in the wording of the verse. The footnote stated: "The Greek word denotes an act of reverence, whether paid to a creature (as here) or to the Creator."[6] The *American Standard Version* translators (of whom Philip Schaff was president) are telling us that Jesus is not the Creator, but a created being (creature).

In **KJV Proverbs 8:22** the Bible says, "The LORD possessed me in the beginning of his way, before his works of old."

This passage, speaking of Jesus, says that he was possessed by God the Father in the beginning of his way.[7] In other words, Jesus existed eternally with the Father. But the NIV says, "The LORD brought me forth as the first of his works, before his deeds of old."[8] Jesus being possessed of the Father in the beginning of his way is totally different theology than the Father bringing Jesus forth as the first of his works. The NIV is calling Jesus a created being. This is exactly what the Jehovah's Witness *New World Translation* tries to do—remove the divinity of Christ.[9] How is the modern version any

---

[6] *American Standard Version: New Testament* (New York: Thomas Nelson, 1900), p. 94.

[7] See E. G. White, *Patriarchs and Prophets* (1890), p. 34.1.

[8] *New International Version* (Grand Rapids, MI: Zondervan Bible Publishers, 1978), p. 687.

[9] Later it will be demonstrated how modern bibles systematically undermine the deity of Christ.

better? Not only is the divinity of Christ undermined in modern versions, but they also tear out hundreds and thousands of words and phrases. So, the Jehovah's Witness bible is a crossed-out bible, but the modern bible is a ripped-up bible—pre-made that way to save the preacher all the drama.

The NIV, for example, has over 60,000 fewer words than the King James Version of the Bible.[10] If all those words were in one place (which they are not), that would be the equivalent of removing everything from 1 Corinthians through Revelation.

KJV Luke 9:56 "For the Son of man is not come to destroy men's lives, but to save them. And they went to another village," is an example of a verse that in the NIV that is not completely gone but may as well be. One could preach a whole sermon on just that verse. Not so in the NIV, which says only: "and they went to another village."[11] The heart of the gospel has been removed from this verse.

Most modern bibles omit at least 16 complete verses in addition to the many words and phrases throughout:[12]

Matthew 17:21
Matthew 18:11
Matthew 23:14
Mark 7:16
Mark 9:44
Mark 9:46
Mark 11:26
Mark 15:28
Luke 17:36
Luke 23:17
John 5:4
Acts 8:37
Acts 15:34
Acts 24:7
Acts 28:29
Romans 16:24

---

[10] KJV: 788,280 (1769 edition of the 1611 King James Bible) – http://www.biblebelievers.com/believers-org/kjv-stats.html Retrieved: 1-27-2016.
KJV: 788,258 – Laurence Vance, Ph.D., *King James, His Bible, and Its Translators* (Pensacola, FL: Vance Publications, 2009), p. 74.
Number of Words in NIV 727,969 – http://wiki.answers.com/Q/How_many_words_in_NIV_Bible Retrieved: 1-27-2016.
http://brandplucked.webs.com/nivmissing64000words.htm Retrieved: 1-27-2016.

[11] *New International Version* (1978), p. 1113.
Also omitted in the ASV, CEV, ERV, ESV, GNB, ISV, MSG, RSV, RV, etc.

[12] In the KJV the verse numbers are all on the left margin, which would make it very easy to spot a missing verse. Most modern bibles mix the verse numbers into the text, in paragraph form, so that the casual reader would not notice the missing verse number.

"Dr. Gordon Fee, a professor at Wheaton College, said in an article in *Christianity Today*, 'The contemporary translations as a group have one thing in common: they tend to agree against the KJV... in omitting hundreds of words, phrases, and verses.' It is interesting that in this article Dr. Fee was promoting the modern versions, yet he realized, as a whole, they are different and they all disagree with the KJV."[13]

How many verses, or portions of verses must be torn from a Bible, before the missing verses are considered a problem? "And Jesus answered him, saying, It is written, That man shall not live by bread alone, ***but by every word of God.***"[14]

"Now what does Satan propose to do? He proposes that he is capable of changing this Bible. These parties that fell understand all about heaven, and that they can bring in the different sentiments from the Bible, and they are going to have a revision of it. You will see they will make revisions of the Bible, but every one of us needs to stand intelligently on the Word. We cannot afford to be careless, but we must have that simplicity of godliness that is a virtue to us. We must have it."[15]

Jesus himself is called the Word: "In the beginning was the Word, and the Word was with God, and the Word was God. The same was in the beginning with God. All things were made by him; and without him was not any thing made that was made. And the Word was made flesh, and dwelt among us, (and we beheld his glory, the glory as of the only begotten of the Father,) full of grace and truth."[16]

Changing God's Word is misrepresenting Jesus himself. "The words that I speak unto you, they are spirit, and they are life."[17] His words are spirit and life. If these Words are changed by human wisdom,

---

[13] Joe Gresham, *Dealing with the Devil's Deception: How to Choose a Bible* (Fort Worth, TX: The Fourth Angel's Publishing, 2001), p. 15.

[14] Luke 4:4

[15] E. G. White, *Manuscript 80-1910*, par. 10.

[16] John 1:1-3, 14

[17] John 6:63

they can no longer be spirit and life. Jesus Christ—the Word—never changes. "Jesus Christ the same yesterday, and to day, and for ever."[18]

"I saw that God had especially guarded the Bible; yet when copies of it were few, learned men had in some instances changed the words, thinking that they were making it more plain, when in reality they were mystifying that which was plain, by causing it to lean to their established views, which were governed by tradition. But I saw that the Word of God, as a whole, is a perfect chain, one portion linking into and explaining another. True seekers for truth need not err; for not only is the Word of God plain and simple in declaring the way of life, but the Holy Spirit is given as a guide in understanding the way to life therein revealed."[19]

---

[18] Hebrews 13:8

[19] E. G. White, *Early Writings* (Nampa, ID: Pacific Press, 1882), p. 220.2.

3 Spiritualism in the Church

"Modern spiritualism... is but a revival in a new form of the witchcraft and demon worship that God condemned and prohibited of old. It is foretold in the Scriptures, which declare that 'in the latter times some shall depart from the faith, giving heed to seducing spirits, and doctrines of devils.'[1]"[2] "As the teachings of Spiritualism are accepted by the churches, the restraint imposed upon the carnal heart is removed, and the profession of religion will become a cloak to conceal the basest iniquity. A belief in spiritual manifestations opens the door to seducing spirits, and doctrines of devils, and thus the influence of evil angels will be felt in the churches."[3]

Clearly foretold is a time when the teachings of spiritualism will come right into the churches. How could this happen? To understand how this occurs, let us consider the birth of spiritualism—in the garden of Eden.

Satan's first step in the deception process was to introduce a new method of Biblical interpretation in which the word of God is questioned: "Yea, hath God said...?"[4]

Eve immediately picked up Satan's higher critical method of interpretation and in reply, left out portions of God's Words:
GOD: "Of every tree of the garden thou mayest **freely** eat:"[5]
EVE: "We may eat of the fruit of the trees of the garden:"[6]

In this restatement Eve introduced to her own mind the doubt that God was really as generous and benevolent as implied in God's actual statement.

---

[1] 1 Timothy 4:1

[2] E. G. White, *Patriarchs and Prophets* (Nampa, ID: Pacific Press, 1890), p. 686.1.

[3] E. G. White, *The Great Controversy* (Nampa, ID: Pacific Press, 1911), p. 603.2.

[4] Genesis 3:1

[5] Genesis 2:16

[6] Genesis 3:2

Next Eve began to add to what God had said:
GOD: "But of the tree of the knowledge of good and evil, thou shalt not eat of it: for in the day that thou eatest thereof thou shalt surely die."[7]
EVE: "But of the fruit of the tree which is in the midst of the garden, God hath said, Ye shall not eat of it, **neither shall ye touch it**, lest ye die."[8]

"Eve had overstated the words of God's command. He had said to Adam and Eve, 'But of the tree of the knowledge of good and evil thou shalt not eat of it; for in the day thou eatest thereof thou shalt surely die.' In Eve's controversy with the serpent, she added the clause, 'Neither shall ye touch it, lest ye die.' Here the subtlety of the serpent was seen. This statement of Eve gave him advantage, and he plucked the fruit, and placed it in her hand, and used her own words, 'He hath said, 'If ye touch it, ye shall die.' You see no harm comes to you from touching the fruit, neither will you receive any harm by eating it.'"[9]

Immediately following, Satan introduced full-blown spiritualism:
1. You are immortal (Ye shall not surely die...)
2. You can attain to deity (Ye shall be as gods...)
Satan's first lies contained direct contradictions of the word of God. These two assertions have formed the foundation of spiritualism ever since, and are never introduced without first initiating doubt in the word of God.

As Satan attempted to attain to Godhood by commanding Jesus to worship him, "Jesus answered and said unto him, **Get thee behind me, Satan: for** [10] it is written, Thou shalt worship the Lord thy God, and him only shalt thou serve."[11] Certainly, Satan chafes at that command more than any other statement in Scripture. He wants the

[7] Genesis 2:17

[8] Genesis 3:3

[9] E. G. White, "Redemption.— No. 1," *Review and Herald,* February 24, 1874, p. 83.

[10] Bold portion missing, in NASB, NIV, ASV, CEV, DRB, GNB, RV, RSV, NWT, etc. The Spirit of Prophecy quotes only KJV as Scripture.

[11] Luke 4:8

worship of the world and even tempted Christ to worship him. Therefore, Satan inspired his agents to remove the hated statement:

NASB Luke 4:8 "Jesus answered him, 'It is written, 'you shall worship the lord your god and serve him only.'"[12] However the statement got removed, I am sure that Satan is well pleased, and doubt is cast on which is the true word of God.

"The work of higher criticism, in dissecting, conjecturing, reconstructing, is destroying faith in the Bible as a divine revelation. It is robbing God's word of power to control, uplift, and inspire human lives."[13]

The most prominent early higher critic to systematically modify Scripture was Origen, who became head of the occult school at Alexandria by A.D. 213. Origen was the first teacher of purgatory, and the father of Arianism—the belief that Jesus is not Divine.

Origen asserts Satan's introductory principle of doubting God's Word: "the Scriptures are of little use to those who understand them as they are written."[14] In modern times Origen's spiritualistic questioning of Scripture is echoed by Helena Petrovna Blavatsky (1831-1891), who established the Theosophical Society. She is considered to be the mother of modern occultism, and claimed that Lucifer is higher and older than Jehovah.[15] Blavatsky states, "Truly, unless we read the 'Old Testament' kabalistically and comprehend the hidden meaning thereof, it is very little we can learn from it."[16] In other words, Blavatsky is echoing the philosophy of Origen—"the Scriptures are of little use to those who understand them as they are written."

---

[12] *New American Standard Bible,* Text ed. (Nashville: Thomas Nelson Publishers, 1977), p. 713.

[13] E. G. White, *The Acts of the Apostles* (Nampa, ID: Pacific Press, 1911), p. 474.1.

[14] John Lawrence Mosheim, D.D., *An Ecclesiastical History, Ancient and Modern, From the Birth of Christ to the Beginning of the Eighteenth Century,* Vol. 1, trans. from original Latin by Archibald Maclaine, D.D. (London: R. Baynes, 1819), p. 278.

[15] H.P. Blavatsky, *The Secret Doctrine,* Vol. 1—Cosmogenesis (London: Theosophical Publishing, 1888), p. 70-71.

[16] H. P. Blavatsky, *Isis Unveiled,* Vol. 2—Theology (New York: J. W. Bouton, 1877), p. 362.

Just like Origen, Blavatsky denies the divinity of Christ, claiming that "there is not a word in so-called sacred scriptures, to show that Jesus was actually regarded as God by his disciples. Neither before nor after his death did they pay him divine honors."[17]

This direct contradiction of Scripture[18] could be expected from a pagan-philosopher-head of the mystical school at Alexandria, or from the mother of modern occultism; but how does this all come right into the Christian church?

Three very influential, supposedly Protestant, bishops named Edward White Benson (future Bishop of Canterbury), Brooke Foss Westcott, and Fenton John Anthony Hort, began by doubting the word of God. This is seen in the words of Westcott, "No one now, I suppose, holds that the first three chapters of Genesis, for example, give a literal history—I could never understand how any one reading them with open eyes could think they did,"[19] and, "I reject the word infallibility—of Holy Scripture overwhelming,"[20] and, in the words of Hort: "If you make a decided conviction of the absolute infallibility of the New Testament... I fear I could not join you."[21]

This rejection of the infallibility of Scripture is in stark contrast to the following: "The Bible, and the Bible alone, is to be our creed, the sole bond of union; all who bow to this holy word will be in harmony. Our own views and ideas must not control our efforts. Man is fallible, but **God's word is infallible**. Instead of wrangling with one another, let men exalt the Lord. Let us meet all opposition as did our Master, saying, 'It is written.' Let us lift up the banner on which is inscribed, The Bible our rule of faith and discipline."[22]

The doubting of Scripture by these bishops led immediately to changing the Words of God. Hort explains the importance of the

---

[17] H. P. Blavatsky, *Isis Unveiled,* Vol. 2—Theology (1877), p. 192-193.

[18] John 20:28

[19] Arthur Westcott, *The Life and Letters of Brooke Foss Westcott,* Vol. 2 (London: MacMillan and Co., 1903), p. 69.

[20] Arthur Westcott, T*he Life and Letters of Brooke Foss Westcott,* Vol. 1 (London: MacMillan and Co., 1903), p. 207.

[21] A. F. Hort, *Life and Letters of Fenton John Anthony Hort,* Vol. 1 (1896), p. 420.

[22] E. G. White, "A Missionary Appeal," *Review and Herald,* December 15, 1885, p. 770.

"trifling alterations" inserted into the Revised Version: "It is quite impossible to judge the value of what appear to be trifling alterations merely by reading them one after another. Taken together, they have often important bearings which few would think at first. The difference between a picture say of Raffaelle and a feeble copy of it is made up of a number of trivial differences... We have successfully resisted being warned off dangerous ground, where the needs of revision required that it should not be shirked...It is, one can hardly doubt, the beginning of a new period in Church history. So far the angry objectors have reason for their astonishment."[23]

The next logical step was the acceptance of full blown spiritualism: "'Among my father's[24] diversions at Cambridge was the foundation of a 'Ghost Society,' the forerunner of the Psychical Society [meaning the S.P.R.][25] for the investigation of the supernatural. Lightfoot, Westcott and Hort were among the members. He was then, as always, more interested in psychical phenomena than he cared to admit.'

"Lightfoot and Westcott both became bishops, and Hort Professor of Divinity."[26]

Their investigations into the supernatural soon led them to attend séances: "But then things began to happen. 'We had grand fun,' Darwin wrote to tell Thomas Huxley. The medium Charles Williams 'made the chairs, a flute, a bell and a candlestick jump about in my brother's dining room, in a manner that astounded everyone, and took away their breath.' It was in the dark, but George Huxley and Hensleigh Wedgewood 'held the medium's hands and feet on both sides all the time...'

"Darwin... 'saw all the chairs, etc., on the table which had been lifted over the heads of those sitting round.' It had been a good séance, Galton told him with understandable satisfaction; and it left Darwin

---

[23] A. F. Hort, *Life and Letters of Fenton John Anthony Hort,* Vol. 2 (London: MacMillan and Co.,1896), p. 138, 139.

[24] A. C. Benson speaking of his father E.W. Benson.

[25] Brackets supplied by Salter. S.P.R. stands for Society for Psychical Research.

[26] William Salter, *The Society for Psychical Research: An Outline of its History* (London: Society for Psychical Research, 1948), p. 4-5.

uneasy: 'how the medium can possibly do what was done passes my understanding.'"[27]

"At a séance with Charles Williams in 1873 a large hand materialized which Myers seized and held in his, feeling it diminish in size until it was no bigger than a baby's, before it melted away altogether. He was at the séance with Darwin,... Arthur Balfour, who had just become a conservative M.P. Another of the Balfour sisters, Eleanor, married Sidgwick in 1875, and worked with the group. The Sidgwicks had several test séances with Slade in 1876.... Nevertheless within four years the society numbered Barrett, Crookes, Oliver Lodge, Rayleigh, Balfor Steward (won over from his earlier scepticism [sic]), J.J. Thomson, J. Venn, F.R.S., and Wallace, among its members; along with many other notabilities, including two bishops [B.F. Westcott and E.W. Benson], William Ewart Gladstone, Arthur Balfour [future Prime Minister of England], John Ruskin, Lord Tennyson, and G.F. Watts."[28]

"in June [Hort] joined the mysterious company of the 'Apostles'.... He remained always a grateful and loyal member of the secret Club, which has now become famous for the number of distinguished men who have belonged to it. In his time the Club was in a manner reinvigorated, and he was mainly responsible for the wording of the oath which binds the members to a conspiracy of silence."[29]

Perhaps you are still wondering what these three bishops had to do with bringing spiritualism into the church. They were the leading translators for the 1881 Revised Version of the Bible.

In 1604, King James wrote a book against the practice of spiritualism, called *Daemonology*.[30] He certainly would not have tolerated the bishops on his translation committee being involved in spiritualism. In 1881, however, a very different atmosphere prevailed. The future Prime Minister of England was attending séances with

---

[27] Brian Inglis, Ph.D., *Natural and Supernatural: a History of the Paranormal* (London: Hodder and Stoughton, 1977), p. 271.

[28] *Ibid.*, p. 318, 322.

[29] A. F. Hort, *Life & Letters of Fenton John Anthony Hort,* Vol. 1 (1896), p. 170, 171.

[30] King James, *A Collection of His Majesties Works* (London: Robert Barker and John Bill, 1616), p. 91.

Darwin and the leading bishops of the Church of England. It was fashionable for most of high society in England, at the time, to be involved in séances. Even if they thought it was sleight of hand by the medium, they would attend to try to prove the manifestation a fraud.

"Many endeavor to account for spiritual manifestations by attributing them wholly to fraud and sleight of hand on the part of the medium. But while it is true that the results of trickery have often been palmed off as genuine manifestations, there have been, also, marked exhibitions of supernatural power. The mysterious rapping with which modern spiritualism began was not the result of human trickery or cunning, but was the direct work of evil angels, who thus introduced one of the most successful of soul-destroying delusions. Many will be ensnared through the belief that spiritualism is a merely human imposture; when brought face to face with manifestations which they cannot but regard as supernatural, they will be deceived, and will be led to accept them as the great power of God."[31]

Speaking of Westcott and Hort's Revised Version, H.P. Blavatsky, says, "Now that the revised version of the gospels has been published and the most glaring mistranslations of the old versions are corrected, one will understand better the words."[32]

So, the mother of modern occultism suggests that one will be able to understand the Bible better with this new version. She further describes what that Bible revision process looked like: "That which for nearly fifteen hundred years was imposed on Christendom as a book, of which every word was written under the direct supervision of the Holy Ghost; of which not a syllable, nor a comma could be changed without sacrilege; is now being retranslated, revised, corrected, and clipped of whole verses, in some cases of entire chapters."[33]

Further, she hated the King James Version and the texts upon which it is based: "that, finally, we have a text, not 900 years old,

---

[31] E. G. White, *The Great Controversy* (1911), p. 553.1.

[32] H. P. Blavatsky, *The Secret Doctrine,* Vol. 1 - Cosmogenesis (1888), p. 570.

[33] H. P. Blavatsky, *Isis Unveiled,* Vol. 2 - Theology (1877), p. 252.

abounding with omissions, interpolations, and premeditated perversions; and that, consequently, as this Masoretic Hebrew text[34] has fossilized its mistakes, and the key to the 'Word of God' is lost, no one has a right to enforce upon so-called 'Christians' the divagations of a series of hallucinated and, perhaps, spurious prophets, under the unwarranted and untenable assumption that the author of it was the 'Holy Ghost.'"[35] "Besides, as the New Testament is noted for its mistranslations and transparent falsifications of texts... The blunders of the Old Testament are as nothing to those of the gospels. Nothing shows better than these self evident contradictions the system of pious fraud upon which the superstructure of the Messiahship rests."[36] "And King James's translators have made such a jumble of it that no one but a kabalist can restore the Bible to its original form."[37]

Considering their interest in the occult, should we be surprised that Westcott and Hort also hated the King James Bible and the text upon which it was based?[38] "I had no idea till the last few weeks of the importance of texts, having read so little Greek Testament, and dragged on with the villainous *Textus Receptus* [39]…. Think of that vile *Textus Receptus* leaning entirely on late MSS. [manuscripts]; it is a blessing there are such early[40] ones."[41] "We have at last hit upon a

---

[34] The Hebrew text upon which the Old Testament of the King James Bible is based.

[35] H. P. Blavatsky, *Isis Unveiled,* Vol. 2 - Theology (1877), p. 470-471.

[36] *Ibid.* p. 133.

[37] *Ibid.* p. 362.

[38] Surely if bible translators are attending séances and in agreement with the mother of modern occultism, it should raise questions in the minds of Christians as to the reliability of their translation. The text of Scripture that occultists hate would likely be the true and pure text. Satan hates the pure word of God.

[39] The Textus Receptus is the Greek text upon which the King James Version New Testament is based.

[40] The early manuscripts to which Hort refers are Codex Sinaiticus and Vaticanus, the Alexandrian manuscripts based on the works of Origen.

[41] A. F. Hort, *Life And Letters of Fenton John Anthony Hort,* Vol. 1 (1896), p. 211.
And believe it or not, the very next sentence in the Hort's biography (after the one quoted above) is: "Westcott, Gorham, C. B. Scott, Benson, Bradshaw, Luard, etc., and I have started a society for the investigation of ghosts and all supernatural appearances and effects, being all disposed to believe that such things really exist, and ought to be discriminated from hoaxes and mere subjective delusions; we shall be happy to obtain any good accounts well authenticated with names."

better plan… which is to set aside this *textus receptus* altogether, and to construct a fresh text."[42]

And where did this plan come from? Just twenty-three years before the Revision was commissioned in 1870, Cardinal John H. Newman wrote to Cardinal Wiseman the following: "The Superior of the Franciscans, Father Benigno, in the Trastevere, wishes us out of his own head to engage in an English Authorized Translation of the Bible [the future Revised Version]. He is a learned man, and on the Congregation of the Index. What he wished was, that we would take the Protestant translation [KJV], correct it by the Vulgate [Catholic Latin bible]… and get it sanctioned here. This might be our first work if your Lordship approved of it."[43]

It is through the revising of the word of God, that we are warned that all nations would drink the wine of Babylon. This is the same process Satan used to introduce spiritualism in the garden of Eden, and he is using it with the same success to introduce spiritualism into the churches today.

"Men act as though they had been given special liberty to cancel the decisions of God. The higher critics put themselves in the place of God, and review the Word of God, **revising** or endorsing it. **In this way, all nations are induced to drink the wine of the fornication of Babylon.** These higher critics have fixed things to suit the popular heresies of these last days. If they cannot subvert and misapply the Word of God, if they cannot bend it to human practices, they break it."[44] "Unless the whole Bible is given to the people just as it reads, it would be better for them not to have it at all."[45]

---

[42] Constantin von Tischendorf, Ph.D., *When Were Our Gospels Written?* (New York: American Tract Society, 1866), p. 21.

[43] Wilfrid Philip Ward, *Life and Times of Cardinal Wiseman*, Vol. 1 (London: Longmans, Green, and Co., 1897), p. 454.

[44] E. G. White, *The Upward Look* (Hagerstown, MD: Review & Herald Publishing Association, 1982), p. 35.5.

[45] E. G. White, *The Spirit of Prophecy,* Vol. 4 (Nampa, ID: Pacific Press, 1884), p. 344.1.

4 Lost Voices

Zacharias began to execute his course of priestly duties, and as he commenced the offering of incense in the house of the Lord, suddenly, an angel of the Lord stood at the right hand of the altar of incense. Trembling with fear, Zacharias heard the angel say, "Fear not, Zacharias: for thy prayer is heard; and thy wife Elisabeth shall bear thee a son, and thou shalt call his name John."[1]

After listening to the angel's full message, Zacharias replied, "Whereby shall I know this? for I am an old man, and my wife well stricken in years. And the angel answering said unto him, I am Gabriel, that stand in the presence of God; and am sent to speak unto thee, and to show thee these glad tidings. And, behold, **thou shalt be dumb, and not able to speak**, until the day that these things shall be performed, **because thou believest not my words**..."[2]

Is it possible that this judgment might fall on others, in modern times, who believe not God's words? Zacharias made his proclamation of unbelief while performing the solemn duties of priest and guardian of the word of God.

Bible translators, of all people, take (or should take) a solemn responsibility to guard the word of God by the most faithful and careful efforts possible. Yet, clearly there has been an effort to change God's Word, "causing it to lean to their established views, which were governed by tradition."[3] In view of the stern warnings in God's Word for anyone changing what it says, surely this would be an ultimate evidence of unbelief.

Perhaps we should let history speak for itself. Kenneth Taylor took some of the most amazing liberties while handling God's Word in the production of his *Living Bible* paraphrase. *Time* magazine, July 24, 1972 records some of the results:

---

[1] Luke 1:13

[2] Luke 1:18-20

[3] E. G. White, *Early Writings* (1882), p. 220.2.

"Mysteriously, halfway through the paraphrase, Taylor lost his voice, and still speaks only in a hoarse whisper. A psychiatrist who examined him suggested that the voice failure was Taylor's psychological self-punishment for tampering with what he believed to be the word of God."[4]

Is this an isolated case, limited perhaps by coincidence, or is there a pattern that can be followed?

Samuel Tregelles was a famous translator on the committee with Westcott and Hort who created the new Greek text used in the revision of 1881. He also served on the Revised Version committee. Philip Schaff describes Tregelles, whom he met at the British Museum, as "scarcely able to speak audibly."[5]

Interestingly enough, Philip Schaff was also on the Revised Version committee and later the chairman of the 1901 American Standard Version, and he was described by his son David Schaff thus: "His eyesight was threatened and his voice so affected that he could not speak in public so as to be heard."[6]

Westcott himself seemed to suffer a similar affliction. "He took his turn of preaching in the chapel, but he dreaded and disliked the duty, and he was quite inaudible to many of the boys....
"His voice was not yet a force in the chapel. It reached but a few, and it was understood by still fewer."[7]

Since it is not that common for people to go dumb, it seems that this must be more than coincidence for so many famous bible translators to have lost their voices.

---

[4] "Religion: A Plowman's Bible?" *Time*, July 24, 1972,

http://www.time.com/time/magazine/article/0,9171,906183,00.html Retrieved: 04-07-2011.

[5] David Schley Schaff, Ph.D., *The Life of Philip Schaff* (New York: Charles Scribner's Sons, 1897), p. 246.

[6] *Ibid.*, p. 171.

[7] Arthur Westcott, *The Life and Letters of Brooke Foss Westcott,* Vol. 1 (1903), p. 198, 272-73.

J. B. Phillips, the author of the Phillips translation, in his own autobiography, ironically named, *The Price of Success*, tells us: "I was still doing a fair measure of speaking in schools and churches until the late summer of 1961. And then quite suddenly my speaking, writing and communication powers stopped."[8]

Frank Lodgson was able to speak as he renounced his involvement in the *New American Standard Bible*, or NASB, June 9, 1973, the audio recording of which is still available today:

"Back in 1956-57 Mr. F. Dewey Lockman of the Lockman Foundation contacted me. He was one of the dearest friends we've ever had for 25 years, a big man, some 300 pounds, snow white hair, one of the most terrific businessmen I have ever met....

"Well, he discovered that the copyright [on the American Standard Version of 1901] was just as loose as a fumbled ball on a football field. Nobody wanted it. The publishers didn't want it. It didn't get anywhere. Mr. Lockman got in touch with me and said, 'Would you and Ann come out and spend some weeks with us, and we'll work on a feasibility report; I can pick up the copyright to the 1901 if it seems advisable....' At any rate we went out and started on a feasibility report, and I encouraged him to go ahead with it.

"I'm afraid I'm in trouble with the Lord, because I encouraged him to go ahead with it. We laid the groundwork; I wrote the format; I helped to interview some of the translators; I sat with the translators; I wrote the preface. When you see the preface to the New American Standard, those are my words...

"some of my friends across the country began to learn that I had some part in it and they started saying, 'What about this; what about that?' Dr. David Otis Fuller in Grand Rapids [Michigan]. I've known him for 35 years, and he would say... 'Frank, what about this? You had a part in it; what about this; what about that?' And at first I thought, now, wait a minute; let's don't go overboard; let's don't be too critical. You know how you justify yourself the last minute. But I finally got to the place where I said, 'Ann, I'm in trouble; I can't refute these arguments; it's wrong; it's terribly wrong; it's frightfully wrong; and what am I going to do about it?' Well, I went through some real soul searching for about four months, and I sat down and wrote one of the most difficult letters of my life, I think.

[8] J.B. Phillips, *The Price of Success* (Wheaton, IL: Harold Shaw Publishers, 1984), p. 193.

"I wrote to my friend Dewey, and I said, 'Dewey, I don't want to add to your problems... but I can no longer ignore these criticisms I am hearing and I can't refute them. The only thing I can do—and dear Brother, I haven't a thing against you and I can witness at the judgment of Christ and before men wherever I go that you were 100% sincere,' (he wasn't schooled in language or anything; he was just a business man; he did it for money; he did it conscientiously; he wanted it absolutely right and he thought it was right; I guess nobody pointed out some of these things to him) 'I must under God renounce every attachment to the New American Standard.'"[9]

The lost voices of bible translators, and the soul wrenching confession of Frank Lodgson testify to the solemn warning of Scripture: "If any man shall add unto these things, God shall add unto him the plagues that are written in this book: And if any man shall take away from the words of the book of this prophecy, God shall take away his part out of the book of life, and out of the holy city..."[10]

---

[9] http://www.av1611.org/kjv/logsdon.html Retrieved: 01-31-2016.

[10] Revelation 22:18-19

5 God Knew All Along

Scripture says that God knows the future; thus, he is able to declare "the end from the beginning, and from ancient times the things that are not yet done."[1] Therefore none of this would have taken him by surprise. In fact, he has revealed it all, ahead of time, in his Word, so that we may have evidence upon which to base our faith.

"For the time will come when they will not endure sound doctrine; but after their own lusts shall they heap to themselves teachers, having itching ears; And they shall turn away their ears from the truth, and shall be turned unto fables."[2]

"The nominal conversion of Constantine, in the early part of the fourth century, caused great rejoicing; and the world, cloaked with a form of righteousness, walked into the church. Now the work of corruption rapidly progressed. Paganism, while appearing to be vanquished, became the conqueror. Her spirit controlled the church. Her doctrines, ceremonies, and superstitions were incorporated into the faith and worship of the professed followers of Christ.
"This compromise between paganism and Christianity resulted in the development of 'the man of sin' foretold in prophecy as opposing and exalting himself above God. That gigantic system of false religion is a masterpiece of Satan's power—a monument of his efforts to seat himself upon the throne to rule the earth according to his will."[3]

Regarding the rise of the anti-Christ, we are told in 2 Thessalonians 2:3-8: "Let no man deceive you by any means: for that day[4] shall not come, except there come a falling away first, and that man of sin be revealed, the son of perdition; Who opposeth and exalteth himself above all that is called God, or that is worshipped; so that he as God sitteth in the temple of God, showing himself that he is God. Remember ye not, that, when I was yet with you, I told you these things? And now ye know what withholdeth that he might be revealed in his time. For the mystery of iniquity doth already work:

---

[1] Isaiah 46:10

[2] 2 Timothy 4:3-4

[3] E. G. White, *The Great Controversy* (1911), p. 49.2-50.1.

[4] The second coming of Jesus.

only he who now letteth will let, until he be taken out of the way. And then shall that Wicked be revealed, whom the Lord shall consume with the spirit of his mouth, and shall destroy with the brightness of his coming."

Notice that the "man of sin," or "mystery of iniquity," Paul says, was already at work in his day (verse 7) and would continue to exist until the second coming (verse 8). Also, he would be a blasphemous power, exalting himself above God and claiming the titles and prerogatives of God—even claiming to be God. There is only one organization on earth, which began developing its power during the time of Constantine and before, that fits this description; but first let us examine more evidence.

Clearly, no one individual would live from the time of Paul to the second coming, so this must be a reference to a position that would be occupied by many individuals. It is also self-evident that no human being could be literally sitting in God's temple, for God's temple is in heaven.[5] Therefore, this individual must be claiming to sit in God's temple, which counterfeit temple must be on this earth. The prophet Daniel also speaks of a little horn power that would exalt himself above all that is called God and last until the second coming and would cast God's sanctuary to the ground. This must also be a reference to that counterfeit temple that would be on earth rather than in heaven.

"And he shall speak great words against the most High [blasphemy], and shall wear out the saints of the most High, and think to change times and laws: and they shall be given into his hand until a time and times and the dividing of time. But the judgment shall sit, and they shall take away his dominion, to consume and to destroy it unto the end. And the kingdom and dominion, and the greatness of the kingdom under the whole heaven, shall be given to the people of the saints of the most High, whose kingdom is an everlasting kingdom, and all dominions shall serve and obey him."[6]

---

[5] Revelation 11:19

[6] Daniel 7:25-27

"Yea, he magnified himself even to the prince of the host, and by him the daily [sacrifice] was taken away, and the place of his sanctuary was cast down."[7] "And the king shall do according to his will; and he shall exalt himself, and magnify himself above every god, and shall speak marvellous things against the God of gods, and shall prosper till the indignation be accomplished: for that that is determined shall be done."[8]

In Revelation 13, John portrays a power with the same characteristics: a beast comes up out of the sea having seven heads and ten horns, with a blasphemous name on its heads,[9] commanding worship,[10] and having a blasphemous mouth.[11]

The woman who rides the beast of Revelation 17 has a name on her forehead—"mystery, Babylon the great, the mother of harlots, and abominations of the earth" which sounds very similar to "mystery of iniquity." This beast also is destroyed at the second coming.[12]

Therefore the "mystery of iniquity" and the "son of perdition" of Thessalonians, the "little horn" of Daniel 7 and 8, the blasphemous power of Daniel 11, the sea beast of Revelation 13, and the woman riding the beast of Revelation 17 are all depicting the same power.

Daniel 7 gives at least ten identifying characteristics[13] of the little horn:

1. It would arise out of the fourth beast or fourth world empire (Rome). Daniel 7:7, 8.

---

7 Daniel 8:11

8 Daniel 11:36

9 Revelation 13:1

10 Revelation 13:3, 4

11 Revelation 13:5. Blasphemy is claiming the title, position, or prerogatives of God. See Mark 2:7 and John 10:33.

12 Revelation 17:14

13 For a much more in-depth treatment of these prophecies, see Martin Klein, *Glimpses of the Open Gates of Heaven,* Daniel 7.

2. It would arise among the ten divisions of the Roman empire (the Roman empire disintegrated into the ten tribes of Western Europe in A.D. 476). Daniel 7:8.
3. It would arise after the ten horns, therefore gaining its political power after A.D. 476. Daniel 7:24.
4. It was to be different from the other ten horns. Daniel 7:24.
5. Although a little horn, it would be more stout, or stronger, than the other ten horns. Daniel 7:20.
6. It would uproot three of the ten horns. Daniel 7:8, 20, 24.
7. It would speak great words against the most high. Daniel 7:25.
8. It would wear out (persecute) God's saints. Daniel 7:25.
9. It would think to change God's times and laws. Daniel 7:25.
10. It would reign for 1260 years.[14] Daniel 7:25.

Additional identifying marks are specified in Revelation chapter 13:

11. A beast in Bible prophecy represents a political power or kingdom.[15] So, this beast represents a kingdom, with a king.
12. This kingdom would receive a deadly wound but the deadly wound would be healed.[16]
13. All the world would wonder after this power as a result of the healing of his deadly wound.[17]
14. The beast would reign 42 months,[18] which is 3 1/2 years, or 1260 days/years, just like the little horn of Daniel 7—proof that both descriptions represent the same power.

---

[14] Daniel 7:25—Reign for a time, times, and dividing of times. A time is a year (Daniel 4:16). A Biblical year is 360 days (see the story of the flood and calculate from the dates given). Therefore, we have here 3 1/2 times or 3 1/2 years. In symbolic Bible prophecy a day represents a year. See Numbers 14:34 and Ezekiel 4:6. Therefore 1260 days represents 1260 years. This prophecy is repeated seven times in Scripture:
Daniel 7:25, "time, times, and a dividing of time"
Daniel 12:7, "time, times, and an half"
Revelation, 11:2 "forty-two months"
Revelation, 11:3 "a thousand two hundred and sixty days"
Revelation, 12:6 "a thousand two hundred and sixty days"
Revelation, 12:14 "time, and times, and half a time"
Revelation, 13:5 "forty-two months."

[15] Daniel 7:17

[16] Revelation 13:3

[17] *Ibid.*

[18] Revelation 13:5

15. He would have a number requiring special wisdom to understand, which must be counted, is the number of a man, and adds up to six hundred and sixty-six.[19]
16. All the world would be led to worship him.[20] The Greek word used for worship in Revelation 13:8 is proskuneō, which can also mean (according to Thayer's Greek Definitions), "to kiss the hand to (towards) one, in token of reverence."

Even more identifying marks are outlined in Revelation 17:

17. A woman in Bible prophecy represents a church.[21] So, the kingdom (beast) would eventually be controlled by a church.[22]
18. This church would be seated on seven hills.[23]
19. She would ride a beast with seven heads and ten horns—indicating the same political power as in chapter thirteen.[24]
20. The woman would be dressed in scarlet and purple.[25]
21. She would have a golden cup in her hand containing abominations.[26]
22. This woman is called a city which reigns over the kings of the earth.[27]

One, and only one power in all of history can answer to these detailed descriptions. If you still have not guessed the power the Bible is warning us about, let us allow history to make the identification. Speaking of the little horn of Daniel 7, which as we

---

[19] Revelation 13:18

[20] Revelation 13:8

[21] 2 Corinthians 11:2; Jeremiah 6:2; Isaiah 51:16; Isaiah 1:21

[22] Revelation 17:3

[23] Revelation 17:9

[24] Revelation 17:3; Revelation 13:1

[25] Revelation 17:4

[26] *Ibid.*

[27] Revelation 17:18

have seen is the same as the little horn of Daniel 8 and the sea beasts of Revelation 13 and 17, Sir Isaac Newton[28] writes: "Kings are put for kingdoms, as above; and therefore the little horn is a little kingdom. It was a horn of the fourth beast,... and therefore we are to look for it among the nations of the Latin Empire [western Europe], after the rise of the ten horns. But, it was a kingdom of a different kind from the other ten kingdoms, having a life or soul peculiar to itself, with eyes and a mouth. By its eyes it was a seer; and by its mouth speaking great things and changing times and laws, it was a Prophet as well as a King. And such a Seer, a Prophet and a King, is the church of Rome."[29]

Does the church of Rome answer to all these identifying marks?

Daniel 7

1. The church of Rome most certainly arose out of the pagan Roman empire. This is why we still call it today, the Roman Catholic Church.
2. This little horn arose in the middle of Western Europe—in Italy.
3. The papacy gained its political power when it took control of Rome from the Ostrogoths in A.D. 538. Prior to this time it did not even have control of its own capital city. In the same year the Roman emperor Justinian, conferred upon the Bishop of Rome authority to be the head of all churches and the corrector of heretics.[30]
4. The ten kingdoms of Western Europe among which it rose were all strictly political in nature. The papacy, however, was a religio-political power—very different from the other ten.
5. Although it was little (today being only 110 acres, and the smallest internationally-recognized independent state), it would be stronger or more stout than the nations of Europe.
6. The papacy was responsible for the annihilation of three of the ten divisions of Western Europe. This identifying mark alone would be sufficient. "The three divisions which were plucked up

---

[28] Sir Isaac Newton (1642-1727), the famous scientist who first quantified the laws of gravity, and arguably the most brilliant mind of modern times, actually wrote more about the Bible than about science. The books of Daniel and Revelation were his particular interest.

[29] Isaac Newton, *Observations upon the Prophecies of Daniel, and the Apocalypse of St. John* (London: J. Darby and T. Browne, 1733), p. 74, 75.

[30] http://biblelight.net/jus-code.htm Retrieved: 01-31-2016.

were the Heruli in 493, the Vandals in 534, and the Ostrogoths in A.D. 538."[31]

7. Speaking great words against the Most High means that it would blasphemously claim the attributes of God, even claiming to be God.[32] One small example of this arrogant claim comes from Pope Gregory XIII's 1582 Decretum Gratiani, Corpus Juris Canonici. An English translation of the Latin text includes the following: "But to believe that our Lord God the Pope, the establisher of said decretal, and of this, could not decree, as he did decree, should be accounted heretical."[33]
8. No other power in history has inflicted more persecution and martyred more Christians than the Church of Rome.[34]
9. God specified that this power would even "think to change times and laws."[35] Indeed, we find that it boldly makes such a claim. God commanded that the seventh day should be kept holy as the Sabbath.[36] But the Catholic church presumes even to change God's ten commandments: "Sunday is a Catholic institution, and its claims to observance can be defended only on Catholic principles.... From the beginning to the end of Scripture there is not a single passage that warrants the transfer of weekly public worship from the last day of the week to the first."[37] "Protestantism, in discarding the authority of the [Roman Catholic] Church, has no good reason for its Sunday theory, and ought, logically, to keep Saturday as the Sabbath."[38] "Since the

---

[31] S. N. Haskell, *The Story of Daniel the Prophet* (Nashville, TN: Southern Publishing Association, 1905), p. 94.

[32] Daniel 11:36

[33] Gregorii XIII. Pont. Max., Decretum Gratiani Emendatum et Notationibus Illustratum Una cum glofsis, Gregorii XIII. Pont. Max. iussu editum. (Rome: In Aedibus Populi Romani, 1582), p. 153. Latin: "Credere autem Dominum Deum nostrum Papam conditorem dictae decret & istius, sic non poruiffe statuere prout statuit, haereti cum censeretur."

[34] David A. Plaisted, "Estimates of the Number Killed by the Papacy in the Middle Ages and Later," (2006), p. 7, 41, https://www.scribd.com/doc/122890407/Estimates-of-the-Number-Killed-by-the-Papacy-David-A-Plaisted.

[35] Daniel 7:25

[36] Exodus 20:8-11

[37] M. Long, "Rampant Sabbatarianism," *Catholic Press,* August 25, 1900, p. 22, biblelight.net/Catholic%Press.jpg Retrieved: 01-31-2016.

[38] John Gilmary Shea, L.L.D., *American Catholic Quarterly Review*, Vol. 8—January, 1883—No. 29 (Philadelphia: Hardy & Mahony, Publishers and Proprietors, 1883), p. 152.

[Catholic] Church has probably influenced Constantine to make the day Sunday a holiday, it can claim the honor of having granted man a rest from his labors every seven days."[39]

10. Just as the Bible prophesied, the papacy maintained its political power for exactly 1260 years, from A.D. 538 to A.D. 1798.[40]

Revelation 13

11. The Bishop of Rome assumed even the title of the Roman emperor—Pontifex Maximus (The Great Bridge Builder).
12. Precisely 1260 years from the assumption of political power at Rome in A.D. 538, Napoleon's general Louis-Alexandre Berthier took the pope captive, on February 15, 1798, bringing an end to the papacy's political power, and delivering the deadly wound.
13. The deadly wound was the loss of political power; therefore, the healing of the wound must, by definition, be the restoration of that political power. On February 12, 1929, the *San Francisco Chronicle* ran a front-page article reporting the events of the previous day with the signing of the Lateran treaty. The article's title had apocalyptic significance: "Heal Wound of Many Years." The same day, Arnaldo Cortesi, writing for the *New York Times* stated: "From 11 o'clock this morning there was another sovereign independent State in the world."[41]
14. Just as the little horn of Daniel 7 reigns for a time, times and the dividing of times, or 1260 years, so the sea beast of Revelation

[39] C.S. Mosna, S.C.J., *Storia della Domenica Dalle Origini Fino Agli Inizi del v Secolo [History of Sunday From its Origins to the Early Fifth Century]* (Rome: Libreria Editrice Dell 'Universita Gregoriana, 1969), p. 366.
Italian: "Avendo la Chiesa influito probabilmente su Constantino per rendere la domenica giorno <<festivo>>, Essa può rivendicarsi l'onore di aver voluto concedere all'uomo una pausa alle sue fatiche ogni sette giorni."

[40] See identifying mark number 12 for more details.

[41] Arnaldo Cortesi, "Pope Becomes Ruler Of A State Again," *New York Times,* February 12, 1929, p. 1.

13 continued 42 months or 1260 days (representing 1260 years[42]).

15. The Catholic periodical *Our Sunday Visitor* (still in print today), on April 18th, 1915, printed an article containing the following statement: "What are the letters on the Pope's crown and what do they signify, if anything? The letters on the Pope's mitre are these: Vicarius Filii Dei, which is Latin for Vicar of the Son of God.... Hence to the Bishop of Rome, as head of the church, was given the title, Vicar of Christ."[43]
    In the 1968 Apostolic Constitutions, which are the highest form of official papal decrees in the Roman Catholic Church and are issued with binding legal authority, Pope Paul VI, refers to the Pope twice with the title Vicarius Filii Dei.[44]
    In a signed statement by Catholic Professor Dr. Quasten, of the Catholic University of America, Washington D.C., to Robert Franklin Correia and Benjamin Mondics, Dr. Quasten writes, "the title Vicarius Filii Dei as well as the title Vicarius Christi is very common as the title for the Pope."[45]
    In Ferraris Ecclesiastical Dictionary, an elaborate Catholic theological work in Latin, under the heading of pope (papa, p. 1828) it mentions the title Vicarius Filii Dei.[46] Many other Catholic documents could be cited,[47] but this should suffice to demonstrate from primary sources that the title is a valid Latin papal title. In Latin various letters have numerical value, and

---

[42] Daniel 7:25—Reign for a time, times, and dividing of times. A time is a year (Daniel 4:16). A Biblical year is 360 days (see the story of the flood and calculate from the dates given). Therefore, we have here 3 1/2 times or 3 1/2 years. In symbolic Bible prophecy a day represents a year. See Numbers 14:34 and Ezekiel 4:6. Therefore we have 1260 days, representing 1260 years. This prophecy is repeated seven times in Scripture:
Daniel 7:25, "time, times, and a dividing of time"
Daniel 12:7, "time, times, and an half"
Revelation, 11:2 "forty-two months"
Revelation, 11:3 "a thousand two hundred and sixty days"
Revelation, 12:6 "a thousand two hundred and sixty days"
Revelation, 12:14 "time, and times, and half a time"
Revelation, 13:5 "forty-two months."

[43] John F. Noll, ed., "Bureau of Information," *Our Sunday Visitor*, April 18, 1915, p. 3.

[44] *Acta Apostolicae Sedis, Commentarium Officiale*, Vol. 60 (Typis Polyglottis Vaticanis, 1968), p. 317-319.

[45] http://biblelight.net/Quasten 20Document 206.11 20x 209.5 20inch.gif Retrieved: 01-31-2016.

[46] http://biblelight.net/1827r.gif Retrieved: 01-31-2016.

[47] http://biblelight.net/666.htm Retrieved 02-09-2016.

these we call Roman numerals. Using the standard letter values, we "count the number of the beast: for it is the number of a man."

Vicarius Filii Dei—Vicar of the Son of God

V - 5
I - 1
C - 100
A - 0
R - 0
I - 1
U - 5 (V and U are the same letter in Latin)
S - 0

F - 0
I - 1
L - 50
I - 1
I - 1

D - 500
E - 0
I - 1

666

At least seven other titles that apply to the papacy or the pope,[48] in a total of three different languages (Greek and Hebrew also have numeric values for letters), add up to 666. God wanted to make it very clear that this could not be coincidence.

Latin DUX CLERI*—Captain of the Clergy

D - 500
U - 5
X - 10

C - 100
L - 50
E - 0
R - 0
I - 1

666

[48] See *Andreas Helwig, *Antichristus Romanus* (Wittenburg: Typis Laurentij Seuberlichs, 1612).
‡ Johannis Gerhardi, SS., *Adnotationes in Apocalypsin* (Germany: Johannis Jacobi Bauhofferi, 1665), p. 119.
§ Alexander Campbell, A Debate on the Roman Catholic Religion (Cincinnati: H. S. Bosworth, 1865), p. 229, 249.
http://biblelight.net/666.htm

Latin LUDOVICUS*—Vicar of the Court

L	-	50
U	-	5
D	-	500
O	-	0
V	-	5
I	-	1
C	-	100
U	-	5
S	-	0
		666

Greek LATEINOS*—"the Latin speaking man" (Latin being the papacy's official language—and no other nation, power or church speaks Latin today.)

L	-	30	lambda
A	-	1	alpha
T	-	300	tau
E	-	5	epsilon
I	-	10	iota
N	-	50	nu
O	-	70	omicron
S	-	200	sigma
		666	

The ancient Greek ITALIKA EKKLESIA‡ is "Italian Church"

I	-	10	iota
T	-	300	tau
A	-	1	alpha
L	-	30	lambda
I	-	10	iota
K	-	20	kappa
A	-	1	alpha
E	-	5	epsilon
K	-	20	kappa
K	-	20	kappa
L	-	30	lambda
E	-	8	eta
S	-	200	sigma
I	-	10	iota
A	-	1	alpha
		666	

The ancient Greek HE LATINE BASILEIA§ is "The Latin Kingdom"

H	-	0	(transliterated)
E	-	8	eta
L	-	30	lambda
A	-	1	alpha
T	-	300	tau
I	-	10	iota
N	-	50	nu
E	-	8	eta
B	-	2	beta
A	-	1	alpha
S	-	200	sigma
I	-	10	iota
L	-	30	lambda
E	-	5	epsilon
I	-	10	iota
A	-	1	alpha
		666	

The Hebrew ROMIITH*‡ means the "Roman Kingdom"

R	-	200	resh
O	-	6	waw (vav)
M	-	40	mem
I	-	10	yod
I	-	10	yod
TH	-	400	taw
		666	

ROMITI, in Hebrew, means the "Roman Man"

R	-	200	resh
O	-	6	waw (vav)
M	-	40	mem
I	-	10	yod
T	-	400	taw
I	-	10	yod
		666	

16. What other figurehead than the pope has religious and political leaders of the world coming to kiss his hand? Never was the worship that the world is giving to the papacy more evident than on April 8, 2005, at the funeral of Pope John Paul II. It was "the single largest gathering in history of heads of state outside the

United Nations,"[49] including 4 kings, 5 queens, 70 presidents and prime ministers, and 14 leaders of other religions. Over 4 million pilgrims arrived in Rome, a city with 3 million residents. The funeral likely had the world's largest TV audience for any event, exceeding 2 billion viewers. And the whole world watched as George Bush Jr. bowed on his knees, before a dead pope, for ten minutes, next to George Bush Sr., Bill Clinton, and Condoleezza Rice. This was the first papal funeral ever attended by a sitting U.S. president.

Revelation 17

17. The papacy is the only such political system in the world where there is this unique combination of a church controlling a state.
18. "In the 300s B.C., a defensive barrier was built, called the Servian Wall around seven hills named: Aventine, Caelian, Capitoline, Esquiline, Palatine, Quirinal, and Viminal. These became the Seven Hills of Rome."[50]
19. For further discussion on the seven heads[51] and ten horns see the book *Glimpses of the Open Gates of Heaven*.[52]
20. Colors for the Catholic church on official occasions are purple and scarlet. God went so far as to describe even the physical appearances of this power. Clearly, by providing all these detailed identifying characteristics, God wanted to leave no question as to the power he was describing.
21. No other church represents themselves as a woman holding a golden cup, and no other church puts such an emphasis in their liturgy on the golden cup. The Bible says that the cup contains abominations. Ezekiel chapter eight lists in ascending order things that God considers greater and greater abominations. The greatest abomination is sun worship masquerading as God's true

---

[49] http://en.wikipedia.org/wiki/Funeral_of_Pope_John_Paul_II Retrieved: 01-31-2016.

[50] David W. Daniels, M.Div., *Why They Changed The Bible: One World Bible For One World Religion* (Ontario, CA: Chick Publications, Inc., 2014), Kindle ed., Kindle Locations 2514-2516.

[51] "Vaticanus B leaves out of the Book of Revelation 'Mystery Babylon the Great,' 'the seven heads are seven mountains upon which the woman (harlot) sits,' and 'the woman is that great city which reigns over the kings of the earth.'"
Floyd Nolen Jones, Th.D., Ph.D., *Which Version is The Bible?* (Goodyear, AZ: Kings Word Press, 2006), p. 114.

[52] Martin Klein, *Glimpses of the Open Gates of Heaven* (Savannah Pictures, 2017), Chapters 13-17.
www.savannahpictures.com

worship.[53] It is precisely the solar disk portrayed emanating from the papal cup—sun worship impersonating the worship of God.

22. There is no other city on earth that can be said to reign over the kings of the earth. We still have a saying today, "all roads lead to Rome."

Roman Catholic Henry Edward Manning, Archbishop of Westminster, sums it up in a most powerful way:
"Now a system like this [Roman Catholicism] is so unlike anything human, it has upon it notes, tokens, marks so altogether supernatural, that men now acknowledge it to be either Christ or Antichrist. There is nothing between these extremes. Most true is this alternative. The Catholic Church is either the masterpiece of Satan or the kingdom of the Son of God."[54]

Thus, God has given abundant evidence warning against this power and the things that it would do against God and his Word. This is not to say that there are not many faithful, godly, people in the Roman Catholic Church who will be saved, for "the times of this ignorance God winked at; but now commandeth all men every where to repent."[55] God is warning against this system, not the individuals who love him and have been honestly deceived. And so, at the very end of time a loving God will send out one final call addressed to his faithful people in apostate churches: "Come out of her, my people, that ye be not partakers of her sins, and that ye receive not of her

---

[53] Ezekiel 8:15-18

[54] Henry Edward Manning, Archbishop of Westminster, *The Fourfold Sovereignty of God* (London: Burns, Oates, and Co., 1871), p. 171-172.
Archbishop Manning was elevated to Cardinal in 1875.

[55] Acts 17:30

plagues."[56] "The Lord is... not willing that any should perish, but that all should come to repentance."[57]

The Scriptures are quite clear that this power would even attempt to change God's times and laws. If it would try to change God's law, written on a table of stone with his own finger, we should not be surprised if we find this same power attempting to change the rest of God's words. Thus, God's Word points to the power that would attempt to change his Word. With this, forgotten facts of history agree: "A Roman Catholic version must be closely conformed to the Latin Vulgate, which the Council of Trent puts on an equal footing with the original text."[58]

John H. Newman[59] writes to Cardinal Wiseman "The Superior of the Franciscans, Father Benigno, in the Trastevere, wishes us out of his own head to engage in an English Authorized Translation of the Bible [the future Revised Version]. He is a learned man, and on the Congregation of the Index. What he wished was, that we would take the Protestant translation [KJV], correct it by the Vulgate [Catholic Latin bible]... and get it sanctioned here. This might be our first work if your Lordship[60] approved of it."[61]

Shortly after his success with introducing Romanism back into Protestant England, through the Oxford movement, Newman openly converted to Catholicism. Clearly, they needed someone of his caliber to continue the process of Romanization. Of course, the Latin Vulgate is the basis of all Catholic bibles, which we shall discuss further in future chapters. Correcting the Protestant Bible by the

---

[56] Revelation 18:4

[57] 2 Peter 3:9

[58] Philip Schaff, D.D., LL.D., *History of the Christian Church*, Vol. 6, 2nd ed. Rev. (New York: Charles Scribner's Sons, 1916), p. 365.

[59] J.H. Newman, converted to Catholicism on October 9, 1845, shortly before this statement was written, on January 17, 1847. Later (May 12, 1879) Newman was made a Cardinal. Newman may have done more than any other individual in history to reverse the Protestant reformation. Under the influence of the Oxford Movement, of which Newman, Edward Bouverie Pusey, and Henry Edward Manning were some of the main instigators, hundreds of Protestant clergy made submission to the papacy. Here he appears to be describing part of how this would be accomplished.

[60] See Matthew 23:8-11.

[61] Wilfrid Phillip Ward, *Life and Time of Cardinal Wiseman,* Vol. 1 (1897), p. 454.

Vulgate meant they were discussing making a *Revised Version* of the *King James Bible* that would harmonize with papal doctrine. At the time of Newman's letter, this idea was still in the planning stages. But, as we shall see, that is exactly what was accomplished in the *Revised Version* of 1881.

Eugene Nida is considered one of greatest modern linguists and was Executive Secretary for Translations for the American Bible Society. He recounts the following experience: "After completing a series of lectures at the Pontifical Biblical Institute in Rome, I chatted with a young Jesuit who expressed his appreciation for what I had said about putting the Scriptures into the every-day language of the people. He insisted that this was the most important development since the Reformation."[62]

The Jesuits are a secretive military order of the Catholic Church formed by Ignatius Loyola in 1539 for the purpose of stopping the Protestant Reformation. If a Jesuit tells you that your Protestant bible translation activity is the most important development since the reformation, what he means is that the Protestant bibles which have introduced changes compatible with papal doctrines are the most important tool they have for bringing Protestantism back under the control of the papacy, and undoing everything the Protestant Reformation accomplished.

Philip Schaff, who was Professor and chair of the Union Theological Seminary in New York, author of the *History of the Apostolic Church*, the three volume *Creeds of Christendom*, the eight volume *History of the Christian Church*, and editor of the 38 volumes of *Ante-Nicene and Post Nicene Fathers*, who was a member of the 1881 *Revised Version* committee and President of the translation committee for the *American Standard Version*, as well as having strong Catholic leanings,[63] penned the following:

---

[62] David W. Daniels, M.Div., *Why They Changed The Bible: One World Bible For One World Religion* (2014), Kindle ed., Kindle Locations 1806–1809.

[63] Schaff apparently had Catholic leanings strong enough to go and kiss the pope's red slipper. Certainly, none of the Protestant reformers ever did such a thing.
See David Schley Schaff, Ph.D., *The Life of Philip Schaff* (1897), p. 53.

"The changes made thus far and communicated by you in confidence are judicious and in the right direction... and should contain the germs of the new theology....
"Every age must produce its own theology....
"Such a theology will give new life to the church, and prepare the way for the reunion of Christendom."[64]

Schaff believes that the changes they were creating contained the germs of new theology which would prepare for the reunion of Christendom. Clearly, the goal of Rome is to bring all churches back under her power. The way this is being accomplished is by changing the Scriptures. This is happening while Protestantism sleeps in its Laodicean blindness, continually asserting that all versions are fine and there are no doctrinal differences. At the Parliament of World Religions Philip Schaff said, "There is a unity of Christian scholarship of all creeds.... This unity has been strikingly illustrated in the Anglo-American Revision [Revised Version of 1881] of the Authorized Version [KJV] of the Scriptures."[65]

If there is a unity of creeds in the Revision, clearly theological changes occurred because Schaff also tells us which Bible is incompatible with the Roman Catholic faith: "The Roman Church will never use Luther's Version or King James's Version, and could not do so without endangering her creed."[66]

The Protestant reformers "took the position that the Bible, and the Bible alone, constituted the rule of faith and doctrine, that the word of God is the only unerring guide for human souls, and that it is unnecessary and harmful to take the words of priests and prelates instead of the word of God."[67]

The Dublin Review, an official Catholic newspaper, regarding the release of the *Revised Version* of 1881 declared, "the New Version

---

[64] David Schley Schaff, Ph.D., *The Life of Philip Schaff* (1897), p. 427, 477-478.

[65] John Wesley Hanson, D.D., *World's Congress of Religions: The addresses and papers delivered before the parliament* (Chicago: International Publishing Co., 1894), p. 616.

[66] Philip Schaff, D.D., LL.D., *History of the Christian Church*, Vol. 6 (1916), p. 365.

[67] E. G. White, "Romanism the Religion of Human Nature," *Signs of the Times*, February 19, 1894 p. 243.

will be the death-knell of Protestantism... One thing at least is certain, the Catholic Church will gain by the New Revision, both directly and indirectly. Directly, because old errors are removed from the translation; indirectly, because the 'Bible-only' principle is proved to be false."[68]

Here they boldly assert that errors have been removed and that the 'Bible-only' principle is proved false by the *Revised Version.* Clearly, they believe that changes have been made that are favorable to Rome.

Reverend Thomas S. Preston of St. Ann's Roman Catholic Church of New York writes, "The brief examination which I have been able to make of the Revised Version of the New Testament has convinced me that the Committee have labored with great sincerity and diligence, and that they have produced a translation much more correct than that generally received among Protestants. It is to us a gratification to find that in very many instances they have adopted the reading of the Catholic Version, and have thus by their scholarship confirmed the correctness of our Bible."[69]

In order to have a One World religion, they must create a One World bible that would be acceptable to all religions. But such a bible is not acceptable with God.

"I marvel that ye are so soon removed from him that called you into the grace of Christ unto another gospel: Which is not another; but there be some that trouble you, and would pervert the gospel of Christ. But though we, or an angel from heaven, preach any other gospel unto you than that which we have preached unto you, let him be accursed."[70]

"The difficulties will be removed from the way of those who search the Scriptures with earnest, humble hearts, praying to the Lord for

---

[68] *Dublin Review*, Third Series, Vol. 6, July - October, 1881 (London: Burns & Oates, 1881), p. 143-144.

[69] Reverend Thomas S. Preston, V.G., Letter to the editor, *The Christian Union,* June 8, 1881, p. 545.

[70] Galatians 1:6-8

wisdom. There is to be no cutting out of Scripture, no mutilating the Word, as the Catholics have done. The Bible is to be searched as a whole. The things in it hard to be understood will become plain through the enlightenment of the Holy Spirit."[71]

[71] E. G. White, *Manuscript 132-1898*, par. 4.

6 Fingerprints of the Anti-Christ

Scripture foretold that an anti-Christ power represented by a little horn would arise and "think to change {God's} times and laws."[1] If this power would be so bold as to attempt to change the portion of God's Word written with his own finger, should we be surprised if the same power changes other parts of Scripture?

The Bible gives a very explicit definition of the anti-Christ: "And every spirit that confesseth not that Jesus Christ is come in the flesh is not of God: and this is that spirit of antichrist, whereof ye have heard that it should come; and even now already is it in the world."[2] "For many deceivers are entered into the world, who confess not that Jesus Christ is come in the flesh. This is a deceiver and an antichrist."[3]

Is it possible that the anti-Christ has left his fingerprints on the manuscripts he has tampered with? Would this give us the insight needed to choose the correct Bible in these times of religious pluralism? With careful investigation it is not difficult to find the fingerprints of the anti-Christ. What better place to start looking for evidence than on the very verses that define the anti-Christ? Changing the definition of the anti-Christ would be top priority for that power, so as to avoid detection. Notice the first of the two verses above that identify the anti-Christ:

KJV 1 John 4:3 "And every spirit that confesseth not that Jesus Christ **is come in the flesh** is not of God: and this is that spirit of antichrist, whereof ye have heard that it should come; and even now already is it in the world."

NIV[4] 1 John 4:3 "but every spirit that does not acknowledge Jesus is not from God. This is the spirit of the antichrist, which you have heard is coming and even now is already in the world."[5]

---

[1] Daniel 7:25

[2] 1 John 4:3

[3] 2 John 1:7

[4] The bold portion is missing in the: ASV, CEV, DRB, ERV, ESV, GNB, MSG, NASB, RSV, RV, NWT, etc.

[5] *New International Version* (1978), p. 1316.

The bold portion is missing in many of the modern versions. This omission changes the very definition of anti-Christ from denying that Jesus is come in the flesh to denying the existence of Jesus. Therefore, a power acknowledging Jesus would escape detection as the anti-Christ, even while denying that Jesus Christ came in the flesh. Is this an unintentional blunder that crept into all these versions, or is this a predictable pattern with recognizable fingerprints?

KJV Romans 1:3 "Concerning his Son Jesus Christ our Lord, which was made of the seed of David **according to the flesh**."

MSG Romans 1:3 "on God's Son. His descent from David roots him in history;"[6]

The bold portion is missing in the GS, Moff, TNIV, WNT, etc.

KJV Acts 2:30 "Therefore being a prophet, and knowing that God had sworn with an oath to him, that of the fruit of his loins, **according to the flesh**, he would raise up Christ to sit on his throne."

NIV Acts 2:30 "But he was a prophet and knew that God had promised him on oath that he would place one of his descendants on his throne."[7]

The bold portion is missing in the NASB, ASV, CEV, DRB, ESV, GNB, RV, RSV, NWT, etc.

KJV 1 Peter 4:1 "Forasmuch then as Christ hath suffered for us **in the flesh**, arm yourselves likewise with the same mind: for he that hath suffered in the flesh hath ceased from sin;"

CEV 1 Peter 4:1 "Christ suffered here on earth. Now you must be ready to suffer as he did, because suffering shows that you have stopped sinning."[8]

---

[6] Eugene H. Peterson, M.A., *The Message* (2002), p. 2031.

[7] *New International Version* (1978), p. 1169.

[8] *The Contemporary Parallel New Testament: Contemporary English Version* (New York: Oxford University Press, 1997), p. 1054.

TLB 1 Peter 4:1 "Since Christ suffered and underwent pain, you must have the same attitude he did; you must be ready to suffer, too. For remember, when your body suffers, sin loses its power,"[9]

The bold portion is missing in the NIV, TNIV, GNB, MSG, etc.

This appears to be an intentional and systematic change to a very important Biblical doctrine.[10]

Hebrews 2:9, 14 assures us that Jesus took part in our human nature: "But we see Jesus, who was made a little lower than the angels for the suffering of death, crowned with glory and honour; that he by the grace of God should taste death for every man. "Forasmuch then as the children are partakers of flesh and blood, he also himself likewise took part of the same; that through death he might destroy him that had the power of death, that is, the devil."

"Clad in the vestments of humanity, the Son of God came down to the level of those he wished to save. In him was no guile or sinfulness; he was ever pure and undefiled; yet he took upon him our sinful nature. Clothing his divinity with humanity, that he might associate with fallen humanity, he sought to regain for man that which, by disobedience, Adam had lost for himself and for the world. In his own character he displayed to the world the character of God."[11]

"Though He had no taint of sin upon His character, yet He condescended to connect our fallen human nature with His divinity. By thus taking humanity, He honored humanity. Having taken our fallen nature, he showed what it might become, by accepting the ample provision He has made for it, and by becoming partaker of the divine nature."[12]

---

[9] *The Living Bible* (1978), p. 993.

[10] Also, *The Living Bible* is introducing the papal doctrine of inflicting penance on your body to gain victory over sin.

[11] E. G. White, "The Importance of Obedience," *The Review and Herald, December 15, 1896,* p. 789.

[12] E. G. White, *Selected Messages,* Vol. 3 (Nampa, ID: Pacific Press, 1980), p. 134.2.

"Satan claimed that it was impossible for human beings to keep God's law. In order to prove the falsity of this claim, Christ left His high command, took upon Himself the nature of man, and came to the earth to stand at the head of the fallen race, in order to show that humanity could withstand the temptations of Satan. He became the Head of humanity, to be assaulted with temptations on every point as fallen human nature would be tempted, that He might know how to succor all who are tempted. On this earth He worked out the problem of how to live in accordance with God's standard of right. Bearing our nature, He was true to God's standard of righteousness, gaining the victory over Satan. He was tempted in all points like as we are, yet He was without sin."[13]

Jesus is presented in Scripture as being fully human and fully divine. The combination of humanity and divinity derives from the fact that the Holy Ghost, or Holy Spirit, who is fully divine, was the father of Jesus,[14] at the incarnation; and Mary, fully human, was his mother. If the mother of Jesus did not have a fully human nature, then Jesus did not come in the flesh. This is exactly what the Roman Church insists in their doctrine of the immaculate conception: "the most blessed Virgin Mary in the first instance of her conception... was preserved free from all stain of original sin.... She was created in a condition more sublime and glorious than that of all natures.... Very different from the rest of mankind."[15]

It is the Roman Catholic church that denies that Jesus came in the flesh. Therefore, we must conclude that the changes we observed previously—removing the truth that Jesus came in the flesh—must have been accomplished by the same organization. No one else would stand to benefit from such a modification.

Who would tamper with the mystery of godliness other than the mystery of iniquity?[16]

---

[13] E. G. White, *The Upward Look* (1982), p. 172.3.

[14] Matthew 1:20

[15] Joseph Faà Di Bruno, D.D., *Catholic Belief,* 2nd ed. (London: Ballantyne Press, 1878), p. 200-203.

[16] 2 Thessalonians 2:7

KJV 1 Timothy 3:16[17] "And without controversy great is the mystery of godliness: **God was manifest in the flesh**, justified in the Spirit, seen of angels, preached unto the Gentiles, believed on in the world, received up into glory."

NIV[18] 1 Timothy 3:16 "Beyond all question, the mystery of godliness is great: **He appeared in a body**, was vindicated by the Spirit, was seen by angels, was preached among the nations, was believed on in the world, was taken up in glory."[19]

Appearing in a body is not the same as being manifest in the flesh. Jesus could appear in a body without being made in our flesh, and taking our nature. Once again, the reference to Jesus coming in the flesh has been removed. Although most Christians reading 1 Timothy 3:16 would assume that Jesus is the one referred to, the modern version has also removed the reference to his divinity by simply calling Jesus "he" instead of "God."

The very next verse (which happens to be in the next chapter) is a solemn warning that at the end of time many would be seduced to accept doctrines of devils: "Now the Spirit speaketh expressly, that in the latter times some shall depart from the faith, giving heed to seducing spirits, and doctrines of devils."[20]

It is indisputable that the Jesuit Douay-Rheims bible contains doctrinal changes that favor papal doctrine. For example, the change in Hebrews 11:21 provides rationale for the worship of relics:

KJV Hebrews 11:21 "By faith Jacob, when he was a dying, blessed both the sons of Joseph; and worshipped, leaning upon the top of his staff."

DRB Hebrews 11:21 "By faith, Iacob dying, blessed every one of the sonnes of Ioseph: and adored the toppe of his rodde."[21]

---

[17] The Spirit of Prophecy quotes only the KJV on this verse.

[18] NASB, ASV, CEV, ESV, GNB, ICB ("the secret of our life of worship is great: He was shown to us in a human body"), RV, RSV, NWT, etc. (These change God to He; the flesh is varied).

[19] *New International Version* (1978), p. 1275-1276.

[20] 1 Timothy 4:1

[21] *Rheims New Testament* (Rhemes: John Fogny, 1582), p. 631.

The change in Genesis 3:15 provides the Roman church with an argument for the veneration of Mary, replacing Jesus with "the Virgin" in the Bible's first Messianic prophecy.

KJV Genesis 3:15 "And I will put enmity between thee and the woman, and between thy seed and her seed; it shall bruise thy head, and thou shalt bruise **his** heel."

DRB Genesis 3:15 "I will put enmyties between thee & the woman, & thy seed and the seed of her: **she** shall bruise thy head in pieces, and thou shalt lie in wait of **her** heele."[22]

To demonstrate that this is indeed the meaning intended by this alteration we shall quote one of many Catholic sources that could be cited:

"Not only most holy Mary is queen of heaven and of the saints, but also of hell and the devils, for she has bravely triumphed over them by her virtues. From the beginning of the world God predicted to the infernal serpent the victory and the empire which our queen would obtain over him, when he announced to him that a woman would come into the world who should conquer him. 'I will put enmities between thee and the woman; she shall crush thy head.' And what woman was this enemy if not Mary, who, with her beautiful humility and holy life, always conquered him and destroyed his forces? St. Cyprian affirms that the mother of our Lord Jesus Christ was promised in that woman: and hence he remarks, that God did not use the words I put, but I will put, lest the prophecy should seem to appertain to Eve. He said, I will put enmity between thee and the woman, to signify that this his vanquisher was not the living Eve, but must be another woman descending from her, who was to bring to our first parents greater blessings, as St. Vincent Ferrer says, than those they had lost by their sin. Mary, then, is this great and strong woman who has conquered the devil, and has crushed his head by subduing his pride, as the Lord added: 'She shall crush thy head.' Some of the commentators doubt whether these words refer to Mary or to Jesus Christ, because in the Septuagint version we read: 'He shall crush thy head.' But in our Vulgate, which is the only version approved by the Council of Trent, it is She, and not He. And thus St.

---

[22] *Douay Old Testament* (Douay: John Cousturier, 1635), p. 9-10.

Ambrose, St. Jerome, St. Augustine, St. John Chrysostom, and many others have understood it. However, this may be, it is certain that the Son by means of the mother, or the mother by means of the Son, has vanquished Lucifer; so that this proud spirit, as St. Bernard tells us, has been ignominiously overpowered and crushed by this blessed Virgin. Hence as a slave conquered in war, he is forced always to obey the commands of this queen."[23]

The Douay bible also provides theological changes to support the papal doctrine of transubstantiation.[24]

KJV Matthew 6:11 "Give us this day our daily bread."

DRB Matthew 6:11 "Give us to day our supersubstantial bread."[25]

It is clear that Catholic bibles have inserted changes supporting papal doctrine which should be totally unacceptable to a Protestant. While the changes just shown are too blatant to be introduced into Protestant versions, could it be that more subtle changes have been introduced into modern bibles that also support papal doctrine?

KJV John 6:33 "For the bread of God is **he** which cometh down from heaven."

The King James Version uses the bread of God that cometh down from heaven as a metaphor for Jesus, but several modern versions follow the Jesuit bible and change "he" to "that"[26] to apply the verse to the 'supernatural' bread being transformed by the priest calling down the literal sacrifice of Jesus at the Mass, turning the participants into virtual cannibals.

---

[23] St. Alphonsus Liguori (1696-1787), C.Ss.R., *The Glories of Mary,* trans. from the Italian, New Rev. ed. (New York: P. J. Kennedy & Sons, 1888), p. 155-156.

[24] Transubstantiation is the doctrine that the priest commands Christ to be created in the host (the wafer taken at communion). This doctrine holds that the wafer is literally changed into a different substance; into the real blood and body of Christ.

[25] *Rheims New Testament* (Rhemes: John Fogny, 1582), p. 15.

[26] DRB, GS, NASB, RSV, RV, etc.

In papal doctrine Mary is placed as co-redemptress with Jesus. Her intercession, they say, is needed to make Jesus willing to save us.

Scripture is very clear in Hebrews 1:3 that Jesus "by himself purged our sins..." But, most modern bibles[27] leave out "by himself," leaving room for the doctrine of Mary contributing something to the forgiveness of sins.

The NASB uses particularly Catholic language in Luke 21:5[28] "And while some were talking about the temple, that it was adorned with beautiful stones and **votive** gifts..."[29]

The **KJV** in **2 Peter 2:9** says, "The Lord knoweth how to deliver the godly out of temptations, and to reserve the unjust **unto the day of judgment to be punished**:"

It seems completely reasonable to our sense of justice that the unjust should be reserved unto the day of judgment to be punished. We would not, however, find it acceptable, or fair judicial practice, to punish them before the evidence is heard and the sentence passed.

The NIV puts it this way: 2 Peter 2:9 "if this is so, then the Lord knows how to rescue godly men from trials[30] and to hold the unrighteous **for the day of judgment, while continuing their punishment**."[31]

So here, the unrighteous are being punished while awaiting judgment. This is nothing other than the papal doctrine of purgatory—an intermediate state of punishment to purge the sinner of guilt through the payment of suffering. The same thing is accomplished in modern versions in Luke 1:72-73:

---

27 ASV, CEV, DRB, ERV, GNB, GS, ISV, MSG, NASB, NIV, RSV, RV, WNT, etc.

28 KJV Luke 21:5 "And as some spake of the temple, how it was adorned with goodly stones and gifts, he said,"

29 *New American Standard Bible,* Text ed. (1977), p. 732.

30 Rescuing godly men from trials is also very different than delivering the godly out of temptations.

31 *New International Version* (1978), p. 1312.
NASB, NKJV (reserve unjust under punishment), ASV, CEV, ESV, GNB, ICB ("Lord will hold evil people and punish them, while waiting for the Judgment Day."), RV, RSV, NEB, etc.

KJV Luke 1:72-73 "To perform the mercy **promised** to our fathers, and to remember his holy covenant; The oath which he sware to our father Abraham."

RV Luke 1:72-73 "To shew mercy towards our fathers, And to remember his holy covenant; The oath which he sware unto Abraham our father."[32]

The King James says the mercy God will perform is the mercy **promised** to the fathers. But, the *Revised Version* (and many other modern versions[33]) has God showing mercy to our fathers. Why would God need to show mercy to our fathers (which are now dead) if they were not in purgatory? To demonstrate conclusively that this is the meaning intended in this alteration, we shall turn to a Catholic source, speaking of this verse:

"For the text was one which, if rendered literally, no one could read without being convinced, or at least suspecting, that the 'fathers' already dead needed 'mercy;' and that 'the Lord God of Israel' was prepared 'to perform' it to them. But where were those fathers? Not in heaven, where mercy is swallowed up in joy. And assuredly not in the hell of the damned, where mercy could not reach them. They must therefore be in a place between both, or neither the one or the other. What? In Limbo or Purgatory? Why, certainly. In one or the other..."[34]

KJV James 5:16 "Confess your **faults** one to another, and pray one for another, that ye may be healed. The effectual fervent prayer of a righteous man availeth much."

Most modern bibles change faults to sins.[35] Regarding this verse, Dean Alford says, "It might appear astonishing, were it not notorious,

---

[32] *Revised Version* (London: C.J. Clay and Son, 1885), p. 43.

[33] ASV, DRB, ESV, GNB, TLB, MSG, NASB, etc. The Spirit of Prophecy quotes only KJV.

[34] Tobias Mullen, *The Canon of the Old Testament* (New York: Fr. Pustet & Co., 1892), p. 271, 272.
http://www.eclipseofthechurch.com/Library/Mullen--Canon_of_OT.pdf

[35] ASV, BBE, CEV, DRB, ERV (the wrong things you have done), ESV, GNB, GW, ICB, ISV, LEB, LITV (deviations from the Law), MSG, NASB, NIV, NKJV (trespasses), RSV, RV, etc.

that on this passage among others is built the Romish doctrine of the necessity of confessing sins to a priest."[36] "Confess your sins to God, who only can forgive them, and your faults to one another."[37]

Catholic prayers consist of multiple repetitions of hail Mary's and our Father's which are specifically forbidden in Scripture.

KJV Matthew 6:7 "But when ye pray, use not vain repetitions, as the heathen do: for they think that they shall be heard for their much speaking."

Some modern versions render this:
NIV[38] Matthew 6:7 "And when you pray, do not keep on babbling like pagans, for they think they will be heard because of their many words."[39]

Babbling like pagans, and vain repetitions are most certainly not the same thing. It would be good, perhaps, not to babble like pagans, but who will be convicted of their vain repetitions by this modified verse? A Catholic would say, I don't babble like the pagans. This interpretation removes from Scripture a very strong condemnation of the Catholic method of praying, thereby supporting papal doctrine.

Paul says, in:
KJV Galatians 5:12 "I would they were even cut off which trouble you."

But the NIV says:
NIV Galatians 5:12 "As for those agitators, I wish they would go the whole way and emasculate themselves!"

To emasculate means to castrate. Paul was speaking of circumcision, not castration. Charles Chiniquy in his book *Fifty Years in the Church of Rome* relates an account of the desolation created by the papal doctrine of celibacy: "One day, as I was amusing

---

[36] Henry Alford, D.D., *The Greek Testament,* Vol. 4, New ed. (Boston: Lee and Shepard, Publishers, 1878), p. 328.

[37] E. G. White, *Steps to Christ* (Nampa, ID: Pacific Press, 1892), p. 37.3.

[38] RSV ("heap of empty phrases."), ICB ("They continue saying things that mean nothing").

[39] *New International Version* (1978), p. 1040.

myself, with a few other young friends, near the house of brother Mark, suddenly we saw something covered with blood thrown from the window, and falling at a short distance from us. At the same instant we heard loud cries, evidently coming from the monk's house: 'O my God! Have mercy on me! Save me! I am lost!'....
"Poor brother Mark had ceased to be a man—he had become an eunuch.
"O cruel and Godless church of Rome! How many souls hast thou deceived and tortured! How many hearts hast thou broken with that celibacy which Satan alone could invent!....
"The twenty-five years that I have been a priest of Rome, have revealed to me the fact that the cries of desolation I heard that day, were but the echo of the cries of desolation which go out from almost every nunnery, every parsonage and every house where human beings are bound by the ties of the Romish Celibacy.
"God knows that I am a faithful witness of what my eyes have seen and my ears have heard, when I say to the multitudes which the Church of Rome has bewitched with her enchantments. Wherever there are nuns, monks and priests who live in forced violation of the ways which God has appointed for man to walk in, there are torrents of tears, there are desolated hearts, there are cries of anguish and despair which say in the words of brother Mark:
"Oh! how miserable and wretched I am!"[40]

Another verse modified in modern versions to teach this doctrine of celibacy is also found in the writings of Paul.

KJV 1Corinthians 7:1 "Now concerning the things whereof ye wrote unto me: It is good for a man **not to touch a woman**."

NIV 1Corinthians 7:1 "Now for the matters you wrote about: It is good for a man **not to marry**."

Paul is not saying that a man should never touch a woman, but that a man should not touch a woman other than his wife, for Paul also says, "Marriage is honourable in all, and the bed undefiled: but whoremongers and adulterers God will judge."[41] These are two

---

[40] Charles Chiniquy, *Fifty Years in the Church of Rome*, Thirtieth ed. (Cleveland: Geo. M. Rewell and Co., 1890), p. 16-21.

[41] Hebrews 13:4

totally different doctrines—one the doctrine Scripture, the other the doctrine of devils. "Now the Spirit speaketh expressly, that in the latter times some shall depart from the faith, giving heed to seducing spirits, and doctrines of devils; Speaking lies in hypocrisy; having their conscience seared with a hot iron; Forbidding to marry..."[42]

Several modern versions also support the Catholic doctrine of penance, or self-punishment.

KJV 1 Corinthians 9:27 "But I keep under my body, and bring it into subjection: lest that by any means, when I have preached to others, I myself should be a castaway."

NIV 1Corinthians 9:27 "**No, I beat my body** and make it my slave so that after I have preached to others, I myself will not be disqualified for the prize."

Many modern versions insert the papal doctrine of a priesthood, trying to make it sound like Paul was a priest.

KJV Romans 15:16 "That I should be the minister of Jesus Christ to the Gentiles, **ministering the gospel of God**, that the offering up of the Gentiles might be acceptable, being sanctified by the Holy Ghost."

ESV Romans 15:16 "to be a minister of Christ Jesus to the Gentiles **in the priestly service of the gospel of God**, so that the offering of the Gentiles may be acceptable, sanctified by the Holy Spirit."

The Scripture directly condemns tradition which Catholicism places above the Bible. Modern bibles support this doctrine by removing this rebuke.

KJV 1 Peter 1:18 "Forasmuch as ye know that ye were not redeemed with corruptible things, as silver and gold, from your vain conversation received **by tradition** from your fathers."

---

[42] 1Timothy 4:1-3

NIV 1 Peter 1:18 "For you know that it was not with perishable things such as silver or gold that you were redeemed from the empty way of life handed down to you from your forefathers."

"A prayerful study of the Bible would show Protestants the real character of the papacy and would cause them to abhor and to shun it; but many are so wise in their own conceit that they feel no need of humbly seeking God that they may be led into the truth. Although priding themselves on their enlightenment, they are ignorant both of the Scriptures and of the power of God. They must have some means of quieting their consciences, and they seek that which is least spiritual and humiliating. What they desire is a method of forgetting God which shall pass as a method of remembering Him. The papacy is well adapted to meet the wants of all these. It is prepared for two classes of mankind, embracing nearly the whole world—those who would be saved by their merits, and those who would be saved in their sins. Here is the secret of its power."[43]

It should come as no surprise that there are Catholic leanings in modern bibles, since most of the recent ones openly included Catholic scholars on their translation committees, and the NASB kept secret the names of those serving on the translation committee. Even in the early versions such as the *Revised Version*, where Roman influence was being hidden, the Catholic leanings of lead translators Brooke Foss Westcott and Fenton John Anthony Hort are easily demonstrable.

Hort states, "I have been persuaded for many years that Mary-worship and Jesus-worship have very much in common in their causes and their results."[44] And, "the pure Romish view seems to me nearer, and more likely to lead to, the truth than the Evangelical."[45]

Regarding the death of Westcott, the following was written by the Sunderland Free Church Council, "We recognise [sic], with deep gratitude to the great Head of the Church, the many Christian qualities and eminent graces which were patent to the most casual

---

[43] E. G. White, *The Great Controversy* (1911), p. 572.2.

[44] A. F. Hort, *Life & Letters of Fenton John Anthony Hort,* Vol. 2 (1896), p. 50.

[45] A. F. Hort, *Life & Letters of Fenton John Anthony Hort,* Vol. 1 (1896), p. 76.

observer of the life of Bishop Westcott. His love to Christ, his genuine piety, his reverent manner, **his catholic spirit**, his spiritual instinct, his social interest, his practical help, his ripe scholarship, and his humble bearing, are a few of the traits which were manifest in him, and which call for our praise to God."[46]

The papacy considers freedom of conscience to be heretical. Thus, the freedom of religion that is fundamental to American liberty is simply tolerated until a change can be affected without danger to Catholicism.[47] Hort hated America and the freedoms it stood for. Speaking of the Civil War he said: "While the war lasts, therefore, I fully sympathize with the South.... I care more for England and for Europe than for America, how much more than for all the niggers in the world! and I contend that the highest morality requires me to do so.... it cannot be wrong to desire and pray from the bottom of one's heart that the American Union may be shivered to pieces."[48]

Is this the fine Christian gentleman that you would choose to translate your bible for you?[49]

KJV Matthew 11:12 "And from the days of John the Baptist until now **the kingdom of heaven suffereth violence**, and the violent take it by force."

NIV Mat 11:12 From the days of John the Baptist until now, **the kingdom of heaven has been forcefully advancing**, and forceful men lay hold of it.

---

[46] Arthur Westcott, *The Life and Letters of Brooke Foss Westcott,* Vol. 2 (1903), p. 413.

[47] "Pope Pius IX, in his Encyclical Letter of August 15, 1854, said: 'The absurd and erroneous doctrines or ravings in defense of liberty of conscience are a most pestilential error—a pest, of all others, most to be dreaded in a state.' The same pope, in his Encyclical Letter of December 8, 1864, anathematized 'those who assert the liberty of conscience and of religious worship,' also 'all such as maintain that the church may not employ force'....
"Says Bishop O'Connor: 'Religious liberty is merely endured until the opposite can be carried into effect without peril to the Catholic world.'"
E. G. White, *The Great Controversy* (1911), p. 564.5-565.1.

[48] A. F. Hort, *Life & Letters of Fenton John Anthony Hort,* Vol. 1 (1896), p. 459.

[49] With the exception of Tischendorf and his Codex Sinaiticus, the work of Westcott and Hort on their new Greek text and the Revised Version has probably influenced modern bibles more than any other person or persons. Their work formed the basis for the NU (Nestle-Aland/United Bible Society) Greek text upon which modern bibles are based.

The Bible is speaking of the violence suffered by God's people, such as the death of John the Baptist. But, the NIV and others justify the advancement of Christianity by force. This is directly opposed to the religion of Christ and is therefore the religion of anti-Christ. "God desires from all His creatures the service of love—homage that springs from an intelligent appreciation of His character. He takes no pleasure in a forced allegiance, and to all He grants freedom of will, that they may render Him voluntary service."[50]

Papal doctrine teaches salvation by works, or by your own merits, rather than the merits of Jesus. Modern versions insert this doctrine in a most blatant way.

KJV Revelation 19:8 "And to her was granted that she should be arrayed in fine linen, clean and white: for the fine linen is the **righteousness of saints.**"

The righteousness of the saints is possessed by them, but only because they received it from Jesus. This verse does not violate that truth, or contradict other Scriptures, but in the NKJV[51] it says:

NKJV Revelation 19:8 "And to her it was granted to be arrayed in fine linen, clean and bright, for the fine linen is the **righteous acts of the saints.**"[52]

The fine linen is the righteous acts of the saints? This is directly contradictory to Scripture: "But we are all as an unclean thing, and all our righteousnesses are as filthy rags; and we all do fade as a leaf; and our iniquities, like the wind, have taken us away."[53] The Bible says (which the NKJV also says) that our righteousnesses are as filthy rages, not fine linen. By following papal doctrine in Revelation

---

[50] E. G. White, *The Great Controversy* (1911), p. 493.2.

[51] Also, the ASV, CEV, ESV, GNB, ISV, NIV, RV, etc. The Spirit of Prophecy quotes only KJV as Scripture.

[52] *New King James Version* (1983), p. 1315.

[53] Isaiah 64:6

19:8, the NKJV[54] is entangled in the irrationality of directly contradicting itself in Isaiah 64:6.

Two contradictory statements cannot both be true, therefore one must be false—or a lie. Since the Bible says that God cannot lie,[55] these modern versions, covered with the fingerprints of the anti-Christ, cannot be the true word of God.

---

[54] Since the NKJV is quite different from most modern versions—does not leave out complete verses and claims to be translated from the same text as the KJV—most of another chapter will be devoted to this version.

[55] Titus 1:2

7 The "Original Manuscripts"

Frequently people will say "in the original it says this" or "the originals don't say that" or "the original manuscripts do not have that phrase" or "the original Hebrew" or "the original Greek," etc. Now, it is certainly not a bad thing for scholars who know the Biblical languages to study the Greek and Hebrew manuscripts, or for Bible students that do not know the original languages to use tools such as lexicons or Bible software, that allow them to ponder various meanings of the Hebrew or Greek words. However, to the lay person, statements such as these tend to give an over-inflated perception of the speaker's scholarliness, or intelligence. In fact, to many it gives the impression that somewhere there exists the original copy of the book of Hebrews, for example, signed and notarized by the hand of Paul. There is far too much latitude of meaning in the phrase "original manuscripts." It is not enough to speak of original manuscripts; but one must ask, what "original manuscripts" are we talking about?

You see, the patriarchs, apostles, and prophets, under the inspiration of the Holy Spirit, wrote down the words of sacred Scripture. In the case of the Old Testament, professional scribes made handwritten copies to distribute and preserve the Words of God. In the case of the New Testament, one of the apostles would send a letter to a church, for example, and Christians, who were not professional scribes, but who valued that counsel and wanted to share and preserve it, would make handwritten copies and send them to other churches, who in turn would also make handwritten copies of God's Words. All the while God was making provision for the preservation of his Word by its proliferation—the Holy Spirit guiding in the copying process and protecting the distribution of Scripture.

As far as we know, we may not have any copy of Scripture that is the actual original copy written by the apostle or prophet himself.[1] Even if we did, how would we recognize it as such? No one today would recognize Paul's handwriting, or signature, for example. This does not mean that we cannot be sure of having the preserved Word of God. He promised that not only did he originate an infallible message

[1] See sub-chapter "Frauds and Forgeries" regarding a manuscript of Matthew that could be original.

in his Word, but that he would protect and preserve that Word uncorrupted. The very fact that we have hundreds and even thousands of copies of Scripture that all agree, (and are even practically identical), from scores of locations and in many languages, bears witness to the accuracy of the preservation of the Word of God. 1 Peter 1:23 says, "Being born again, not of corruptible seed, but of incorruptible, by the word of God, which liveth and abideth for ever." The word of God, the Bible says, is incorruptible seed, which lives and abides forever. That means his Word is eternal and infallible.

In the meantime, Satan set about to destroy the word of God. "I saw that God had especially guarded the Bible; **yet when copies of it were few, learned men had in some instances changed the words**, thinking that they were making it more plain, when in reality they were mystifying that which was plain, by causing it to lean to their established views, which were governed by tradition. But I saw that the Word of God, as a whole, is a perfect chain, one portion linking into and explaining another. True seekers for truth need not err; for not only is the Word of God plain and simple in declaring the way of life, but the Holy Spirit is given as a guide in understanding the way to life therein revealed."[2]

Dean[3] Burgon, speaking of the Vatican, Sinaitic, and Beza manuscripts, "solemnly assures us, and 'without a particle of hesitation, that they are three of the most scandalously corrupt copies extant;' that they 'exhibit the most shamefully mutilated texts which are anywhere to be met with;' that they 'have become... the depositaries of the largest amount of fabricated readings, ancient blunders, and intentional perversion of truth, which are discoverable in any known copies of the Word of God.'"[4]

Clearly, intentional changes have occurred in some manuscripts. Indeed, this is what we previously observed Paul telling us was

---

[2] E. G. White, *Early Writings* (1882), p. 220.2.

[3] "Dean" is his title, not his first name, which is John.

[4] Philip Mauro, *Which Version? Authorized or Revised?* (Boston: Scripture of Truth Depot, 1924), p. 48-49.

happening in his day.[5] Paul even went so far as to imply that someone might attempt to counterfeit a letter from him.[6] He instructed the Thessalonians not even to believe a letter purporting to be from him if it claimed that Jesus was coming in their day.

The question would naturally follow: which manuscripts have been preserved, and which have been tampered with? Let us begin with some basics as we answer this question.

Today the word manuscript often means an unpublished book even though that book may exist only on a computer and is therefore not handwritten. However, the word manuscript, in reference to historical copies of Scripture means handwritten. Manu– comes from the word manual—by hand; script, meaning writing. Thus, we see that these copies of Scripture were hand copied before the advent of printing. It was a time-consuming, painstaking effort to proliferate Scripture in this manner, but God had promised to protect and preserve his Word.

Manuscripts are divided by scholars according to the type of writing used. Uncial manuscripts are those written in an all capital style of Greek writing. This style of writing is supposed to be older than the miniscules which is more like a cursive style of Greek writing. The Hebrew manuscripts do not have all-caps or cursive styles of writing. Of course, the Old Testament was originally written in Hebrew (with the exception of Daniel 2:4-7:28, and some portions of Ezra, which were written in Aramaic); and the New Testament was originally written in Greek. Besides the manuscripts that contained only Scripture, there are also lectionary manuscripts, which were lesson books, containing commentary on the verses, hymns, and Scripture readings. The verses quoted in the lectionaries can be compared in wording to the verses from the other manuscripts. In fact, Bible verses are so widely quoted in them that almost the entire New

---

[5] 2 Corinthians 2:17 "For we are not as many, which corrupt the word of God: but as of sincerity, but as of God, in the sight of God speak we in Christ."

[6] 1 Thessalonians 2:1-3 "Now we beseech you, brethren, by the coming of our Lord Jesus Christ, and by our gathering together unto him, That ye be not soon shaken in mind, or be troubled, neither by spirit, nor by word, nor by letter as from us, as that the day of Christ is at hand. Let no man deceive you by any means: for that day shall not come, except there come a falling away first, and that man of sin be revealed, the son of perdition."

Testament could be compiled from the lectionaries. The papyri are manuscripts that came from Egypt where the paper was made from papyrus reed rather than vellum which came from animal skins. Scholars also divide manuscripts into families with those manuscripts having similar textual characteristics sharing the same family. Generally, manuscripts are divided into three families:[7]

1. Traditional texts (also called the Majority Text, Byzantine Text, or later, Textus Receptus or the Received Text, and Masoretic Text for the Hebrew)[8];
2. Alexandrian texts;
3. Western texts.

The majority text is so-named, because it comprises over 5000 manuscripts, which is by far the bulk of all extant manuscripts; and it is called Traditional, because it was the most commonly used through the centuries,[9] right up until 1881.[10] The Alexandrian manuscripts are named this because they came from Alexandria, Egypt. The Western texts are those that originated in Rome.

Scholars often lump the Western and the Alexandrian texts together, calling them collectively, the Critical Text, because these are the texts that contain the most variations, and are therefore used for higher critical interpretations which claim to reconstruct what was really said in the originals. Interestingly, there are only a few dozen manuscripts that make up these two classifications.

---

[7] "Some include a fourth family called Caesarean, but other scholars say this is not a separate family, but part of the Alexandrian, or a mixture of Alexandrian/Western. Pamphilus and Eusebius, two of the Gnostic philosophers from Alexandria, founded the library of Caesarea, bringing with them biblical writings, patristic writings, and Origen's works."
Thomas Holland, Th.D., *Crowned with Glory: The Bible from Ancient Text to Authorized Version* (San Jose: Writers Club Press, 2000), p. 10, 33-34.

[8] Sometimes the early copies of this text-type are also called Constantinopolitan or Antiochian.

[9] Except in Roman Catholicism.

[10] In 1881 the Revised Version was published based almost exclusively on the two Alexandrian manuscripts—Vaticanus and Siniaiticus. Since then, almost all versions have followed the same pattern.

Manuscript Families[11]

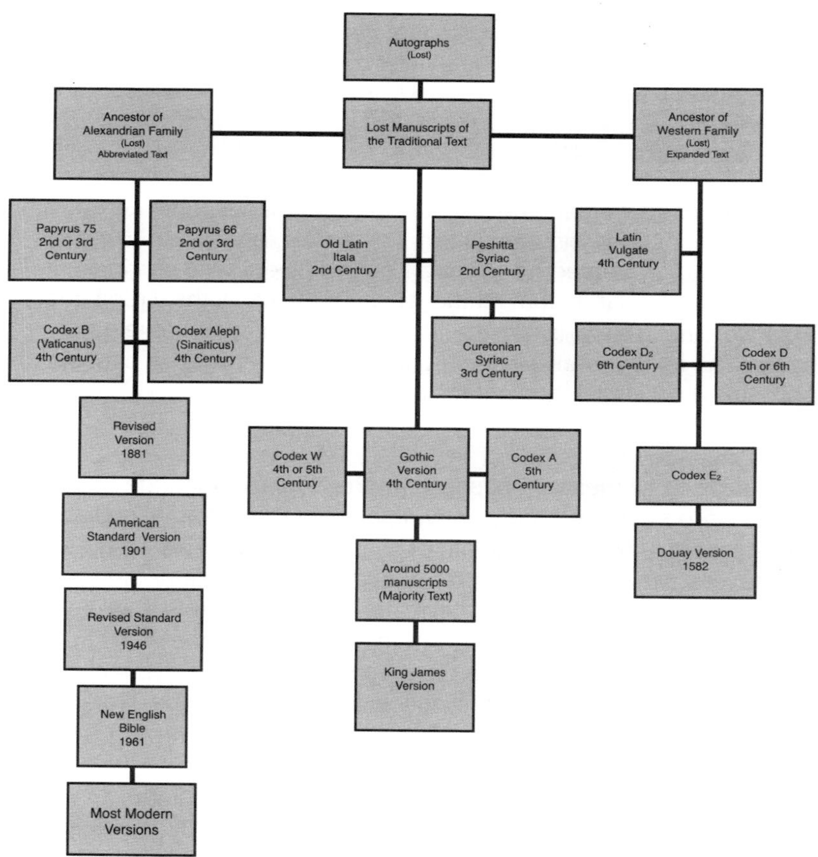

[11] *Total Onslaught: The Battle of the Bibles,* Walter Veith, Ph.D., (Amazing Discoveries, 2004), 4:00, http://amazingdiscoveries.tv/media/125/213-battle-of-the-bibles/

To give them the benefit of the doubt, we will combine the Western and the Alexandrian texts together, into the Critical Text,[12] in the following chart:

	Total	Traditional	Critical	% Traditional
Papyri	88	75	13	85%
Uncials	267	258	9	97%
Minuscules	2,764	2,741	23	99%
Lectionaries	2,143	2,143	0	100%
	5,262	**5,217**	**45**	**99%**[13]

From this chart we can see that fully 99% of manuscripts agree with the traditional text, and only about 1% are Alexandrian or Western. Clearly God preserved his Word as he promised. One striking feature of this chart is that all the lectionaries follow the Traditional Text wording. This tells us what the early church used on a daily basis. The texts that were being corrupted were forged in schools of philosophy by infidel theologians and did not come into wide use until much later.

In addition to all these manuscripts in the original language, many Bibles were translated, very early, into several ancient languages, some probably before the death of all the apostles. This included the Syriac Peshitta, the Curetonian Syriac, the Vetus Itala or old Latin (not to be confused with the later Latin Vulgate of the Catholic church), Ulfilas Gothic (early German), the 1,244 Armenian manuscripts, the Ethiopic, the Georgian, the Coptic (Egyptian), and the Slavonic, which all primarily follow the wording of the Traditional Text.[14]

Would it make more sense for God to preserve 99% of the manuscripts, or only 1%? This clearly begins to answer the question

---

[12] "It was from this type of manuscript that Jerome translated the Latin Vulgate which became the authorized Catholic Bible for all time."
B.G. Wilkinson, Ph.D., *Our Authorized Bible Vindicated* (1930; Facsimile Repr., New York: Teach Services, 2006), p. 22.

[13] D.A. Waite, Th.D., Ph.D., *Defending the King James Bible, A Fourfold Superiority: Texts, Translators, Technique, Theology*, 3rd ed. (Collingswood, NJ: The Bible for Today, 2006), p. 56.

[14] Bruce Metzger, Ph.D., *The Early Versions of the New Testament* (New York: Oxford University Press, 1977), p. 324-327.

of which manuscripts have been preserved and which have been altered.[15]

However, the most powerful clue as to which manuscripts were corrupted comes from the prophetic framework of the Bible itself. As we discussed in the chapter "God Knew All Along," the Bible outlines, in advance, identification marks of a "little horn" power that would even think to change God's laws.[16] This power, which for centuries, made war upon the word of God, is the prime suspect for the introduction of changes favorable to its doctrine.

Therefore, one would not look for an uncorrupted Bible among the Western manuscripts, as these came from Rome, the capital city of the little horn power.[17] This power, in fact, claims that their Latin Vulgate translation is better than the original Greek manuscripts. "The Council of Trent had declared the Vulgate 'not only better than all other Latin translations, but better than the Greek text itself in those places where they disagree.'"[18]

We still have available William Fulke's defence of the Protestant Bible, which is now over 400 years old (first printed in 1583): "What your vulgar Latin translation hath left out in the latter end of the Lord's prayer in St. Matthew, and in the beginning and midst of St. Luke, whereby that heavenly prayer is made imperfect, not comprehending all things that a Christian man ought to pray for,

---

[15] Although God miraculously preserved his Word, there were times in history when Satan very nearly succeeded in accomplishing its eradication. "I was shown a time when Satan especially triumphed. Multitudes of Christians were slain in a dreadful manner, because they would preserve the purity of their religion. The Bible was hated, and efforts were made to rid the earth of it. The people were forbidden to read it, on pain of death; and all the copies which could be found were burned. But I saw that God had a special care for His Word. He protected it. **At different periods there were but a very few copies of the Bible in existence**, yet He would not suffer His Word to be lost, for in the last days copies of it were to be so multiplied that every family could possess it. I saw that when there were but few copies of the Bible, it was precious and comforting to the persecuted followers of Jesus. It was read in the most secret manner, and those who had this exalted privilege felt that they had had an interview with God, with His Son Jesus, and with His disciples. But this blessed privilege cost many of them their lives. If discovered, they were taken to the headsman's block, to the stake, or to the dungeon to die of starvation."
E. G. White, *Early Writings* (1882), p. 214.2.

[16] See Daniel 7.

[17] The Latin Vulgate is the major manuscript in this category.

[18] Benson Bobrick, Ph.D., *Wide as the Waters, The Story of the English Bible and the Revolution it Inspired* (New York: Simon & Schuster, 2001), p. 189-190.

besides many other like omissions, whether of purpose, or of negligence, and injury of time, yet still by you defended, I spare to speak of in this place."[19]

During the Protestant reformation, wars were fought and people gave their lives over the issue of which Bible manuscripts were correct. Protestants unanimously rejected the Latin Vulgate because of its corruptions. "Wycliffe's Bible had been translated from the Latin text [Latin Vulgate], **which contained many errors**. It had never been printed, and the cost of manuscript copies was so great that few but wealthy men or nobles could procure it; and, furthermore, being strictly proscribed by the church, it had had a comparatively narrow circulation."[20]

We would also not expect to find uncorrupted copies of Scripture in Alexandria. The early Christian church had its headquarters at Antioch, not Alexandria. In fact, Alexandria was the center of the pagan philosophy of Gnosticism, which today we would call spiritism or occultism.

"Christianity was to enter a new field through the leadership of Paul, strong herald of the cross. In Antioch, the capital of the Roman province of Syria, was to be found a new center for the gospel. When Jerusalem, the original headquarters, was destroyed, the leadership passed to Antioch, where it remained for some time."[21] Antioch and Alexandria were always antagonists, Antioch having no sympathy for Alexandria's mystical interpretations of Scripture.[22] Interestingly, the Alexandrian manuscripts are really Catholic manuscripts. The two main manuscripts from the Alexandrian family are the Codex

---

19 William Fulke, D.D., *A Defence of the Sincere and True Translations of the Holy Scriptures* (London: Henrie Bynneman, 1583), p. 57-58.

20 E. G. White, *The Great Controversy* (1911), p. 245.2.

21 B.G. Wilkinson, Ph.D., *Truth Triumphant: The Church in the Wilderness* (Mountain View, CA: Pacific Press, 1944), p. 23.

22 "In the great christological controversies of the fourth and following centuries Alexandria and Antioch were always antagonists, Alexandria representing a mystical transcendentalism and promoting the allegorical interpretation of the Scriptures; Antioch insisting on the grammatico-historical interpretation of the Scriptures, and having no sympathy with mystical modes of thought." Albert Henry Newman, *A Manual of Church History*, Vol. 1 (Philadelphia: American Baptist Publication Society, 1900), p. 297.

Vaticanus and the Codex Sinaiticus. The Vaticanus is so named because it was discovered in the Vatican library around 1475,[23] just in time to counter the Protestant reformation.

"The fall of Constantinople before the armies of the Moslem Turks opened to Western Europe the empire's libraries with their thousands of manuscripts. The nations west of Constantinople awoke from the sleep of centuries. For nearly a thousand years the ecclesiastical power of Rome had eliminated the study of Greek language and literature. 'Knowledge of the Greek language died out in Western Europe....'
"The greatest treasure accruing to the world by the fall of Constantinople was the recovery of multiplied manuscripts of the Greek New Testament. The vast majority of these manuscripts were the Received Text. Having had only the Latin Bible of Rome, called the Vulgate, the western world in general lacked the exact words written by the apostles of the revelations of Jesus."[24]

The reformation begun by John Wycliffe,[25] already underway for over 70 years, was stirring a desire for a knowledge of Scripture. The reception of ancient Greek manuscripts of the New Testament, in Western Europe, from those fleeing the invasion of the Turks into Constantinople in 1453, made obvious the corruptions of the Latin Vulgate. Suddenly the papacy had need of a Greek manuscript that agreed better with their Latin translation. Within 25 years the Vatican manuscript was listed in the Vatican library. "Frauds and forgeries to advance the power and prosperity of the church have in all ages been esteemed lawful by the papal hierarchy."[26] Dr. Scot McKendrick the Head of Western Manuscripts, British Library, London, commenting on the appearance of the Vatican manuscript for a 2012 documentary film, said, "Vaticanus has a very strange appearance. When you look at it as a manuscript expert, although you know that people tell you that it's a fourth century manuscript, it

---

[23] The earliest record of the Codex Vaticanus is 1475 when it was listed in the Vatican library's catalog.
Tares Among the Wheat, directed by Christian J. Pinto (Adullam Films, LLC, 2012), 2:25:40.

[24] B.G. Wilkinson, Ph.D., *Truth Triumphant: The Church in the Wilderness* (1944), p. 383, 384.

[25] John Wycliffe lived 1323-1384.

[26] E. G. White, *The Great Controversy* (1911), p. 576.1.

actually looks like a fifteenth century manuscript, and there's one very simple reason for that, is that almost the entire text has been over-written by a fifteenth century scribe. Not only that, he's added in fifteenth century decoration, titling and so forth, so it has a very strange appearance."[27]

"It is easy to understand why the Codex Vaticanus would be cherished at the Vatican; for its corruptions are what make it valuable to the leaders of the papal system."[28]

Even if this manuscript is from the early fourth century as many scholars claim—one of Eusebius' fifty bibles, commissioned by Constantine—this was the time of greatest compromise with paganism, accomplished primarily by these two men. "The nominal conversion of Constantine, in the early part of the fourth century, caused great rejoicing; and the world, cloaked with a form of righteousness, walked into the church. Now the work of corruption rapidly progressed. Paganism, while appearing to be vanquished, became the conqueror. Her spirit controlled the church. Her doctrines, ceremonies, and superstitions were incorporated into the faith and worship of the professed followers of Christ."[29] Early Christianity was based solely on Scripture; therefore, a new bible would be one way to accomplish the insertion of paganism into Christianity, on this scale.

The Codex Sinaiticus was named for its discovery on the traditional Mt. Sinai. This sounds orthodox until you realize that the traditional Mt. Sinai is not the true Mt. Sinai; since Scripture says that Mt. Sinai is in Arabia.[30] The traditional site of Sinai is most certainly not in Arabia. Second, the location of its discovery on traditional Mt. Sinai was in a Catholic monastery.[31]

---

[27] *Tares Among the Wheat*, directed by Christian J. Pinto (2012), 2:24:27-2:25:40.

[28] Philip Mauro, *Which Version? Authorized or Revised?* (1924), p. 50.

[29] E. G. White, *The Great Controversy* (1911), p. 49.2.

[30] Galatians 4:25

[31] B.G. Wilkinson, Ph.D., *Our Authorized Bible Vindicated* (1930), p. 255.
Apparently, this historical connection of St. Catherine's Monastery with Catholicism is in the process of being rewritten as most modern sources refer to St. Catherine's as an Orthodox Monastery.

To demonstrate further that the Catholic church endorses the Sinaitic manuscript (after having spent more than a thousand years trying to destroy the Bible), Pope Gregory XVI, wrote an autograph letter to Constantin von Tischendorf, the discoverer of the manuscript, extolling its virtue: "In the meantime he [Tischendorf] had discovered the Sinaitic manuscript, and it had been published in sumptuous form under the patronage of the Czar, and a copy had been presented to the Pope. The latter wrote an autograph letter to Tischendorf, 'in which he expressed his highest appreciation, yes, his admiration of this publication.'"[32]

"Dean Burgon, whom we shall have occasion to quote largely because of his mastery of the entire subject, after having spent five and a half years 'laboriously collating the five old uncials throughout the Gospels,' declared at the completion of his prodigious task that— 'So manifest are the disfigurements jointly and exclusively exhibited by the two codices (Vatican and Sinaitic) that, instead of accepting them as two independent witnesses to the inspired original, we are constrained to regard them as little more than a single reproduction of one and the same scandalously corrupt and comparatively late copy.'"[33]

"The impurity of the text exhibited by these codices is not a question of opinion, but of fact... In the Gospels alone Codex B (Vatican) leaves out words or whole clauses no less than 1,491 times. It bears traces of careless transcription on every page. Codex Sinaiticus [Aleph] abounds with errors of the eye and pen.... On many occasions 10, 20, 30, 40 words are dropped through very carelessness. Letters and words, even whole sentences, are frequently written twice over, or begun and immediately cancelled; while that gross blunder, whereby a clause is omitted because it happens to end in the same words as the clause preceding, occurs no less than 115 times in the New Testament."[34]

---

[32] George E. Merrill, D.D., *The Story Of The Manuscripts* (Boston: Boston Stereotype Foundry, 1881), p. 75.

[33] Philip Mauro, *Which Version? Authorized or Revised?* (1924), p. 41-42.

[34] *Ibid.*, p. 151.

Even *Wikipedia* says, “Compared to Alexandrian text-type manuscripts, the distinct Byzantine readings tend to show a greater tendency toward smooth and well-formed Greek, they display fewer instances of textual variation between parallel Synoptic Gospel passages, and they are less likely to present contradictory or ‘difficult’ issues of exegesis.”[35]

Princeton Professor, Bruce Metzger, in speaking of the Sinaitic manuscript says: “In the light of such carelessness in transcription, it is not surprising that a good many correctors (apparently as many as nine) have been at work on the manuscript.... Tischendorf's edition of the manuscript enumerates some 14,800 places where some alteration has been made to the text.... By the use of the ultra-violet lamp, Milne and Skeat discovered that the original reading in the manuscript was erased at a few places and another written in its same place by the same scribe.”[36]

The problem is that almost all modern versions are translated from Westcott and Hort's Greek text, for the early ones; and the Nestle-Aland (abbreviated NU, which stands for Nestle-Aland/United Bible Society) for the later ones. Both these published Greek texts follow, almost exclusively, the Codex Sinaiticus and Codex Vaticanus. The Nestle-Aland also closely follows the Westcott and Hort Greek text.

Nestle states that “the Vatican manuscript is to be preferred above every other manuscript.”[37] “Canon Cook in his book *Revised Version of the First Three Gospels*, says,... ‘The Vatican Codex, sometimes alone, but generally in accord with the Sinaitic, is responsible for nine-tenths of the most striking innovations of the R.V. [Revised Version]’”[38] “The Westcott and Hort text is substantially the Roman Catholic Vaticanus (B). No Bible student has ever handled it except private Catholic scribes.”[39]

---

[35] http://en.wikipedia.org/wiki/Byzantine_text-type Retrieved 2-4-2015.

[36] Bruce Metzger, Ph.D., *Manuscripts of the Greek Bible: An Introduction to Palaeography* (Oxford: Oxford University Press, 1981), p. 77.

[37] Peter Ruckman, Ph.D., *The Christian Handbook of Manuscript Evidence* (Pensacola, FL: Pensacola Bible Press, 1970), p. 25.

[38] Philip Mauro, *Which Version? Authorized or Revised?* (1924), p. 66-67.

[39] Peter Ruckman, Ph.D., *The Christian Handbook of Manuscript Evidence* (1970), p. 24.

Codex Vaticanus and Sinaiticus[40] are the primary authorities scholars appeal to for the missing verses, and indeed, most departures from the wording of the King James Bible.

Tischendorf explained the intention of supplanting the Textus Receptus: "we have at last hit upon a better plan... which is to set aside this *textus receptus* altogether, and to construct a fresh text."[41] One wonders who the "we" are since this plan was not realized by Tischendorf, but by Westcott and Hort two decades later.

"The recent printed editions of the Greek New Testament [NU], which we can buy, give a text which never existed as a manuscript of the New Testament. They are all reconstructions based on their editor's choice of readings from manuscripts they had at their disposal, or which they elected to concentrate on."[42]

John Burgon, a contemporary of Westcott and Hort and one of the foremost textual scholars of the day, in speaking of their new Greek text, stated, "Who was to imagine that an utterly untrustworthy new Greek Text, constructed on mistaken principles,—(say rather, on no principles at all,)—would be the fatal result? To speak more truly, who could have anticipated that the opportunity would have been adroitly seized to inflict upon the Church the text of Drs. Westcott and Hort, in all its essential features,—a text which, as will be found elsewhere largely explained, we hold to be the most vicious recension of the original Greek in existence..... it was deliberately invented.
"Who will venture to predict the amount of mischief which must follow, if the New Greek Text which has been put forth by the men who were appointed to revise the English Authorized Version, should become used in our Schools and in our Colleges."[43]

---

[40] Along with the less frequently used Codex Alexandrinus, another Alexandrian manuscript.

[41] Constantin von Tischendorf, Ph.D., *When Were Our Gospels Written?* (1866), p. 21.

[42] J. K. Elliott, "The Original Text of the Greek New Testament," *Fax Theologica* 8 (1988), p. 6. As cited in William Einwechter, Th.M., *English Bible Translations: By What Standard?* (Pensacola, FL: Chapel Library, 2010). p. 31.
http://www.chapellibrary.org/files/5014/0485/0884/ebtb.pdf

[43] John William Burgon, B.D., *The Revision Revised* (1883), p. 114, 273, 345.

Remember that the two manuscripts (Vaticanus and Sinaiticus), which scholars call the oldest and best, and on which Westcott and Hort based their new Greek text, were lost to the world for more than one thousand, and almost fifteen hundred years, respectively. If these two manuscripts represent God's pure Word, "then God's church was without His word for the greatest portion of its existence. How could anyone, except those with Roman Catholic sympathies, accept such a ludicrous notion that God allowed His word to be lost for nearly 1,500 years, after which He handed it over to the Pope for safekeeping?"[44]

The King James Bible, on the other hand, is based on the Textus Receptus, which is the text used by all Christians (except the

---

[44] Joe Gresham, *Dealing with the Devil's Deception: How to Choose a Bible* (2001), p. 35.

Catholic church) since the days of the Apostles.[45]

"Fundamentally there are only two streams of Bibles. The first stream which carried the Received Text in Hebrew and Greek, began with the Apostolic churches, and reappearing at intervals down the Christian Era among enlightened believers, was protected by the wisdom and scholarship of the pure church in her different phases; by such as the church at Pella in Palestine where the Christians fled, when in A.D. 70 the Romans destroyed Jerusalem; by the Syrian Church of Antioch which produced eminent scholarship; by the Italic Church in northern Italy; and also at the same time by the Gallic

---

[45] **The Majority Text's use in History**

1. All Apostolic Churches
2. Churches in Palestine
3. Syrian church at Antioch
4. The Peshitta Syriac Version (A.D. 150) was based on it
5. Papyrus #75
6. Itallic church of Northern Italy (A.D. 150)
7. Gallic church of Southern France (A.D. 177)
8. Celtic church of Great Britain
9. Churches of Scotland and Ireland
10. Pre-Waldensian churches
11. Waldensian churches (A.D. 120 - 1700's)
12. Gothic Version of the fourth century
13. Codex W of Matthew from 4th or 5th century was based on this text
14. Gospels of Codex A from the 1st century
15. Majority of all NT manuscript (99%) are of this type.
16. Greek Orthodox church used this text.
17. Greek Orthodox church still uses this text and rejects the critical text.
18. All churches of reformation used this text.
19. Erasmus 1516
20. Complutensian Polyglot Bible of 1522
21. Luther's German Bible
22. Tyndale's Bible (1525)
23. Olivetan's French Bible (1535)
24. Coverdale's Bible (1535)
25. Matthew's Bible (1537)
26. Tavener's Bible (1539)
27. The Great Bible (1539-1541)
28. The Stephanus Greek New Testament (1546-1551)
29. The Geneva Bible (1557-1560)
30. The Bishop's Bible (1568)
31. Spanish Version (1569)
32. Beza Greek New Testament (1598)
33. Czech version (1602)
34. Italian version of Diodati (1607)
35. King James Version (1611)
36. Elzevir Greek New Testament (1624)
37. The Received text is the text that has survived in continuity from the very beginning of the New Testament.

D.A. Waite, Th.D., Ph.D., *Defending the King James Bible, A Fourfold Superiority* (2006), p. 45-48.

Church in southern France and by the Celtic Church in Great Britain; by the pre-Waldensian, the Waldensian, and the churches of the Reformation. This first stream appears, with very little change, in the Protestant Bibles of many languages, and in English, in that Bible known as the King James Version, the one which has been in use for three hundred years [over 400 now] in the English speaking world. These [manuscripts] have in agreement with them, by far the vast majority of numbers. So vast is this majority that even the enemies of the Received Text admit that nineteen-twentieths and some ninety-nine one-hundredths of all Greek [manuscripts] are for the Received Text.

"The second stream is a small one of a very few [manuscripts]. These last manuscripts are represented:

(a) In Greek:–The Vatican MS., or Codex B, in the library at Rome; and the Sinaitic, or Codex Aleph, its brother [in the Russian Museum in Moscow].

(b) In Latin:– The Vulgate or Latin Bible of Jerome.

(c) In English:– The Jesuit Bible of 1582, which later with vast changes is seen in the Douay, or Catholic Bible.

(d) In English again:– In many modern Bibles which introduce practically all the Catholic readings of the Latin Vulgate which were rejected by the Protestants of the Reformation; among these, prominently, are the Revised Versions."[46]

Perhaps, the next time you hear someone referring to the "original manuscripts" you may want to politely inquire to which "originals" he refers.

[46] B.G. Wilkinson, Ph.D., *Our Authorized Bible Vindicated* (1930), p. 12, 13.

8 The Canon, the Apocrypha, and the Septuagint

The Canon[1]

Since the Catholic Church claims to be the universal church, they profess to be the organization that has given us the Bible. This claim is completely false; in fact, exactly the opposite is true. It was this power that for centuries tried to eradicate the Bible and keep people from owning, understanding, or reading Scripture.[2] Speaking of the Catholic Church, the famous protestant reformer and Bible translator, William Tyndale said, "Far from having given us the Scriptures, it is you who have hidden them from us; it is you who burn those who teach them, and if you could, you would burn the Scriptures themselves."[3] Even the most cursory knowledge of history will reveal this, despite the fact that history is often suppressed, or even re-written. Though many would not agree that the papacy preserved Scripture for us, yet even in Protestant schools it is oft repeated that the Bible was compiled through a messy process of church councils in which it was determined what would be included and what would be left out of the Bible. While it is true that there were church councils (Catholic church councils) that voted additional books (which we call the Apocrypha[4] today) into their bible, this is not how

---

[1] Canon: the list or collection of sacred books accepted as genuine.

[2] "Satan had urged on the papal priests and prelates to bury the word of truth beneath the rubbish of error, heresy, and superstition; but in a most wonderful manner it was preserved uncorrupted through all the ages of darkness."
E. G. White, *The Great Controversy* (1911), p. 69.2.

[3] J. H. Merle D'Aubigne, D.D., *History of the Reformation of the Sixteenth Century,* Vol. 5 (Edinburgh: Oliver and Boyd, 1853) p. 180.

[4] The reasons the Apocryphal books cannot be a part of Scripture are as follows: "1. Not one of them is in the Hebrew language, which was alone used by the inspired historians and poets of the Old Testament. 2. Not one of the writers lays any claim to inspiration. 3. These books were never acknowledged sacred Scriptures by the Jewish Church, and therefore were never sanctioned by our Lord. 4. They were not allowed a place among the sacred books, during the first four centuries of the Christian Church. 5. They contain fabulous statements, and statements which contradict not only the canonical Scriptures, but also themselves; as when, in the two Books of Maccabees, Antiochus Epiphanes is made to die three different deaths in as many different places. 6. It inculcates doctrines at variance with the Bible, such as prayers for the dead and sinless perfection. 7. It teaches immoral practices, such as lying, suicide, assassination, and magical incantation. For these and other reasons, the Apocryphal books, which are all in Greek, except one which is extant only in Latin, are valuable only as ancient documents, illustrative of the manners, language, opinions and history of the East."
Alexander McClure, *The Translators Revived; A Biographical Memoir of the Authors of the English Version of the Holy Bible* (New York: Charles Scribner, 1853), p. 186-187.

the Bible was compiled. Scripture itself testifies internally to the validity and composition of the canon.

"For the prophecy came not in old time by the will of man: but holy men of God spake as they were moved by the Holy Ghost."[5] It was not the will of man that brought forth the words of Scripture and therefore is most certainly not the will of man that preserves or compiles the books of Scripture. All this was under the control and therefore the foreknowledge of God Almighty. "For this cause also," Paul says, "thank we God without ceasing, because, when ye received the word of God which ye heard of us, ye received it not as the word of men, but as it is in truth, the word of God...."[6] It is the word of God, not the word of men.

Scripture declares that the oracles of God were committed to the Jews. The books of Scripture were communicated to us, by God, through Jewish writers.[7] "What advantage then hath the Jew? or what profit is there of circumcision? Much every way: chiefly, because that **unto them were committed the oracles of God**."[8]

At the time the New Testament was being written, the Old Testament canon was already established as Scripture and even referred to as the Old Testament. "But their minds were blinded: for until this day remaineth the same veil untaken away in the reading of the old testament; which veil is done away in Christ."[9] Therefore the New Testament writers understood that their writings were composing the New Testament.

Jesus himself refers to the three sections that made up the Hebrew Old Testament, or Tanakh: "And he said unto them, These are the words which I spake unto you, while I was yet with you, that all things

---

[5] 2 Peter 1:21

[6] 1 Thessalonians 2:13

[7] **"When God's written word was given through the Hebrew prophets**, Satan studied with diligence the messages concerning the Messiah."
E. G. White, *Prophets and Kings* (Nampa, ID: Pacific Press, 1917), p. 686.1.

[8] Romans 3:1-2

[9] 2 Corinthians 3:14

Torah (Five Books of Moses)
Genesis
Exodus
Leviticus
Numbers
Deuteronomy
Nevi'im (Prophets)
Joshua
Judges
Samuel (1st + 2nd)
Kings (1st + 2nd)
Isaiah
Jeremiah
Ezekiel
The 12 Minor Prophets:
Hosea
Joel
Amos
Obadiah
Jonah
Micah
Nahum
Habakkuk
Zephaniah
Haggai
Zechariah
Malachi

Ketuvim (Writings)
Psalms
Proverbs
Job
Song of Songs
Ruth
Lamentations
Ecclesiastes
Esther
Daniel
Ezra + Nehemiah
Chronicles (1st + 2nd)

must be fulfilled, which were written in the **law of Moses**, and in **the prophets**, and in **the psalms**, concerning me."[10]

The Hebrew Old Testament consisted first of the books (or law) of Moses, second the prophets, and finally the psalms (or writings).

The Tanakh is an acronym for these three divisions, first the Torah, or first five books of Moses, second the Nevi'im or prophets, and third the Ketuvim or writings.

It is popular to claim that the Bible that Jesus used was a Greek translation of the original Hebrew, since the common trade language at the time was Greek. The above statement from Jesus disproves this idea since the Greek translation does not have the three divisions of the Hebrew Bible. Jesus was referring to the Hebrew Scriptures.

In Matthew 5:18 Jesus says, "For verily I say unto you, Till heaven and earth pass, one jot or one tittle shall in no wise pass from the law, till all be fulfilled." The jot and the tittle are the smallest marks of Hebrew characters. Once again, Jesus is making reference to the Hebrew Old Testament, not a Greek translation.

Another allusion of Christ to the Hebrew Scriptures occurs in Luke 11:51-52: "From the blood of Abel unto the blood of Zacharias, which perished between the altar and the temple: verily I say unto you, It shall be required of this generation. Woe unto you, lawyers! for ye have taken away the key of knowledge: ye entered not in yourselves, and them that were entering in ye hindered."

Jesus refers to the blood of all the martyrs slain. Interestingly, in English Abel begins with A and Zacharias with Z—from A to Z. Jesus was, in fact, meaning from the beginning to the end. Abel was the first martyr ever slain, and Zacharias was the last martyr recorded in the Hebrew Scriptures. What book records his death? 2 Chronicles, the last book in the Tanakh. Why is this significant? Because the Greek translation of the Hebrew Old Testament was not in the same order—it ended with Malachi, as our Bibles do today. Once again, Jesus is referring to the original Hebrew Scriptures, not the Greek

---

[10] Luke 24:44

translation. This will be important when we get to the subject of the Septuagint.

"From the earliest times the faithful in Israel had given much care to the education of the youth. The Lord had directed that even from babyhood the children should be taught of His goodness and His greatness, especially as revealed in His law, and shown in the history of Israel. Song and prayer and lessons from the Scriptures were to be adapted to the opening mind. Fathers and mothers were to instruct their children that the law of God is an expression of His character, and that as they received the principles of the law into the heart, the image of God was traced on mind and soul. Much of the teaching was oral; **but the youth also learned to read the Hebrew writings**; and the parchment rolls of the Old Testament Scriptures were open to their study....

"The child Jesus did not receive instruction in the synagogue schools. His mother was His first human teacher. From her lips and from the scrolls of the prophets, He learned of heavenly things. **The very words which He Himself had spoken to Moses for Israel**[11] **He was now taught at His mother's knee.** As He advanced from childhood to youth, He did not seek the schools of the rabbis. He needed not the education to be obtained from such sources; for God was His instructor."[12]

The New Testament writers, as we have seen, were aware of the fact that they were writing Scripture.[13] There were no church councils, decades or centuries after their deaths, to decide which books went into the Bible. The apostles knew that their message was inspired by God himself. The disciples were eyewitnesses[14] of the things they were recording. There were plenty of people who could have disproved this claim had it not been true. Matthew, John[15], and Peter were numbered among the twelve apostles. James was an

---

[11] The very words that Christ had spoken to Moses, were spoken in Hebrew, not Greek.

[12] E. G. White, *The Desire of Ages* (1898), p. 69.2-70.1.

[13] 1 Thessalonians 2:13

[14] Luke 1:2; 2 Peter 1:16; 1 John 1:1-3

[15] John wrote the Gospel of John, 1st, 2nd, 3rd John, and the Revelation.

apostle and the brother of Jesus, though not of the twelve.[16] Jude was the brother of James. All these were eyewitnesses of the events. Mark was probably John Mark, also an eyewitness, although, perhaps younger than the rest. Luke,[17] the physician who travelled with Paul, though not among the twelve, was a disciple who lists himself as an eyewitness of Christ's life.[18] This leaves only Paul, the apostle to the Gentiles. Were his writings considered part of Scripture? The apostle Peter, speaking of Paul, says the following: "And account that the longsuffering of our Lord is salvation; even as our beloved brother Paul also according to the wisdom given unto him hath written unto you; As also in all his epistles, speaking in them of these things; in which are some things hard to be understood, which they that are unlearned and unstable wrest, as they do also **the other scriptures**, unto their own destruction."[19]

Peter, under the inspiration of the Holy Spirit, calls the writings of Paul Scriptures. Therefore, the entire New Testament was assembled as a complete canon of Scripture while the apostles were yet alive. Any church councils centuries later that were deciding what should be in the Bible were only usurping the authority that they claimed. Thus, the books they added are apocryphal and not a part of the canon of Scripture.

A most astonishing prophecy buried in the symbolism of the sanctuary in the wilderness ordains the books of the canon before they were formed "declaring the end from the beginning."[20] In Exodus 25:31-34, the Bible describes the candlestick that was to be

---

[16] Apparently, James the son of Alphaeus, one of the twelve (perhaps the brother of Matthew, who had a father by the same name—Mark 2:14), and James the son of Zebedee (brother of John the beloved—Matthew 10:2-4), were different from James the brother of Christ (Galatians 1:19—also called Thaddaeus or Lebbaeus, see Matthew 10:3, Luke 6:16). When listed with the twelve James the brother of Christ is called the brother of Judas rather than the son of Alphaeus as the other James is called. Apparently, Jude was a step-brother of Jesus as he is listed in Jude 1:1 simply as the brother of James rather than a brother of Jesus. His name is possibly included in the list in Mark 6:3 as Juda. He may also be the Judas listed with the twelve (not Judas Iscariot).
See also Mark 3:13-19; Luke 6:13-16; Acts 1:13.

[17] Luke wrote the gospel of Luke and the book of Acts.

[18] Luke 1:2

[19] 2 Peter 3:15-16

[20] "Declaring the end from the beginning, and from ancient times the things that are not yet done, saying, My counsel shall stand, and I will do all my pleasure:"
Isaiah 46:10

in the sanctuary. "And thou shalt make a candlestick of pure gold: of beaten work shall the candlestick be made: his shaft, and his branches, his bowls, his knops, and his flowers, shall be of the same. "And six branches shall come out of the sides of it; three branches of the candlestick out of the one side, and three branches of the candlestick out of the other side. Three bowls made like unto almonds, with a knop and a flower in one branch; and three bowls made like almonds in the other branch, with a knop and a flower: so in the six branches that come out of the candlestick. And in the candlestick shall be four bowls made like unto almonds, with their knops and their flowers."

The bowls were shaped like almonds; the almond being the fruit, the flower giving rise to the fruit, and the bud (knop) leading to the flower. The three almonds on every side-branch each had their corresponding bud and flower; creating a total of three items: bud, flower, and fruit, repeated three times, in each of the six branches. This means that there were nine different items on one branch. If we add up the items on three branches, we find there are twenty-seven items on one side of the candlestick; with twenty-seven items on the other side. In the candlestick (the main stalk in the center), there are four bowls like almonds with their knops and flowers. Therefore, there are four sets of three items, or 12 items on the middle stalk. If you add the 12 items from the middle stalk to the 27 items from the first side of the candlestick, you have 39 items, with 27 items remaining on the second side. There are 39 books in the Old Testament and 27 books in the New Testament. Scripture says in Psalm 119:105, "Thy word is a lamp unto my feet, and a light unto my path."

The Apocrypha

The sanctuary candlestick had seven branches whereas the Jewish[21] menorah today typically has nine branches. Assuming the same decorations on the two extra branches, would give eighteen additional items for the nine-branched menorah. Interestingly, and perhaps not coincidentally, counting the extra-Biblical books distributed between the three primary manuscripts[22] used for almost all modern bibles, we find there are eighteen apocryphal books.[23]

---

[21] When the Jews were clamoring for the crucifixion of Jesus, they made two oaths: 1. "his blood be upon us and upon our children" and 2. "we have no king but Caesar."
Thankfully, the blood of Jesus paid the penalty for the sins of all men, whether they like it, know it, believe it, or not. "Therefore, as by the offence of one judgment came upon all men to condemnation; even so ***by the righteousness of one the free gift came upon all men*** unto justification of life." Romans 5:18
"My little children, these things write I unto you, that ye sin not. And if any man sin, we have an advocate with the Father, Jesus Christ the righteous:
And ***he is the propitiation for our sins***: and not for ours only, ***but also for the sins of the whole world***." 1 John 2:1-2
In this sense his blood is upon the sins of the Jews, to reconcile them to God. Of course, they must individually accept his life if those sins are not to be imputed back to them. As a nation, however, they are no longer God's chosen people, as they continue to reject the one name under heaven "whereby we must be saved." Acts 4:12
See Martin Klein, *Glimpses of the Open Gates of Heaven*, Daniel 9. Sadly, they also claimed no king but Caesar. The Pope claims all the titles given to Caesar, such as Pontifex Maximus; thus, he is the Caesar. Not only have they claimed Caesar as their king, but they have accepted Caesar's bible, and the nine-branched symbol for it. (The Jewish Publication Society bible primarily follows the Catholic manuscripts.)

[22] Codex Sinaiticus, Codex Vaticanus, and Codex Alexandrinus.

[23] Aleph is the abbreviated name for the Sinaitic Codex; B stands for the Vaticanus; and A represents Alexandrinus.

1. Tobith (Aleph, B)
2. Judith (Aleph, B)
3. 1 Maccabees (Aleph, A)
4. 2 Maccabees (Aleph, A)
5. 3 Maccabees (Aleph, A)
6. 4 Maccabees (Aleph, A)
7. Wisdom (of Solomon) (Aleph, B)
8. Sirach/Ben Sira/Ecclesiasticus (Aleph, A, B)
9. Baruch (B)
10. Epistle of Barnabus (Aleph)
11. Shepherd of Hermas (Aleph)
12. Epistle of Jeremiah (In catholic Bibles, last chapter of Baruch; separate in B) (B)
13. 1 Clement (A)
14. 2 Clement (A)
15. Odes (contains Prayer of Manasseh) (A)
16. Epistle to Marcellinus (A)
17. 1 Esdras (Aleph, B)
18. 2 Esdras (Aleph, B)

(Footnote continued on next page.)

It is very clear that these books are not only spurious, but also highly adapted to Catholic doctrine. For example, in the Epistle of Barnabas chapter 15, we find the following: "Your present Sabbaths are not acceptable to Me, but that is which I have made, [namely this,] when, giving rest to all things, I shall make a beginning of the eighth day, that is, a beginning of another world. Wherefore, also, we keep the eighth day with joyfulness, the day also on which Jesus rose again from the dead. And when He had manifested Himself, He ascended into the heavens."

This is clearly an attempt to provide theological justification for the change of the day of worship from the Biblical Saturday sabbath to the papal Dies Domini, or Day of the Sun (Sunday). The Catholic Church boldly claims that this change is their mark of authority[24] for being above Scripture: "The Church is above the Bible; and this transference of Sabbath observance from Saturday to Sunday is proof positive of that fact."[25]

The book of Barnabas also contains the following, in chapter 10: "Moreover, 'You shall not,' he says, 'eat the hare.' Wherefore? 'You shall not be a corrupter of boys, nor like such.' Because the hare multiplies, year by year, the places of its conception; for as many years as it lives so many it has. Moreover, 'You shall not eat the hyena.' He means, 'You shall not be an adulterer, nor a corrupter, nor be like to them that are such.' Wherefore? Because that animal annually changes its sex, and is at one time male, and at another female. Moreover, he has rightly detested the weasel. For he means, 'You shall not be like to those whom we hear of as committing wickedness with the mouth, on account of their uncleanness; nor

---

The 1993 NRSV with Apocrypha, by Zondervan, though differing slightly in the books included, also contains eighteen Apocryphal books.
Twelve of these books are included in the Catholic Latin Vulgate and the English Jesuit Douay-Rheims bible, along with additions to the books of Esther, Jeremiah and Daniel.

[24] "The Bible says, 'Remember that thou keep holy the Sabbath day.' The Catholic Church says: 'No! By my divine power I abolish the Sabbath day, and command you to keep holy the first day of the week.' And, lo! the entire civilized world bows down in reverent obedience to the command of the holy Catholic Church."
Father Enright, CSS. R. to E.E. Franke, January 11, 1892, in "An Adventist Minister on Sunday Laws," *American Sentinel,* June 1, 1893, p. 173.

[25] "Sabbath Observance," *The Catholic Record,* September 1, 1923, p. 4, http://biblelight.net/c-record.htm. Retrieved 02-09-2016.

shall you be joined to those impure women who commit iniquity with the mouth. For this animal conceives by the mouth.'"

"This must rank as the poorest biological exposé ever written."[26] Not only is this outrageous nonsense, but it is also completely obscene.

Why would it matter that these corruptions are here, since most people are not reading the Epistle of Barnabas? It matters in that this book is contained in the famous Codex Sinaiticus, which is quoted, along with the Vatican manuscript, in the margins of most modern Bibles as "the oldest and best manuscripts" and upon which almost all modern bible versions are based. Should we trust the rest of a manuscript that contains such perversions? Should we trust commentators and translators who call this the oldest and best?

The Bible says "If any man shall add unto these things, God shall add unto him the plagues that are written in this book: And if any man shall take away from the words of the book of this prophecy, God shall take away his part out of the book of life, and out of the holy city, and from the things which are written in this book."[27]

The very word Apocrypha, which means hidden or secret book, is incongruent with the message of Scripture for Jesus said, "I spake openly to the world... and in secret have I said nothing."[28]

"I then saw the word of God pure and unadulterated, and that we must answer for the way we received the truth proclaimed from that word. I saw that it had been a hammer to break the flinty heart in pieces, and a fire to consume the dross and tin, that the heart might be pure and holy. I saw that the Apocrypha was the hidden book, and that the wise of these last days should understand it. I saw that the Bible was the standard book, that will judge us at the last day. I saw that heaven would be cheap enough, and that nothing was too dear to sacrifice for Jesus, and that we must give all to enter the

---

[26] Walter Veith, Ph.D., "Bible Versions: Does it matter which Bible we use?," *Faith on the Line*, Fall 2009, p. 11, http://pdf.amazingdiscoveries.org/Newsletters/2009%20fall%20Newsletter-LQ.pdf Retrieved 02-09-2016.

[27] Revelation 22:18-19

[28] John 18:20

kingdom. I heard an angel say, 'Think ye God will place His seal where there is an idol? No, no.'"[29]

Some have advanced the idea that the Testimony of Jesus is endorsing the Apocrypha with this statement. Nothing could be further from the truth. The contrast is being made between the Apocrypha, or hidden book, and the Bible or the standard book by which we shall be judged. Many have made an intellectual idol out of the critical text of Scripture, which is nothing more than the Vatican and Sinaitic manuscripts, containing the Apocrypha. The solemn warning is given that God will not place his seal in the mind of a person who sets up this idol. This must be understood by God's people in these last days.

Further evidence that this is the meaning intended comes from a most negative statement regarding the New Testament Apocrypha: "Nothing supernatural occurred during the first thirty years of his [Jesus'] life at Nazareth which would attract the attention of the people to himself. The apocraphy [apocrypha] of the New Testament attempts to supply the silence of the Scriptures in reference to the early life of Christ, by giving a fancy sketch of his childhood years. These writers relate wonderful incidents and miracles, which characterized his childhood, and distinguished him from other children. They relate fictitious tales, and frivolous miracles, which they say he wrought, attributing to Christ the senseless and needless display of his divine power, and falsifying his character by attributing to him acts of revenge, and deeds of mischief, which were cruel and ridiculous.

"In what marked contrast is the history of Christ, as recorded by the evangelists, which is beautiful in its natural simplicity, with these unmeaning stories, and fictitious tales. They are not at all in harmony with his character. They are more after the order of the novels that are written, which have no foundation in truth; but the characters delineated are of fancy creating."[30]

---

[29] E. G. White, *Manuscript Releases,* Vol. 16 (Nampa ID: Pacific Press, 1990), p. 34.3.

[30] E. G. White, "Life of Christ.—No. 2," *Youth Instructor,* April 1, 1872, p. 29.

The Septuagint

Lately it is popular to quote from, or refer to, the Septuagint; perhaps the speaker wants to sound scholarly, or maybe it is just because it is the popular thing to do, or most likely the speaker is simply unaware of the facts. Most people really have no idea what the Septuagint is, and even most Bible scholars are ignorant of many salient details.

To begin with, the name Septuagint is short for the Latin title *Versio Septuaginta Interpretum*, meaning "translation of the seventy interpreters," and abbreviated LXX. It is a Greek translation of the Hebrew Old Testament, supposed to have been translated around 285-250 B.C. in Alexandria, Egypt. According to the legend, translation was accomplished by 72[31] Jewish scholars (six from each tribe), in 72 days, at the request of Ptolemy II Philadelphus. Since Greek was the trade language of Jesus' day, scholars claim that this is the Bible that Jesus used and quoted from, rather than the Hebrew.

Most of the details of this story come from an ancient document called the Letter of Aristeas. This letter was written by Aristeas to his brother Philocrates claiming to be written during the reign of Ptolemy II Philadelphus. According to the letter, the royal librarian, Demetrius of Phalerum, convinced Ptolemy to appeal to the high priest at Jerusalem to send translators to Alexandria, for the purpose of translating the Hebrew Scriptures into Greek for the library. This is the only document from which these details seem to originate. Apparently, the letter was extant by the first century B.C., as Philo of Alexandria (c. 20 B.C. – A.D. 50), a Jewish Gnostic philosopher, refers to 72 interpreters. Flavius Josephus, the Jewish historian (c. A.D. 37-100) also relates the story of Aristeas.[32]

The problem is, "Aristeas blunders in naming Demetrius of Phalerum (c.345 – c.283 BC) as a member of the court and keeper of Ptolemy II Philadelphus's (285 – 247 BC) library. The latter part of Demetrius' life was spent in the court of Ptolemy Soter, not Philadelphus.

---

[31] Do not ask why the name is the "translation of the seventy interpreters," when there were supposed to be 72 translators. This is one of the smallest inconsistencies of the story.

[32] Floyd Nolen Jones, Th.D., Ph.D., *The Septuagint: A Critical Analysis,* 6th ed. (Woodlands, TX: Kings Word Press, 2000), p. 5-6.

Moreover, having lost favor with Philadelphus, Demetrius was banished by that monarch. Indeed, he was never the royal librarian. The author further indicts himself when just prior to the banquet given in honor of the translators he states: 'it happens to be the anniversary of our naval victory over Antigonus.' This is a major blunder. The writer has either transformed a decisive defeat of the Egyptian navy at the battle of Cos (c.260 B.C.) into a victory or this is a reference to an actual victory at Andros around B.C. 245. Regardless, both of these battles occurred long after the c.283 decease of Demetrius....
"Such historical errors recorded in the Letter of Aristeas disclose the undeniable fact that the work is not of the time period it claims.... Surely enough has already been said to alert the reader to the true nature of 'Aristeas.'"[33]

The letter of Aristeas appears to have been written about 150 years after the time period it claims to be from, and was exposed as legend as early as 1705, by Humphry Hody,[34] a Protestant Professor of Greek at Oxford (1698-1706). Oddly, though scholars agree that the letter is fiction, most of the details, oft repeated, regarding the origin of the Septuagint, still come from this letter.

The sacred responsibility of preserving and copying Scripture was entrusted to the sons of Levi.[35] All the scribes in the Bible were of the tribe of Levi,[36] therefore they would not be six from each tribe as in the popular mythology. Also, by the date given for the letter of

---

[33] Floyd Nolen Jones, Th.D., Ph.D., *The Septuagint: A Critical Analysis* (2000), p. 6.

[34] Humphry Hody, D.D., *Bibliorum Textibus Originalibus, versionibus Graecis, et Latina Vulgata*, Bk. 4, (Oxford: Oxford University, 1705).

[35] Malachi 2:7-8; Deuteronomy 31:24-25

[36] See Ezra 7:6, 10-11.
"One notable exception was the King from the tribe of Judah (Gen. 49:8-10; Psa. 78:67-71). Upon his ascension to the throne, the King was to take the Scriptures which the Levites were protecting and write out a copy himself. He was to keep it with him at all times so that he could govern God's people according to God's laws, justice, and wisdom.
"God revealed this through Moses when prophesying to Israel that it would some day have a king: 'And it shall be, when he [the king] sits upon the throne of his kingdom, that he shall write him a copy of this law in a book out of that which is before the priests the Levites: And it shall be with him, and he shall read therein all the days of his life: that he may learn to fear the LORD his God, to keep all the words of this law and these statutes, to do them' (Deuteronomy 17:18-19)"
Floyd Nolen Jones, Th.D., Ph.D., *The Septuagint: A Critical Analysis* (2000), p. 8.

Aristeas, the tribes of the northern kingdom of Israel were non-existent.

The quality of translation in the Septuagint varies widely from book to book, from fairly good in the Pentateuch, to incompetent in Isaiah, and the Psalms not much better. Esther, Job, and Proverbs are not faithful translations, but paraphrases.[37] An important detail to note regarding the Septuagint is that it contains the Apocrypha.

The Septuagint contains many serious problems that we could not accept as the faithfully preserved word of God. "The majority of LXX manuscripts give 167 as the age of Methuselah at the birth of his son, Lamech (the Hebrew reads 187—Genesis 5:25). However, if Methuselah were 167 at the birth of Lamech, Lamech 188 at the birth of Noah and Noah 600 at the Flood (as recorded in the LXX), Methuselah would have been 955 at the date of the Flood. Since he lived to be 969 (the lifespan given by both), the LXX becomes entangled in the absurdity of making Methuselah survive the Flood by 14 years!

"The constructor of the scheme in the LXX lengthens the chronology of the Patriarchs after the flood by 720 years. He also graduates the length of lives of the patriarchs throughout the entire register, both those before and after the flood. The curious result is that with the three exceptions of Enoch, Cainan, (whose life exceeds that of his father by only five years) and Reu (whose age at his death is the same as that of his father), every one of the Patriarchs from Adam to Abraham is made to die a few years younger than his father. Could anything be more manifestly artificial?

"After analyzing the disparity between these discordant ages of the patriarchs in both the LXX and the Samaritan Pentateuch with regard to the Hebrew, C.F. Keil concluded that the Hebrew text was the only reliable account: 'That the principal divergences of both texts from the Hebrew are intentional changes, based upon chronological theories or cycles, is sufficiently evident from their internal character.... No such intention is discernible in the numbers of the Hebrew text: consequently every attack upon the historical character

---

[37] Floyd Nolen Jones, Th.D., Ph.D., *The Septuagint: A Critical Analysis* (2000), p. 8-9.

of it [sic] numerical statements has entirely failed, and no tenable argument can be adduced against their correctness.'"[38]

Keil is telling us that the Hebrew Old Testament is the only reliable text, and therefore the LXX and the Samaritan Pentateuch cannot be trusted.

The Septuagint is like the missing link in evolution. Everyone assumes it is there somewhere, but no one can seem to find it. Remember, the Septuagint is supposed to be a Greek translation of the Hebrew Old Testament from around 250 B.C. that Jesus quoted from, when on earth. However, when someone quotes to you from the Septuagint today, they are actually quoting from the Sinaiticus and the Vaticanus (4th century A.D. at the earliest). Now, why would someone quote from fourth century A.D. manuscripts when they could quote from a 250 B.C. manuscript,[39] if older is better? Because they have not found the 250 B.C. manuscript. It is the mythical predecessor to the Sinaiticus and Vaticanus that everyone assumes is there, and no one can find.

So, the Catholic church capitalized on the forged Letter of Aristeas, and its story of the Septuagint, to give validity to their corrupted Greek manuscripts, making them sound as if they were copies of the Bible that Jesus used. Essentially, the earliest "Septuagint" is the fifth column of Origen's Hexapla, or six columned bible, circa A.D. 245.[40]

So, what is the origin of these corrupted Greek manuscripts?

---

[38] Floyd Nolen Jones, Th.D., Ph.D., *The Septuagint: A Critical Analysis* (2000), p. 10-13.

[39] The only really significant B.C. manuscripts discovered are the Dead Sea Scrolls. They are certainly not considered copies of the Septuagint. Rather, they support the Majority Text. This is the reason it took scholars 50 years to finally publish parts of the Dead Sea Scrolls. Though first discovered in 1946, nothing was published until the 1990's.
In the meantime, they had time to discover more scrolls with extra-Biblical material so they would not have to focus on the big embarrassment that their "oldest and best" manuscripts—Sinaiticus and Vaticanus—did not agree with the oldest scrolls ever discovered.

[40] H.B. Swete, D.D., *An Introduction to the Old Testament in Greek* (Cambridge: University Press, 1902), p. 63.
"For proof of this identification, see the LXX designation at the top of the 5th column in Swete on the designated page."
Floyd Nolen Jones, Th.D., Ph.D., *The Septuagint: A Critical Analysis* (2000), p. 19.

The Cisterns of Egypt

"For my people have committed two evils; they have forsaken me the fountain of living waters, and hewed them out cisterns, broken cisterns, that can hold no water.... And now what hast thou to do in the way of Egypt, to drink the waters of Sihor?"[41]

Five men stand out in prominence who corrupted a handful of manuscripts:

1. Justin Martyr
2. Tatian
3. Clement of Alexandria
4. Origen
5. Eusebius

Justin Martyr

"The year in which the Apostle John died, A.D. 100, is given as the date in which Justin Martyr was born. Justin, originally a pagan and of pagan parentage, afterward embraced Christianity and although he is said to have died at heathen hands for his religion, nevertheless, his teachings were of a heretical nature. Even as a Christian teacher, he continued to wear the robes of a pagan philosopher.

"In the teachings of Justin Martyr, we begin to see how muddy the stream of pure Christian doctrine was running among the heretical sects fifty years after the death of the apostle John. It was in Tatian, Justin Martyr's pupil, that these regrettable doctrines were carried to alarming lengths, and by his hand committed to writing."[42]

Tatian

"After the death of Justin Martyr in Rome, Tatian returned to Palestine and embraced the Gnostic heresy. This same Tatian wrote a Harmony of the Gospels which was called the Diatessaron, meaning four in one. The Gospels were so notoriously corrupted by his hand that in later years a bishop of Syria, because of the errors, was obliged to throw out of his churches no less than two hundred

---

[41] Jeremiah 2:13, 18

[42] B.G. Wilkinson, Ph.D., *Our Authorized Bible Vindicated* (1930), p. 16.

copies of this Diatessaron, since church members were mistaking it for the true Gospel."[43]

Irenaeus says that Tatian invented a system of invisible Aeons (or gods); believed that marriage was corruption and fornication; and paraphrased words of the apostles to improve their style.[44]

Clement of Alexandria

"We come now to Tatian's pupil known as Clement of Alexandria, A.D. 200. He went much farther than Tatian in that he founded a school at Alexandria [Egypt] which instituted propaganda along these heretical lines. Clement expressly tells us that he would not hand down Christian teachings, pure and unmixed, but rather clothed with precepts of pagan philosophy."[45]
"He habitually mistakes apocryphal writings for inspired Scripture... with corrupted copies always at hand and before him."[46]

"His influence in the depravation of Christianity was tremendous. But his greatest contribution, undoubtedly, was the direction given to the studies and activities of Origen, his famous pupil."[47]

Origen

"When we come to Origen, we speak the name of him who did the most of all to create and give direction to the forces of apostasy down through the centuries. It was he who mightily influenced Jerome, the editor of the Catholic Latin Bible known as the Vulgate. Eusebius worshiped at the altar of Origen's teachings. He claims to have collected eight hundred of Origen's letters, to have used Origen's six-column Bible, the Hexapla, in his Biblical labors. Assisted by Pamphilus, he restored and preserved Origen's library."[48]

---

[43] B.G. Wilkinson, Ph.D., *Our Authorized Bible Vindicated* (1930), p. 16.

[44] Thomas Holland, Th.D., *Crowned With Glory* (2000), p. 29.

[45] B.G. Wilkinson, Ph.D., *Our Authorized Bible Vindicated* (1930), p. 16.

[46] John William Burgon, B.D., *The Revision Revised* (1883), p. 336.

[47] B.G. Wilkinson, Ph.D., *Our Authorized Bible Vindicated* (1930), p. 16.

[48] *Ibid.*, p. 17.

Origen became head of the school at Alexandria by A.D. 213, was the first teacher of purgatory, and the father of Arianism.[49] Origen taught that the soul existed from eternity before it inhabited a body, he emasculated himself,[50] and he wrote the Hexapla, a six-columned bible in which we first find the "Septuagint" in its fifth column.

Origen said that "the Scriptures are of little use to those who understand them as they are written."[51]

Interestingly, Helena Petrovna Blavatsky,[52] a Luciferian[53] who established the Theosophical Society, and is considered to be the mother of modern occultism, agrees with Origen. "Truly, unless we read the 'Old Testament' kabalistically and comprehend the hidden meaning thereof, it is very little we can learn from it."[54]

Not only this, but Blavatsky considered the Septuagint and the Vulgate to be correct and the Protestant Bible (KJV) to be in error. This should be a huge warning to Christians who insist that there are no doctrinal changes in modern bibles, as the Septuagint is the basis of most modern Bibles (at least the Old Testament portion[55]).

Blavatsky states, "the text of the English (Protestant) Bible is, in disagreement, as usual, with those of the Septuagint and the Vulgate. Thus, while in the former one reads (in Deuter. xxxii., 8 and 9) 'When the MOST HIGH (not Jehovah) divided to the nations their inheritance he set the bounds of the people according to the number of the children of Israel,' in the Septuagint the text reads 'according

---

[49] Arianism is the belief that Jesus is a created being and not divine.

[50] Matthew 5:30; See Deuteronomy 23:1.

[51] John M'Clintock, D.D., James Strong, S.T.D., *Cyclopedia of Biblical, Theological, and Ecclesiastical Literature*, Vol. 7 (1877), p. 430.

[52] Blavatsky (1831-1891), mother of modern occultism and the one who greatly influenced Alice A. Bailey to become the most prolific occult writer ever.

[53] H.P. Blavatsky, *The Secret Doctrine*, Vol. 1—Cosmogenesis (1888), p. 70-71.

[54] H. P. Blavatsky, *Isis Unveiled,* Vol. 2 - Theology (1877), p. 362.

[55] The Septuagint is a Greek translation of the Hebrew Old Testament. The New Testament is also contained in the Sinaitic and Vatican copies of the Septuagint. It is considered to have been added to the Septuagint later.

to the number of the Angels' (Planet-Angels), which is more concordant with truth and fact."[56]

Eusebius

Eusebius was a devotee of Origen, collecting 800 of Origen's letters, and using Origen's Hexapla in his teachings and works. Eusebius was also a strong Arian, and presided over the Council of Nicaea of A.D. 325. He was commissioned by Constantine the Great to create 50 ecumenical bibles, from Origen's bible, to help make Christianity acceptable to the pagans. Many authorities believe that the Sinaiticus and Vaticanus are two of those 50 Bibles.[57]

"The nominal conversion of Constantine, in the early part of the fourth century, caused great rejoicing; and the world, cloaked with a form of righteousness, walked into the church. Now the work of corruption rapidly progressed. Paganism, while appearing to be vanquished, became the conqueror. Her spirit controlled the church. Her doctrines, ceremonies, and superstitions were incorporated into the faith and worship of the professed followers of Christ."[58]

An unholy trinity was formed between the Emperor Constantine, the bishop Eusebius and Pope Sylvester I. Pope Sylvester was the first person to call Sunday "the Lord's day," Eusebius was the first bishop to advance a theological argument claiming the transference of the Bible sabbath to Sunday, and Constantine was the first civil ruler to legislate Sunday observance.

"The royal mandate not proving a sufficient substitute for divine authority, Eusebius, a bishop who sought the favor of princes, and

---

[56] H. P. Blavatsky, *The Secret Doctrine,* Vol. 1 - Cosmogenesis (1888), p. 576.

[57] "Eusebius of Caesarea (260-340), the first church historian, assisted by Pamphilus or vice versa, issued with all its critical marks the fifth column of the Hexapla, with alternative readings from the other columns, for use in Palestine. The Emperor Constantine gave orders that fifty copies of this edition should be prepared for use in the churches."
Ira M. Price, Ph.D., *The Ancestry of Our English Bible* (Philadelphia: The Sunday School Times Co., 1907), p. 70.
"Constantine himself ordered fifty Greek Bibles from Eusebius, Bishop of Caesarea, for the churches in Constantinople. It is quite possible that Aleph and B are two of these fifty."
A. T. Robertson, M.A., D.D., LL.D., LITT.D., *Introduction to Textual Criticism of N. T.* (London: Hodder & Stoughton, 1925), p. 80.

[58] E. G. White, *The Great Controversy* (1911), p. 49-50.

who was the special friend and flatterer of Constantine, advanced the claim that Christ had transferred the Sabbath to Sunday. Not a single testimony of the Scriptures was produced in proof of the new doctrine. Eusebius himself unwittingly acknowledges its falsity and points to the real authors of the change. 'All things,' he says, 'whatever that it was duty to do on the Sabbath, these **we** have transferred to the Lord's Day.'"[59]

"And he shall speak great words against the most High, and shall wear out the saints of the most High, and think to change times and laws..."[60]

Frauds and Forgeries

"Frauds and forgeries to advance the power and prosperity of the church have in all ages been esteemed lawful by the papal hierarchy."[61]

The Donation of Constantine is the name traditionally applied to a document purporting to have been addressed by Constantine to Pope Sylvester I. Since the eleventh century it has been used as a powerful argument in favor of the papal claims. Lorenzo Valla proved that this document could not possibly have been written in the fourth century, during the time of Constantine. Today both Catholic and Protestant scholars agree that it was a forgery, fabricated between the eighth and ninth centuries.

"About the close of the eighth century, papists put forth the claim that in the first ages of the church the bishops of Rome had possessed the same spiritual power which they now assumed. To establish this claim, some means must be employed to give it a show of authority; and this was readily suggested by the father of lies. Ancient writings were forged by monks. Decrees of councils before unheard of were discovered, establishing the universal supremacy of the pope from

---

[59] E. G. White, *The Great Controversy* (1911), p. 574.

[60] Daniel 7:25

[61] E. G. White, *The Great Controversy* (1911), p. 576.1.

the earliest times. And a church that had rejected the truth greedily accepted these deceptions."[62]

The Decretals of Isidore (False Decretals) were an elaborate forgery of 700 pages mixed with authentic historic documents to give credibility. The Decretals involved a series of letters from early figures like Clement (first century), through to Gregory the Great (6th and 7th centuries). In Gratian's eleventh century compilation of canon law, out of approximately 330 quotations of sources of authority that he gives in support of papal power, 313 are from the False Decretals. The decretals deceived for over 600 years. Calvinist scholar, David Blondell, finally exposed the fraud in 1628.

The Dictatus Papae of Pope Gregory VII (1020-1085), is the most notorious forgery ever acknowledged by Catholic historians. Among other falsehoods in its 27 points he declared:
"The Pope can be judged by no one on earth. The Roman church has never erred, nor can it err until the end of time. The Pope alone can... dethrone emperors and kings, and absolve their subjects from allegiance. All princes are obliged to kiss his feet."[63]

"For seven centuries the Greeks had called Rome the home of forgeries. Whenever they tried talking with Rome, the Popes brought out forged documents... which the Greeks, naturally, had never seen.
"Gregory went way beyond the Donation of Constantine, he had a whole school of forgers right under his nose, turning out document after document, with the papal seal of approval, to cater for his every need.
"Pope Gregory (and, later, Urban II) might require justification for some action against a prince or bishop. Very well, these prelates literally produced the appropriate document. No need for research; it was all done on the premises.
"Many earlier documents were touched up to make them say the opposite of what they said originally. Some of these earlier documents were themselves forgeries.... This instant method of

---

[62] E. G. White, *The Great Controversy* (1911), p. 56.1.

[63] Peter DeRosa, *Vicars of Christ: the Dark Side of the Papacy* (New York: Crown Publishers, 1988), p. 58.

inventing history was marvelously successful, especially as the forgeries were at once inserted into canon law.... Thus was accomplished the quietest and longest lasting of all revolutions: it was all done on paper."[64]

Charles Spurgeon documented that the Vatican was using fake relics, "so far back as 1828, this trade was going on... with pieces of bones of sheep, and hares or of human bones,... taken from the catacombs, but such as were probably those of pagans, certainly not of saints and martyrs whose names they affixed to them....
"The Jesuits play a prominent part in these transactions, as they do in most Catholic affairs."[65]

In 1912 Charles Dawson discovered the Piltdown Man, hailed as the missing link of evolution. Forty years later, Piltdown Man was demonstrated a hoax. Dawson was assisted by Jesuit priest Teilhard de Chardin. Harvard Professor Stephen Jay Gould published his hypothesis (in 1980) that de Chardin may have conspired with Dawson to create the deception.[66]

Jesuit priest Georges Lemaitre developed the Big Bang theory in 1931. Nineteenth century British historian, Thomas Carlyle stated succinctly, "Jesuitism has poisoned the wellsprings of truth in the whole world."[67]

What does all this fraud and forgery have to do with the Septuagint? The Codex Sinaiticus is considered one of the oldest copies of the Septuagint in existence. Parts of the manuscript are now held by four institutions: The British Library, Leipzig University Library, St. Catherine's Monastery at Mount Sinai, and the National Library of Russia.[68] In 2009 the British Library finished the *Codex Sinaiticus Project* aimed at fully examining the famous manuscript, and

---

[64] Peter DeRosa, *Vicars of Christ: the Dark Side of the Papacy* (1988), 59.

[65] Charles Spurgeon, *Geese in their Hoods* (Huntsville, AL: Whitehorse Publications, 1997), p. 118-119.

[66] Stephen Jay Gould, Ph.D., *The Panda's Thumb* (New York: W. W. Norton and Company, 1980), p. 110-114.

[67] *Tares Among the Wheat*, directed by Christian J. Pinto (2012), 1:40:30.

[68] http://www.bl.uk/projects/codex-sinaiticus-project Retrieved 02-09-2016.

reuniting the manuscript electronically. Prior to the project's completion in a 2008 video interview, Dr. Juan Garces, one of the curators of the *Codex Sinaiticus Project* stated that, "The great role of this project is to produce this history, which hasn't been written, as we all agree, well enough. I hope in 2009, July, we will be able to tell the full story."[69]

Oddly, once the project was published, most of the documented evidence regarding the Sinaiticus was omitted. They even ignored Tischendorf's own assertion that he found it in a waste basket,[70] instead, claiming that the monastery monks brought it to his notice. One would think that a project of this magnitude from an institution of this caliber would present all available historical data. The fact that the charge of forgery forms a major part of the history of the Codex Sinaiticus was passed by without mention—suppressed, as it has been for more than a century and a half.

The story begins in 1855 at the University of Leipzig in Germany when Europe's most distinguished paleographer, Constantine Simonides, got into a heated debate with scholars over a manuscript of the Sheperd of Hermas which he was presenting, making enemies with Constantin von Tischendorf. Tischendorf had already discovered a part of the Sinaiticus manuscript in 1844, but had only published its transcribed contents, and to that time had kept secret the location of its discovery. The probable reason for Tischendorf's anger with Simonides in this debate will become apparent later in the story.

Simonides owned a private collection of over 5000 ancient manuscripts, part of which he inherited from his uncle. These works

---

[69] *Tares Among the Wheat*, directed by Christian J. Pinto (2012), 2:22:40.

[70] "It was in April, 1844, that I embarked at Leghorn for Egypt... the desire which I felt to discover some precious remains of any manuscripts, more especially Biblical of a date which would carry us back to the early times of Christianity was realized beyond my expectations. It was at the foot of Mt. Sinai, in the convent of St. Catherine that I discovered the pearl of all my researches.
"I perceived in the middle of the great hall a large and wide basket full of old parchments and the librarian... told me that two heaps of papers like this had been already committed to the flames. What was my surprise to find amid this heap of papers a considerable number of sheets of a copy of the Old Testament in Greek which seemed to me to be one of the most ancient that I had ever seen."
Constantin von Tischendorf, Ph.D., *When Were Our Gospels Written* (1866), p. 27-28; 34-35.

he presented at libraries and universities throughout Europe. He generally believed that his own knowledge of ancient languages was superior to those around him, although he did not have a reputation for arrogance. "As a scholar Simonides was equally in the thick of debates about ancient manuscripts. He had presented his work before kings, nobles, foreign ministers, diplomats. He'd sold a number of manuscripts to the British museum and other prominent institutions of Europe. So, he was involved in the highest levels of the academic world at that time."[71]

"Dr. Simonides is a Greek by birth and he speaks and writes the classic language of his forefathers with fluency, purity and elegance....

"From [his] uncle Simonides thoroughly acquired the art of paleography, and became so great a proficient therein that few surpass him either in the practice of it, or in the diagnosis of manuscripts."[72] "Tischendorf was only the senior of Simonides by five years and in the science of paleography had neither his knowledge nor his experience."[73]

Tischendorf originally found the Sinaitic manuscript in 1844. Strangely, though Tischendorf was supposedly a Protestant, he met with the Pope one year before the manuscript was first found, "I was also favored with many letters of introduction from Prince John of Saxony to his personal friends of high rank; and in addition with a very flattering note from the Archbishop Affre, of Paris, directed to Gregory XVI. The latter, after a prolonged audience granted to me, took an ardent interest in my undertaking."[74]

"I here pass over in silence, the interesting details of my travels—my audience with the Pope, Gregory XVI, in May, 1843—my intercourse with Cardinal Mezzofanti that surprising and celebrated

---

[71] *Tares Among the Wheat*, directed by Christian J. Pinto (2012), 1:57:15 - 1:57:41.

[72] "Biblical Criticism," *The Homilist*, Feb., Mar., Apr., 1862, as cited in Constantine Simonides, *The Periplus of Hannon* (London: Trubner and Co., 1864), p. 52.

[73] James A. Farrer, *Literary Forgeries* (London: Longmans, Green and Co., 1907), p. 50.

[74] George E. Merrill, D.D., *The Parchments of the Faith* (Philadelphia: American Baptist Publication Society, 1894), p. 176.

linguist."[75] "Mezzofanti honored me with some Greek verses composed in my praise."[76] Another person Tischendorf met at the Vatican was Jesuit Cardinal Angelo Mai, the Cardinal Librarian for the Vatican Library. Speaking of Mai, Cardinal Wiseman stated, "there is not a single century of the Christian era, from the second to the seventeenth, from which he has not produced important and previously unknown works... he had transcribed all with his own hand... entirely by himself."[77] Apparently, Mai was in charge of producing important and previously unknown works from earlier centuries.

In 1859, fifteen years after his initial discovery, Tischendorf returned to Mt. Sinai to find the rest of the manuscript, which he published in 1860. As soon as it was published, a copy was presented to the Pope who expressed his highest appreciation for the document: "In the meantime he had discovered the Sinaitic manuscript, and it had been published in sumptuous form under the patronage of the Czar, and a copy had been presented to the Pope. The latter wrote an autograph letter to Tischendorf, 'in which he expressed his highest appreciation, yes, his admiration of this publication.'"[78] This was the same Pope that was still continuing the inquisition and denouncing Bible societies and the Bibles they distributed as promoting the gospel of the devil.[79]

In 1860 Dr. Simonides was shown a copy of Tischendorf's newly published work. Simonides immediately stated that the work was not an ancient manuscript as Tischendorf claimed, but was his own manuscript, which he created in 1840, at Mt. Athos,[80] intended by

---

[75] Constantin von Tischendorf, Ph.D., *When Were Our Gospels Written?* (1866), p. 27.

[76] George E. Merrill, D.D., *The Parchments of the Faith* (1894), p. 176.

[77] Nicholas Wiseman, Th.D., *Recollections of the Last Four Popes, and of Rome in their Times* (London: Hurst and Blackett, 1858), p. 492-493.

[78] George E. Merrill, D.D., *The Story Of The Manuscripts* (1881), p. 75.

[79] The Bibles they were distributing were the King James Bible.
"The present Pope, Gregory XVI, and his predecessor, Pope Leo XII, denounced all Bible societies, declaring that by the Bibles they distributed 'they converted the Gospel of Christ into a human gospel, or what is still worse, the gospel of the devil.'"
John Dowling, A.M., *The Burning of the Bibles* (Philadelphia: Nathan Moore, 1843), p. 15.

[80] Mt. Athos is a mountain in Northern Greece that is home to 20 Eastern Orthodox monasteries, many of them housing important ancient manuscripts.

himself and his uncle as a gift to Czar Nicholas I of Russia, without any intention to deceive.

The press picked up the story, "We understand that in literary circles a rumor prevails that the manuscript now publishing by the Russian government, under the direction of M. Tischendorf, purporting to be a MS. [manuscript] Bible of the fourth century, is not an ancient manuscript, but is an entirely modern production, written by a gentleman now alive, who will shortly take measures to establish his claim to the authorship. The manuscript is known as the *Codex Sinaiticus*, and has attracted a large amount of attention throughout Europe. Should the rumor prove to be correct, as we believe it will, the disclosures that will follow must be of the greatest interest to archaeology."[81]

Samuel Tregelles, who would later sit on the Revised Version translation committee, sided with Tischendorf and wrote that "the story of Simonides… is as false and absurd as possible."[82]

In response Simonides published his defense in *The Guardian* on September 3, 1862, "When, about two years ago, I saw the first fac-similes of Tischendorf, which were put into my hand at Liverpool, by Mr. Newton, a friend of Dr. Tregelles, I at once recognized my own work, as I immediately told him."[83]

"To prove his claims, Simonides challenged Tischendorf to a public debate, yet Tischendorf refused to take part."[84] Simonides stated, "The real test of the genuineness of the Codex Sinaiticus is neglected. The public were assured that in *May* Tischendorf was to be in London, armed with a portion at least of his great Codex. I have waited in England hoping to have the opportunity of meeting him,

---

[81] *The Literary Gazette,* No. 161, July 27, 1861, as cited in Constantine Simonides, *The Periplus of Hannon* (1864), p. 52.

[82] B. Harris Cowper, *Journal of Sacred Literature & Biblical Record, 1862,* Vol. 2 (London: Williams & Northgate, 1863), p. 491.

[83] J.K. Elliott, *Codex Sinaiticus and the Simonides Affair* (Thessaloniki: Patriarchal Institute for Patristic Studies, 1982), p. 29.

[84] *Tares Among the Wheat,* directed by Christian J. Pinto (2012), 2:02:44.

face to face, to prove him in error; but May has come and gone, and the discoverer has not appeared.
"Let the favorers of the antiquity of the MS. persuade him to come *at once*, and brave the ordeal, or else for ever hold his peace."[85]

"Dr. Simonides always maintained... that the Mt. Athos Bible [Codex Sinaiticus] written in 1840 for the Emperor of Russia was not meant to deceive anyone... that it was Professor Tischendorf's ignorance and inexperience which rendered him so easily deceived, where no deception was intended."[86]

"Mt. Athos was the location where Simonides claimed he had created the Codex. He provided many details for how the manuscript had been written and how it came to be at Mt. Sinai. He also provided many names of those in the Greek world who he said could confirm that he created the manuscript. But, strangely, most of these details were never investigated, either by the supporters of Tischendorf, or by the newspapers of the time."[87]

Despite Tischendorf's silence, the newspapers began siding with him in denouncing Simonides.[88] "The attacks were almost fanatical and often unreasonable."[89]

Yet, Simonides was not without supporters: The *Literary Churchman* stated, "For ourselves, we must profess entire impartiality.... Though we were quite ready from the first to admit the importance of the discovery of Tischendorf, we are not prepared, at this moment, to say, with Dr. Tregelles, that the statements of Simonides are 'as

---

[85] B. Harris Cowper, *Journal of Sacred Literature & Biblical Record, 1863,* Vol. 3 (London: Williams & Northgate, 1863), p. 496.

[86] B. Harris Cowper, *Journal of Sacred Literature & Biblical Record, 1863,* Vol. 3 (1863), p.481.

[87] *Tares Among the Wheat*, directed by Christian J. Pinto (2012), 2:11:45-2:12:22.

[88] Protestant historian, Wylie about the same time wrote regarding the Jesuit influence on media. "There are two institutions in especial to which the Jesuits will lay siege. These are the Press and the Pulpit. The press of Great Britain is already manipulated by them to an extent of which the public but little dream. The whole English press of the world is supervised, and the word is passed round how writers, speakers, and causes are to be handled, and applause or condemnation dealt out as it may accord with the interests and wishes of Rome."
J.A. Wylie, LL.D., *The Jesuits: Their Moral Maxims, and Plots Against Kings, Nations and Churches* (London: Hamilton, Adams, & CO., 1881), p. 93-94.

[89] *Tares Among the Wheat*, directed by Christian J. Pinto (2012), 2:03:55.

false and absurd as possible.' Tischendorf applies these terms,[90] false and absurd, just now to Tregelles himself."[91]

James Farrer, in his 1907 work, *Literary Forgeries*, wrote that the controversy "cannot be said to have been settled by the mere opinions of Tregelles or Bradshaw... [who] examined the Codex two months before Simonides had made his claim to it as his work, so that they had no reason to examine it with suspicion."[92]

"Simonides was working at the time with a man named Joseph Mayer (1803-1886), who was the founder of the Mayer Museum in Liverpool."[93] Mayer requested him to come to the museum to examine some ancient Egyptian manuscripts he had purchased sometime earlier. They were first century fragments of the gospel of Matthew dating within 15 years of Christ's ascension. "This proved that Matthew was the first gospel, not Mark, and that it was originally written in Greek."[94] Additionally, he discovered a first century manuscript that contained the Johannine Comma (1 John 5:7). This, of course proved all the higher critical scholars to be in error,[95] which would not help the papal cause.

"The few believers in Simonides represented him as a man whose towering genius had aroused the envy, alike of Grecian professors, German students, and English librarians, and banded them together in a conspiracy to crush him."[96]

---

[90] Tischendorf had attacked Tregelles because Tregelles had said, "On one point I believe that I differ materially from Tischendorf as to the writing of the MS. He thinks that he sees traces of various hands having been employed, in such a way that a change of writer must have frequently taken place. I believe that the difference is to be attributed to the scribe having more or less ink in his style, the ink being more or less thick, and the surface of the vellum slightly varying." Letter of Tregelles, *The Guardian*, August 13, 1862 as cited in J.K. Elliott, *Codex Sinaiticus and the Simonides Affair* (1982), p. 24.

[91] *Literary Churchman*, December 16, 1862 as cited in J.K. Elliott, *Codex Sinaiticus and the Simonides Affair* (1982), p. 34.

[92] James A. Farrer, *Literary Forgeries* (1907), p. 64.

[93] *Tares Among the Wheat*, directed by Christian J. Pinto (2012), 2:13:20.

[94] *Tares Among the Wheat*, directed by Christian J. Pinto (2012), 2:14:00.

[95] J.K. Elliott, *Codex Sinaiticus and the Simonides Affair* (1982), p. 122-123, 133, 142, 151-152.

[96] *The London Review*, 1862, Vol. 5 (London: Cox and Wyman, 1862), p. 538.

"Professor Tischendorf having visited the Holy Land, returned to Europe with a voluminous manuscript that he obtained from the library of the Monastery of Mount Sinai, the earliest known copy of the Bible. In time one of the parts fell into the hands of Simonides, who at once recognized it as a MS [manuscript] he had himself executed. He made his assertion public that... the Codex Sinaiticus... had been written by himself... but Tischendorf and the learned men of Germany... refused to recognize the claims of Simonides and continued its publication.
"Things went on this way,—some persons believing Simonides, some Tischendorf, when suddenly a Greek Archimandrite[97] [Kallinikos]... wrote to the English papers from Alexandria, corroborating the statement of Simonides."[98]

He stated that he had seen Simonides writing the manuscript on Mt. Athos. Kallinikos called Tischendorf "the master and pupil of all guile, and all wickedness."[99] "I repeat, that the MS. in dispute is the work of the unwearied Simonides, and of no other person. A portion of this was secretly removed from Mt. Sinai, by professor Tischendorf, in 1844. The rest, with inconceivable recklessness, he mutilated and tampered with, according to his liking, in the year 1859. Some leaves he destroyed, especially such as contained the Acrostics of Simonides."[100]

Apparently, the reason for such vast numbers of "corrections" to the manuscript is because Tischendorf was modifying Simonides' manuscript (which originally followed the Traditional Text), to match better with the Catholic manuscripts—the burnt and missing pages removing Simonides' marks of authorship. This would explain the need for the story of the discovery in a waste basket of kindling, which never made any sense. If you use papers to start a fire, you do not generally pull partially burned portions back out to save—they are typically completely consumed. Many of the manuscript pages

---

[97] Archimandrite—head of a large monastery, or group of monasteries, in the Greek Orthodox Church.

[98] *The Brighton Observer*, December 26, 1862 as cited in Constantine Simonides, *The Periplus of Hannon* (1864), p. 56.

[99] J.K. Elliott, *Codex Sinaiticus and the Simonides Affair* (1982), p. 88.

[100] *The Literary Churchman*, November 2, 1863 as cited in B. Harris Cowper, *Journal of Sacred Literature & Biblical Record, 1864,* Vol. 5 (London: Williams and Norgate, 1864), p. 227.

are partially burned, apparently necessitating the need for a story about a fire, yet, Tischendorf never mentions rescuing partially burned manuscripts from the fire—which seems like an important detail. This may be why even Tischendorf's own story of the waste basket seems to be suppressed.

Kallinikos stated, "I further declare that the codex which Dr. Tischendorf obtained is the identical codex which Simonides wrote... inasmuch as I saw it in the hands of Tischendorf and recognized the work."[101] He also claimed that the Codex had been washed with lemon juice and herbs to weaken the appearance of the letters and to give it a more ancient look.[102] He said, "you will greatly sin in foisting on the world a new MS as an old one, and especially a MS containing the Holy Scriptures. Injury to the Church must accrue from all this, even from the evidently numerous corrections of the MS."[103]

In response, the supporters of Tischendorf insisted that the claim was made up by Simonides and that Kallinikos was a fictional character. Yet, "to this day the monks at Mt. Sinai deny Tischendorf's story, and his claim that he found the manuscript in a rubbish basket."[104]

Simonides stated, "What, then, have you to oppose to the evidence of living men... O zealous defender of the pseudo-Sinaitic Codex? If you are still incredulous, I say to you, remain faithful in your faithlessness.... I have proclaimed the truth.... for I will answer as I should to the All-seeing God in the Day of Judgment. Therefore... I have spoken, I have no sin. Wholly yours, C. Simonides."[105]

When Simonides presented at Leipzig, most of the scholars had embraced the Sheperd of Hermas as valid, but Tischendorf pronounced it a forgery, because it differed from the Latin

---

[101] B. Harris Cowper, *Journal of Sacred Literature & Biblical Record, 1863,* Vol. 3 (1863), p. 212.

[102] J.K. Elliott, *Codex Sinaiticus and the Simonides Affair* (1982), p. 77-78.

[103] *The Literary Churchman*, December 16, 1862 as cited in J.K. Elliott, *Codex Sinaiticus and the Simonides Affair* (1982), p. 76.

[104] *Tares Among the Wheat,* directed by Christian J. Pinto (2012), 2:19:00.

[105] B. Harris Cowper, *Journal of Sacred Literature & Biblical Record, 1863,* Vol. 3 (1863), p. 231.

version.[106] The Sheperd of Hermas had only been known from the Latin translations. In 1855 when Simonides presented the first Greek manuscript of Hermas ever discovered, Tischendorf had already taken the Codex from Sinai, which contained the Sheperd of Hermas in Greek. This fact was at the time unknown to Simonides. Since Simonides had the only known manuscript of Hermas in Greek,[107] it would make sense that he would include it in the manuscript he was creating, and provides strong evidence of the truth of Simonides' story. Tischendorf apparently had already altered the Greek copy of Hermas in the Codex to match the Latin [Catholic] versions. By presenting an original Greek manuscript of Hermas, in Leipzig, Simonides would have threatened Tischendorf's entire scheme, hence his anger and the charge that Simonides had forged the Greek Hermas.

Simonides said, "the manuscript Hermas was correct... and that the common Latin translations from which it differed had been made not in accordance with the Greek originals but to suit the views of the Latin translators, who had put into the mouth of... Hermas doctrinal opinions... eminently calculated to strengthen the position of the [Catholic] Church... to which the translators belonged."[108] "As some of the chief dogmas of the Latin Church were severely attacked by an exposure of the fraud in the Latin translations, Simonides gained much ill-will among the members of that Church."[109]

"Simonides would publish a final work in 1864, before leaving England for good. In it he reaffirmed his claims about Sinaiticus, and included the testimonies of those who believed him. Yet his enemies in the press continued to insist that he was merely a liar and a forger. The charge of forgery was never proven against Simonides."[110] The charge of forgery against Tischendorf's Codex Sinaiticus was never disproven.

---

[106] *Tares Among the Wheat*, directed by Christian J. Pinto (2012), 2:34:00.

[107] James A. Farrer, *Literary Forgeries* (1907), p. 64.

[108] *Tares Among the Wheat*, directed by Christian J. Pinto (2012), 2:35:20.

[109] J.K. Elliott, *Codex Sinaiticus and the Simonides Affair* (1982), p.183.

[110] *Tares Among the Wheat*, directed by Christian J. Pinto (2012), 2:33:25.

The British Library's Codex Sinaiticus Project fails to mention any details related to the charges of forgery against the Codex. Despite its shady history and questionable origin, this Codex is lauded as the oldest and best.

As stated in the BBC documentary, *Codex Sinaiticus*, the theological effect of the Codex Sinaiticus was to undermine faith in the preserved and infallible word of God: "On closer inspection the text of the Codex Sinaiticus is littered with revisions. It is history's most altered Biblical manuscript; and within those changes lie its real theological secrets.
"It has approximately 23,000 corrections, in all that survives. Which is an extraordinary rate of correction. It means that there are on average about 30 corrections on each page.
"Given the quality of the calligraphy, scholars were surprised to find so many changes. Many scribes wrote for money. They wrote quickly which meant they sometimes made errors. But, 23,000 corrections can't be explained in this way. There have to be theological reasons too. If the Biblical text could vary it couldn't be the immutable word of God. What the Codex Sinaiticus was revealing was the instability of the story....
"Here was a manuscript that offered unique insights into Scripture and which made scholars reevaluate the Bible that Victorian Christians had relied on.
"The King James Bible, sturdy and black on the shelves was thought to be perfect, inerrant, by many people across the English-speaking world, which was mostly Bible believing Protestants. But the fact of the matter was that scholars had known that the translations were all based on rather shaky evidence, shaky texts."[111]

[111] *Tares Among the Wheat*, directed by Christian J. Pinto (2012), 2:28:55.

"Rome decreed that the light of God's Word should be extinguished,[112] and the people should be shut up in darkness. But Heaven had provided other agencies for the preservation of the church."[113]

[112] To this day, Rome is heavily in control of the distribution and publishing of bibles based on the Codex Sinaiticus. Leo Hindery, managing partner of Intermedia Partners, which purchased Thomas Nelson Publishers, the largest Christian publishing house in the world, in an interview with Tom Southwick, 2001, explained the source of his success: "'What gave you the ambition to go from you know, sort of blue collar jobs to wanting to become, I guess, a businessman?' 'Lots of demons, lots of devils that have always caused me to want to succeed. I was blessed with some intellect, some intellectual curiosity as well, that just drove me... a lot of my early influences came from the Jesuits, I was Jesuit trained at both the high school level and at college. I always knew that I wanted to be something special. I don't mean that self-servingly, but I did want to succeed and be well thought of. I give a lot of the early, early, credit to the Jesuits.'
"In 2011 Intermedia Partners sold possession of Thomas Nelson to Ruppert Murdoch, most famous for his ownership of Fox News. Murdoch is also a Knight of the Pontifical Order of St. Gregory; knighted by the Pope for his service to Rome. Through Thomas Nelson, Murdoch..., publishes the NKJ[V]..., and through Zondervan, he publishes the NIV... Murdoch also owns Harper Collins, that publishes the Satanic Bible, for the church of Satan."
Tares Among the Wheat, directed by Christian J. Pinto (2012), 2:48:00.

[113] E. G. White, *The Great Controversy* (1911), p. 97.1.

9 The Church in the Wilderness

In his Word, God depicts his true church, not as the church that has political acceptance and power, but as a pure woman who must flee into the wilderness in order to find refuge from the powers that were persecuting and trying to kill her.[1]

"Some will ask, should not we look to the church which for ages has been the favored of kings and nations to find the true church instead of looking to a people who for centuries were never the dominant church, and who many times were obscure? Let the prophet John answer this question: 'The woman [church] fled into the wilderness.' (Revelation 12:6) In order to recognize the true church, it is imperative that we fix our eyes upon those Christian bodies which have largely been forgotten in the works of history.
"Divine revelation teaches that the light which was to shine upon the last generation of men would be a continuation and an enlargement of the light which shone upon the Church in the Wilderness throughout almost thirteen centuries; namely, the 1260-year period."[2]

"The Church in the Wilderness did not arrive at the truth by opposition to prevailing dogmas and heresies. Its faith was not a faith newly received. The religious beliefs of its members were an inheritance from the days of the apostles. To them men owe the preservation of the Bible. Contrary to almost universal belief, the Church in the Wilderness embraced the true missionary churches during the long night of the Dark Ages. It held aloft the torch of education while the rest of the world about it was falling into the darkness of ignorance and superstition. Its territory was not circumscribed. On the contrary, its influence penetrated into all parts of the known world."[3]

"The Church in the Wilderness, surrounded by savage tribes and battling against barbaric darkness, has been painted by its enemies without its victories. Driven often by opposition to mountain retreats, it was saved from the corrupting influences of ecclesiastical and

---

[1] See Revelation 12.

[2] B.G. Wilkinson, Ph.D., *Truth Triumphant: The Church in the Wilderness* (1944), p. 10.

[3] *Ibid.*, p. 11.

political power. In many parts of the world, all the way from Ireland in the west to China in the east, there were centers of truth. The leaders in these centers were united in their desire to remain in the faith, and to perpetuate from generation to generation the pure truths of the gospel handed down from the days of the apostles. Their records have been systematically destroyed."[4]

"Within the generation following the apostles, if not even before the death of John, the New Testament had been translated into that most beautiful of all Latin texts, the Italic version, often called Itala. For centuries scholars of the Celtic church quoted from the Itala."[5]

"Shortly after the death of the apostles, the New Testament was translated into Syriac. This noble version, called the Peshitta, meaning "simple," had for centuries a wide circulation in the East."[6]

"The Bibles produced by the Syrian scribes presented the Syrian text of the school of Antioch, and this text became the form which displaced all others in the Eastern churches and is, indeed, the Textus Receptus (Received Text) from which our Authorized Version [KJV] is translated."[7]

"Lucian [c. 250-312] was really a learned man; his work on the text of the Old Testament... soon became famous; he was a Hebrew scholar, and his version was adopted by the greater number of the churches of Syria and Asia Minor. He occupied himself also with the

---

[4] B.G. Wilkinson, Ph.D., *Truth Triumphant: The Church in the Wilderness* (1944), p. 12-13.

[5] *Ibid.*, p. 28.
See also:
W.S. Gilly, D.D., *Vigilantius and His Times* (London: Seeley Burnside, and Seeley, 1844), p. 116;
Frederick Nolan, LL.D., F.R.S.L., *An Inquiry into the Integrity of the Greek Vulgate* (London: R & R Gilbert, 1815), p. 17;
George T. Stokes, D.D., *Ireland and the Celtic Church* (London: Hodder and Stoughton, 1886), p. 27, 28.

[6] *Ibid.*, p. 26.
See also:
John William Burgon, B.D., *The Revision Revised* (1883), p. 9.
Francis Crawford Burkitt, M.A., D.D., *Early Eastern Christianity* (New York: E.P. Dutton & Co., 1904), p. 41.

[7] De Lacy O'Leary, D.D., *The Syriac Church and Fathers*, p. 49 as cited in B.G. Wilkinson, Ph.D., *Truth Triumphant: The Church in the Wilderness* (1944), p. 59.

New Testament. His exegesis differs widely from that of Origen. In Antioch allegorical interpretation was not in fashion."[8]

"Lucian and his school gathered and edited a definite and complete Bible. It was a collection of the books from Genesis to Revelation. Well-known writers like Jerome, Erasmus, and Luther, and, in the nineteenth century, John William Burgon and Fenton John Anthony Hort, whether friends or opponents, agree that Lucian was the editor who passed on to the world the Received Text—the New Testament text which was adopted at the birth of all the great churches of the Reformation. Not a single church born of the Reformation, such as Lutheran, Calvinistic, Anglican, Baptist, Presbyterian, Methodist, Congregational, or Adventist, adopted any other Bible than that whose New Testament text came down from Lucian.

"The Papacy passed on to the world an indefinite and incomplete Bible. While it recognized to a certain extent the books from Genesis to Revelation, it added to them seven other books not considered canonical by the authorities quoted above. In the Latin Vulgate of the Papacy it adopted a New Testament text with passages radically different from the same in the Received Text. It also made the decrees of the councils and the bulls of the popes equal to the books of the Bible. In other words, with the Roman Catholic Church, the Scriptures are still in the making. The Papacy exalts the church above the Bible. Cardinal Gibbons says, 'The Scriptures alone do not contain all the truths which a Christian is bound to believe.'"[9]

Besides the Syrian Church, God was raising others to preserve and transmit his Word. The Waldenses, also called the Vaudois, or Leonists trace their origins all the way back to apostolic times. Even though their writings were systematically destroyed, their enemies admitted to their ancient origins. Reinerius Saccho, an officer of the Inquisition (c. 1254), charged with exterminating heretics, who dared to believe God's Word—such as the Waldenses, wrote a treatise as to why they were dangerous. The first reason he gives is their ancient origin:

---

[8] Louis Duchesne, LITT.D., *Early History of the Christian Church*, Vol. 1 (New York: Longmans, Green and Co., 1912), p. 362.

[9] B.G. Wilkinson, Ph.D., *Truth Triumphant: The Church in the Wilderness* (1944), p. 59-60.

"First, because it is more lasting; for some say that it hath endured from the time of Pope Sylvester; others from the time of the apostles; Second, because it is more general. For there is scarcely any country where this sect has not been. Third, because when all other sects beget horror in the hearers by the presumption of their blasphemies against God, this of the Leonists hath a great appearance of loving kindness: because they live justly before men and believe all things well concerning God and all the articles which are contained in the creed; only they blaspheme the Roman Church and the clergy..."[10]

"Gilles says, 'This Vaudois people have had pastors of great learning... versed in the languages of the Holy Scriptures... and very laborious... especially in transcribing to the utmost of their ability, the books of Holy Scripture, for the use of their disciples.'"[11]

"'The church in the wilderness,' and not the proud hierarchy enthroned in the world's great capital, was the true church of Christ, the guardian of the treasures of truth which God has committed to His people to be given to the world...
"The Waldenses were among the first of the peoples of Europe to obtain a translation of the Holy Scriptures. **Hundreds of years before the Reformation they possessed the Bible in manuscript in their native tongue. They had the truth unadulterated**, and this rendered them the special objects of hatred and persecution. They declared the Church of Rome to be the apostate Babylon of the Apocalypse, and at the peril of their lives they stood up to resist her corruptions. While, under the pressure of long-continued persecution, some compromised their faith, little by little yielding its distinctive principles, others held fast the truth. Through ages of

---

[10] Reinerius Saccho, cir. 1254, "Contra Waldenses," as cited in Margarino de la Bigne, *Maxima Bibliotheca Veteran Patrum,* Tomus Vigesimusquintus, [*Great Encyclopedia of the Ancient Fathers,* Vol. 25] (Lugduni: Apud Anissonios, 1677), p. 264.
Latin: "Prima est, Quia est diuturnior. Aliqui enim dicunt, quod durauerit a tempore Sylvestri: aliqui, a tempore Apostolorum. Secunda, quia est generalior. Fere enim nulla est terra, in qua haec secta non sit. Tertia, quia cum omnes aliae sectae immanitate blasphemiarum in Deum, audientibus horrerem inducant, haec scilicet Leonistarum, Magnam habet speciem pietaris: eo quod coram hominibus iuste uiuant, bene omnia de Deo credant & omnes articulos, qui in Symbolo continentur; solummodo Romanam Ecclesiam blasphemant, & Clerum..."

[11] Alexis Muston, D.D., *The Israel of the Alps*, Vol. 2, trans. John Montgomery, A.M. (London: Blackie and Son, 1866), p. 448.

darkness and apostasy there were Waldenses who denied the supremacy of Rome, who rejected image worship as idolatry, and who kept the true Sabbath. Under the fiercest tempests of opposition, they maintained their faith. Though gashed by the Savoyard spear, and scorched by the Romish fagot, they stood unflinchingly for God's word and His honor."[12]

It was the Waldenses that had the true, unadulterated manuscripts, not Rome. Indeed, from the forward of the Jesuit 1582 *Rheims New Testament*, we see Rome's hatred for the Bibles of the Waldenses and Protestants, such as Wycliffe. "More than tvvo hundred yeres agoe, in the daies of Charles the fifth, the Frenche king, vvas it put forth faithfully in Frenche, the sooner to shake out of the deceiued peoples hãdes [hands], the false heretical translations of a secte called Vv*aldenses.* In our ovvn countrie...no vulgar translation [was] commonly vsed or occupied of the multitude, yet they vvere extant in English euen before the troubles that Vvicleffe and his follovvers raised in our Church.... straite [straight] prouision vvas made, that no heretical version set forth by Vvicleffe, or his adherentes, should be suffered, nor any other in or after his time be published or permitted to be readde."[13]

On the other hand, the preface of the 1611 King James Version also highlights the controversy between the Bibles: "Now the Church of Rome... So much are they afraid of the light of the Scriptures... that they will not trust the people with it, not as it is set foorth [sic] by their owne sworne men, no not with the Licence of their owne Bishop and Inquisitors. Yea, so vnwilling they are to communicate the Scriptures to the peoples understanding in any sort, that they are not ashamed to confesse, that wee forced them to translate it into English against their wills. This seemeth to argue a bad cause, or a bad conscience, or both. Sure we are, that it is not he that hath good gold, that is afraid to bring it to the touch-stone, but he that hath the counterfeit; neither is it the true man that shunneth the light, but the malefactour, lest his deedes should be reproued: neither is it the plaine dealing Merchant that is vnwilling to haue the waights, or the meteyard

[12] E. G. White, *The Great Controversy* (1911), p. 64.2-65.2.

[13] John Fogny, preface to the *Rheims New Testament* (Rhemes: John Fogny, 1582).

brought in place, but he that vseth deceit. But we will let them alone for this fault, and returne to translation."[14]

"By patient, untiring labor, sometimes in the deep, dark caverns of the earth, by the light of torches, the sacred Scriptures were written out, verse by verse, chapter by chapter. Thus the work went on, the revealed will of God shining out like pure gold; how much brighter, clearer, and more powerful because of the trials undergone for its sake, only those could realize who were engaged in the work. Angels from Heaven surrounded these faithful workers."[15]

As the dark shadows of the middle ages were pressed back by the light of dawn, John Wycliffe,[16]—morning star of the reformation—for the first time, brought the Bible to the common person—in English. At the time, all he had access to was the Catholic Latin Vulgate. The treasures of Constantinople had not yet burst upon Europe.

"Wycliffe's Bible had been translated from the Latin text, which contained many errors. It had never been printed, and the cost of manuscript copies was so great that few but wealthy men or nobles could procure it, and, furthermore, being strictly proscribed by the church, it had had a comparatively narrow circulation. In 1516, a year before the appearance of Luther's theses, Erasmus had published his Greek and Latin version of the New Testament. Now for the first time the Word of God was printed in the original tongue. In this work many errors of former versions were corrected, and the sense was more clearly rendered."[17]

"Endowed by nature with a mind that could do ten hours work in one, Erasmus, during his mature years in the earlier part of the sixteenth century, was the intellectual dictator of Europe. He was ever at work, visiting libraries, searching in every nook and corner for the profitable. He was ever collecting, comparing, writing and publishing. Europe was rocked from end to end by his books which exposed the ignorance of the monks, the superstitions of the priesthood, the

---

[14] The Translators, preface to the *King James Bible* (London: Robert Barker, Printer to the Kings most Excellent Maiestie, 1611).

[15] E. G. White, *The Great Controversy* (1911), p. 69.1.

[16] John Wycliffe lived 1323-1384.

[17] E. G. White, *The Great Controversy* (1911), p. 245.1.

bigotry, and the childish and coarse religion of the day. He classified the Greek MSS. [manuscripts], and read the Fathers.
"It is customary even to-day with those who are bitter against the pure teachings of the Received Text, to sneer at Erasmus. No perversion of facts is too great to belittle his work. Yet while he lived, Europe was at his feet. Several times the King of England offered him any position in the kingdom, at his own price; the Emperor of Germany did the same. The Pope offered to make him a cardinal. This he steadfastly refused, as he would not compromise his conscience. In fact, had he been so minded, he perhaps could have made himself Pope. France and Spain sought him to become a dweller in their realm, while Holland prepared to claim her most distinguished citizen.
"Book after book came from his hand. Faster and faster came the demands for his publications. But his crowning work was the New Testament in Greek. At last after one thousand years, the New Testament was printed (A.D. 1516) in the original tongue."[18]

"There were hundreds of manuscripts for Erasmus to examine, and he did; but he used only a few. What matters? The vast bulk of manuscripts in Greek are practically all the Received Text.... Moreover, the text he chose had such an outstanding history in the Greek, the Syrian, and the Waldensian Churches, that it constituted an irresistible argument of God's providence."[19]

"Indeed almost all the important variant readings known to scholars today were already known to Erasmus more than 450 years ago and discussed in the notes.... Erasmus dealt with such problem passages as the conclusion of the Lords' Prayers (Matt. 6:13), the interview of the rich young man with Jesus (Matt. 19:17-22), the ending of Mark (Mark 16:9-20), the angelic song (Luke 2:14), the angel, agony, and bloody sweat omitted (Luke 22:43-44), the woman taken in adultery (John 7:53-8:11), and the mystery of Godliness (1 Tim. 3:16)."[20]

---

[18] B.G. Wilkinson, Ph.D., *Our Authorized Bible Vindicated* (1930), p. 53-54.

[19] *Ibid.*, p. 54.

[20] Edward F. Hills, Th.D., *The King James Version Defended* (Des Moines, IA: Christian Research Press, 1984), p. 198,199.

Erasmus even had access to information about, and renderings from, the Vatican manuscript (which readings he rejected as corrupt), via the Papal librarian Paul Bombasius, "as early as 1521" and later from Sepulveda.[21]

Erasmus had available the texts of the Waldenses, the Syrian Bibles, and the Greek manuscripts from Constantinople. From these treasures, Erasmus published the first Greek New Testament ever printed.

"This text is and has been for 300 [over 400 now] years the best known and most widely used. It has behind it all the Protestant scholarship of nearly three centuries."[22]

"Satan had urged on the papal priests and prelates to bury the Word of truth beneath the rubbish of error, heresy, and superstition, but in a most wonderful manner it was preserved uncorrupted through all the ages of darkness. It bore not the stamp of man, but the impress of God."[23]

---

[21] William P. Grady, M.Ed., *Final Authority,* (Schererville, IN: Grady Publication, 1993), p. 113. Frederic George Kenyon, B.A., GBE, KCB, FSA, *Our Bible and the Ancient Manuscripts,* 3rd ed. (London: Eyre and Spottiswood, 1897), p. 133.

[22] B.G. Wilkinson, Ph.D., *Our Authorized Bible Vindicated* (1930), p. 73-74.

[23] E. G. White, *The Great Controversy* (1911), p. 68.3.

10 The Glorious King James Version

God's promise to preserve his pure Word was dramatically fulfilled in the 1611 publication of the Authorized Version of the Bible, more commonly known, today, as the King James Version. "The words of the LORD are pure words: as silver tried in a furnace of earth, purified seven times. Thou shalt keep them, O LORD, thou shalt preserve them from this generation for ever."[1]

On January 16, the second day of the Hampton Court Conference of 1604, Dr. John Rainolds proposed to King James I that a new translation of the Bible be undertaken. Sixteen years earlier, "In 1588, the year when the Spanish Armada sailed to its destruction, there had appeared from this monarch's pen *A Paraphrase Upon the Revelation of the Apostle S. Iohn.* It was republished in 1603, the year of his accession to the English throne. The royal theologian not only considered himself to be the head of the Anglican Church but also dared to call the pope the Antichrist. Revelation 13, King James explained pointedly, as 'the Popes arising: His description: His rising caused by the ruine of the fourth Monarchie the Romane Empire: The rising of the false and Papisticall Church; her description; her conformitie with her Monarch the Pope.'"[2]

Perhaps the Pope and the Jesuits would have tolerated a Protestant monarch publishing such a thing, as most Protestants at the time were thundering these kinds of things against the papacy, but the news of a new translation of the Bible by the same monarch, was too large a threat to be ignored. Within three months of the decision to translate what would become the King James Version of the Holy Bible, "On May 1, 1604, the five Gunpowder conspirators, Robert Catesby, Thomas Winter, Thomas Percy, a distant relation and steward to the Duke of Northumberland, John Wright, and Guido [also known as Guy] Fawkes, after having sworn each other to

---

[1] Psalm 12:6-7

[2] Edwin de Kock, *The Truth About 666 and the Story of the Great Apostasy* (Edinburgh, TX: Edwin de Kock, 2011), p. 64.

secresy [sic], received the host at the hands of John Gerard a Jesuit."[3]

Part of a much larger Jesuit conspiracy,[4] they planned to put an end to the new translation of the Bible, by assassinating not only King James but also the entire English government by blowing up the Parliament house with gunpowder, during session. "One of the conspirators, Thomas Percy, was promoted in June 1604, gaining access to a house in London that belonged to John Whynniard, Keeper of the King's Wardrobe. Fawkes was installed as a caretaker and began using the pseudonym John Johnson, servant to Percy. The contemporaneous account of the prosecution (taken from Thomas Wintour's confession) claimed that the conspirators attempted to dig a tunnel from beneath Whynniard's house to Parliament... If the story is true, however, by December 1604 the conspirators were busy tunnelling [sic] from their rented house to the House of Lords. They ceased their efforts when, during tunnelling [sic], they heard a noise from above. Fawkes was sent out to investigate, and returned with the news that the tenant's widow was clearing out a nearby undercroft, directly beneath the House of Lords.
"The plotters purchased the lease to the room.... Unused and filthy, it was considered an ideal hiding place for the gunpowder the plotters planned to store."[5]

Initially twenty barrels of gunpowder, and on July 20, 1605, sixteen more barrels were deposited in the cache. The threat of the plague delayed the opening of the Parliament session until November 5. In the providence of God, "On the evening of October 26, Lord Monteagle received an anonymous letter warning him to stay away, and to 'retyre youre self into yowre contee whence yow maye expect the event in safti for... they shall receyve a terrible blowe this parleament.'"[6] Monteagle's suspicions were aroused and he showed

---

[3] Arthur Tozer Russell, B.C.L., *The Memoirs of the Life Works of Lancelot Andrewes* (London: Saunders, Otley and Co., 1863), p. 178.

[4] "It ought to be remembered that all the avowed conspirators belonged to the Jesuit faction." Arthur Tozer Russell, B.C.L., *The Memoirs of the Life Works of Lancelot Andrewes* (1863), p. 192.

[5] https://en.wikipedia.org/wiki/Guy_Fawkes Retrieved 9-15-15.

[6] https://en.wikipedia.org/wiki/Thomas_Knyvet,_1st_Baron_Knyvet Retrieved 4-13-16.

the letter to King James. "The King ordered Sir Thomas Knyvet to conduct a search of the cellars underneath Parliament, which he did in the early hours of November 5. Fawkes had taken up his station late on the previous night, armed with a slow match and a watch given to him by Percy 'becaus he should knowe howe the time went away.' He was found leaving the cellar, shortly after midnight, and arrested. Inside, the barrels of gunpowder were discovered hidden under piles of firewood and coal."[7]

The King James Bible is the greatest threat to the power of the papacy. "The printing of the English Bible has proved to be by far the mightiest barrier ever reared to repel the advance of Popery, and to damage all the resources of the Papacy."[8] "The Roman Church will never use Luther's Version or King James's Version, and could not do so without endangering her creed."[9] The Jesuits, speaking of the Protestant Bible, described it thus, "Then the Bible, that serpent which, with head erect and eyes flashing fire threatens us with its venom shall be changed again into a rod, as soon as we are able to seize it. Oh then mysterious rod! We will not again suffer thee to escape from our hands. For you know too well that for three centuries past this cruel asp has left us no repose. You well know with what folds it entwines us, and with what fangs it gnaws us."[10]

The Bible's power, feared by its enemies, is the power to transform those who submit to its claims, and love its precepts. The written words of the King James translators have had a greater influence on this world than any other literary work the planet has ever seen. It has changed the course of nations, and altered history in a way the translators could have never fathomed. It has transmitted the precious Gospel message to more souls than all other agencies combined. Only in eternity will its power be comprehended.

The King James translators of the Bible achieved what has never been accomplished before, or since. Although the translators are

---

[7] https://en.wikipedia.org/wiki/Guy_Fawkes Retrieved 9-15-15.

[8] Alexander McClure, *The Translators Revived; A Biographical Memoir of the Authors of the English Version of the Holy Bible* (1853), p. 71

[9] Philip Schaff, D.D., LL.D., *History of the Christian Church,* Vol. 6 (1916), p. 365.

[10] Jacopo Leone, *The Jesuit Conspiracy: The Secret Plan of the Order* (London: Chapman and Hall, 1848), p. 98-99.

mostly unknown, and their masterpiece is either unappreciated or maligned; though the importance of their accomplishment is not comprehended; though every power of hell and demons has been arrayed against this book, yet their legacy survives as the living Word of God—the best-selling book of all time.

"Priests, atheists, skeptics, devotees, agnostics, and evangelists are generally agreed that the Authorised [sic] Version of the English Bible is the best example of English literature that the world has ever seen.... Everyone who has a thorough knowledge of the Bible may truly be called educated; and no other learning or culture, no matter how extensive or elegant, can, among Europeans and Americans, form a proper substitute. Western civilisation [sic] is founded on the Bible.... The Elizabethan period—a term loosely applied to the years between 1558-1642—is properly regarded as the most important era in English Literature.... But the crowning achievement of those spacious times was the Authorised [sic] Translation of the Bible, which appeared in 1611.... Now as the English-speaking people have the best Bible in the world, and as it is the most beautiful monument ever erected with the English alphabet, we ought to make the most of it, for it is an incomparably rich inheritance, free to all who can read. This means that we ought invariably in the church and on public occasions to use the Authorised [sic] Version; all others are inferior."[11]

The translation began in 1604 with the appointment of 54 men to the translation committee. Forty-seven ended up serving, and the translation process was completed in seven years. From the sparse information surviving regarding these men, we find almost incomprehensible talent and ability, certainly only because they were endowed by the power of God with skill for the task at hand. Without praising the human instrument, it is valuable to remind ourselves of what God can accomplish through ailing, erring mortals who have dedicated their services to God. "Out of mere human beings who worked and even quarreled in company came the miraculous perfection of the Authorized Version."[12]

---

[11] William Lyon Phelps, Ph.D., Professor of English Literature, Yale University, *Human Nature in the Bible* (New York: Charles Scribner's Sons, 1922), p. ix-xi.

[12] Ward Allen, *Translating for King James* (Nashville, TN: Vanderbilt University Press, 1969), p. ix.

The Bible records the skill God gave to Bezaleel to build the ark of the covenant. "Then wrought Bezaleel and Aholiab, and every wise hearted man, in whom the LORD put wisdom and understanding to know how to work all manner of work for the service of the sanctuary, according to all that the LORD had commanded."[13] "And Bezaleel made the ark of shittim wood: two cubits and a half was the length of it, and a cubit and a half the breadth of it, and a cubit and a half the height of it: And he overlaid it with pure gold within and without, and made a crown of gold to it round about."[14] If God imparted special wisdom and understanding to the artisans making the ark that would contain the Words of God, how much more would he impart skill and guidance to those translators who bowed to the Word of God, rather than altering it to suit their opinions.

Sir Lancelot Andrewes was the chief and guiding translator of the King James Bible. "This was the man who was acknowledged as the greatest preacher of the age... who was the most brilliant man in the English Church... The man was a library, the repository of sixteen centuries of Christian culture, he could speak fifteen modern languages and six ancient."[15] While studying at Cambridge University, "Once a year, at Easter, he used to pass a month with his parents. During this vacation, he would find a master, from whom he learned some language to which he was before a stranger. In this way after a few years, he acquired most of the modern languages of Europe."[16] His knowledge of Latin, Greek, Hebrew, Chaldee, Syriac and Arabic was so advanced "that he may well be ranked in first place, to be one of the rarest linguists in Christendom."[17] People commented on his serenity, and the sense of grace that hovered around him. He frequently spent five hours each morning in prayer.[18] "It is because people like Lancelot Andrewes flourished in the first

---

[13] Exodus 36:1

[14] Exodus 37:1-2

[15] Adam Nicolson, FRSL, FSA, *God's Secretaries: The Making of the King James Bible* (New York: Harper Collins, 2003), p. 33.

[16] Alexander McClure, *The Translators Revived; A Biographical Memoir of the Authors of the English Version of the Holy Bible* (1853), p. 78.

[17] Arthur Tozer Russell, B.C.L., *Memoirs of the Life and Works of Lancelot Andrewes* (1863), p. 532.

[18] *Ibid.*, p. 526.

decade of the seventeenth century—and do not now—that the greatest translation of the Bible could be made then, and cannot now."[19] Lancelot's brother Roger was also a famous linguist and likewise served on the translation committee.

The earnest and solemn Thomas Holland was admired by all who heard of him. He was distinguished for his preaching and his zeal for purity of faith. "Whenever he took a journey, he first called together the Fellows of his College, for his parting charge, which always ended thus,—'I commend you to the love of God, and to the hatred of all popery and superstition!'"[20]

Also serving was Richard Bancroft, Archbishop of Canterbury, and Dr. Thomas Sparke educated at Magdalen College, Oxford; where he earned four degrees. John Spencer was elected Greek lecturer at Oxford, at nineteen years of age.

Much information about these men has been covered in the dust of history. We have more information available about the translator John Bois, than others, because the original notes he took on the translation process survived to be discovered some 300 years later, and a biography of his life was written by his contemporary, Anthony Walker. John Bois was apparently a child prodigy in intellect. His father being an eminent Greek and Hebrew scholar, Bois could read the Hebrew Bible at age five.[21] Bois was admitted to university at age 14 (where most students of the day were not admitted until age 21 or 22). At the University he finished Greek I in about a week (which usually took one year) and finished Greek II & III in something over a month (which usually took two years).[22] John Bois translated part of Revelation and was on the committee to review the final copy of the Bible, which took three-quarters of a year.

---

[19] Adam Nicolson, FRSL, FSA, *God's Secretaries: The Making of the King James Bible* (2003), p. 33.

[20] Alexander McClure, *The Translators Revived; A Biographical Memoir of the Authors of the English Version of the Holy Bible* (1853), p. 137.

[21] *Ibid.*, p. 200.

[22] Anthony Walker, S.T.P., *Life of John Bois* (1728), as reprinted in Ward Allen, *Translating for King James* (1969), p. 130-133.

One translator, John Laifield, was a skilled architect, and "his judgment was much relied on for the fabric of the tabernacle and temple."[23] Laifield had also been to the New World.

Two translators were mathematicians: William Bedwell and Henry Savile. Savile was tutor in Greek and mathematics to Queen Elizabeth.[24]

Lawrence Chaderton "spent some years in the study and practice of the law,"[25] prior to his conversion to Protestantism, when he returned to school to study theology. Dr. Chaderton lived 29 years beyond the publication of the King James Bible, dying at the age of one hundred and three. Famed for his preaching, even at a great age, "while our aged saint was visiting some friends in his native county of Lancashire, he was invited to preach. Having addressed his audience for two full hours by the glass, he paused and said,—'I will no longer trespass on your patience.' And now comes the marvel; for the whole congregation cried out with one consent,—'For God's sake, go on, go on!' He, accordingly, proceeded much longer, to their great satisfaction and delight."[26]

Of Dr. John Rainolds, president of Corpus Christi College, Oxford, and the one who put forth the suggestion of undertaking the translation, it was said, "He alone was a well furnished library, full of all faculties, of all studies, of all learning; the memory, the reading of that man were near to a miracle."[27]

The youngest, Daniel Fairclough, was only twenty-six years old, when the Bible translators were nominated. The oldest, Hadrian Saravia, was eighty-one when the translation was completed. Hadrian published a treatise against papal primacy to answer the Jesuit Gretser.

---

[23] Alexander McClure, *The Translators Revived; A Biographical Memoir of the Authors of the English Version of the Holy Bible* (1853), p. 97.

[24] *Ibid.*, p. 165.

[25] *Ibid.*, p. 107.

[26] *Ibid.*, p. 115.

[27] Laurence Vance, Ph.D., *King James, His Bible, and Its Translators* (2009), p. 16.

Their method of translation has never since been attempted, much less surpassed. The translators were divided into six companies: two at Cambridge, two at Oxford and two at Westminster. There was an average of seven men per company. Every man in the company translated separately the section assigned to that division. Then each of the seven would bring his version together and they would go over all seven and take only the best parts of each. Then each group would give the resulting translation to each of the other five companies to be reviewed by every individual in the group. Finally, two from every division went over everything the final time, so that, by the end, every word was gone over at least fourteen times.[28] Then, copies were sent to all the bishops of the Church of England who knew the original tongues, to be reviewed. Even during the translation process any scholar on the continent with knowledge of the languages of Scripture was able to provide input on difficult passages.

With modern Bibles, the primary consideration is financial, as evidenced by the copyright. Therefore, no modern translation has ever accomplished this careful and thorough collaboration. Typically, a modern translation committee will assign each section to the various committee members, who submit their sections to be combined with everyone else's sections for the final review before publishing.

"It's worth noting the emphasis the King James translators placed, not only on the readable text of the King James Bible, but also its sound. Before the King James Bible was published and after the initial translation work was completed, a re-working took place, *The Story of English* describes this unique process,"[29] "they were to go through the text, re-working it so that it would not only read better but sound better, a quality for which it became famous throughout the English-speaking world."[30]

---

[28] Alexander McClure, *The Translators Revived; A Biographical Memoir of the Authors of the English Version of the Holy Bible* (1853), p. 69.

[29] Terry Watkins, Th.D., "Is the King James Bible Harder to Read?," http://www.av1611.org/kjv/kjv_easy.html Retrieved: 02-12-2016.

[30] Robert McCrum, William Cran, and Robert MacNeil, *The Story of English*, 3rd Rev. ed. (New York: Penguin Books, 2002), p. 112.

"The fine-tuning done by the KJV translators was done to magnify the following qualities: Intensify meter, add alliteration, secure brevity, ensure continuity, introduce a separate-from-sinners' vocabulary, give a transparent view of the Greek and Hebrew, polish the synchronization of letter sounds, syllabication, and syntax to enhance memorization, comprehension, and parasympathetic rhythms."[31]

For this reason, it is much easier to memorize from the King James Version than from modern versions. In fact, with the wide acceptance of modern translations, Bible memorization has all but ceased.

A commonly circulated bias against the King James Bible is the belief that the language is seventeenth century English and therefore difficult to read. Though its style and word usage are admittedly different than the everyday English we currently use, objective evidence is lacking by those making this assertion. The truth is that the data shows otherwise.

Dr. Rudolf Flesch, authority on readability studies and originator of the famous Flesch-Kincaid readability standards, makes a very significant statement regarding the King James Bible: "The best example of very easy prose (about 20 affixes per 100 words) is the King James Version of the Bible."[32] D.A. Waite, Jr. did an exhaustive word by word readability comparison between the King James Bible and six popular modern translations,[33] measuring the readability with computer analysis. "I wanted to first discover, then document the truth whatever it was. When I began this research project three years ago, I had no idea what the truth was. I had been just as confused by modern Bible version propaganda as everyone else. I don't suppose I believed everything that I heard, but I thought there must be some truth to all the claims. Quite frankly I was surprised at the results! Maybe you will be too."[34]

---

[31] Riplinger, M.A., M.F.A., *In Awe of Thy Word* (Ararat, VA: AV Publications, 2003), p. 17.

[32] Rudolf Flesch, Ph.D., *The Art of Plain Talk* (New York: Harper & Brothers,1946), p. 43.

[33] RSV, NKJV, NASB, ASV, NRSV, NIV.

[34] D.A. Waite, Jr., M.A., M.L.A., *The Comparative Readability of the Authorized Version* (Collingswood, NJ: The Bible for Today, 1996), p. 4.

"Only one version had a book on the college sophomore level (grade 14). And that version was not the KJV! Only one version had a Bible book on the college freshman level (grade 13). And that version was not the KJV! Despite what we may have heard elsewhere, the KJV did not have a single Bible book on the college level! Which versions, then, did? The college level culprits were two renderings of 2 Peter crafted by the NASV [NASB] (sophomore) and the NKJV (freshman)."[35] In fact, the Gunning's Fog Index showed that the KJV had the highest number of books at or below seventh grade reading level (35%), and highest number (98.5%) of books at or below tenth grade level, making it the easiest, not the hardest to read. The NASB came in as hardest to read. The Flesh-Kincaid reading ease showed the same thing: the KJV had the most number of books rating either fairly easy or, easy to read. The NASB had the least. The King James Bible was the easiest to read. In fact, the KJV is easier to read than an average children's book.

[35] D.A. Waite, Jr., M.A., M.L.A., *The Comparative Readability of the Authorized Version* (1996), p. 58.

Kind of Text	Grade	Words/Sentence	Syllables/Word	9+ letter words
Tech Journals	19	22	2	26%
Wall Street Journal	15	23	1.7	23%
New York Times	12	26	1.5	13%
USA Today	9	18	1.5	10%
People Magazine	8	14	1.5	10%
Children's Books	7	14	1.3	8%
KJV New Testament	7	18	1.3	3%
Pro Scribe Guidelines for Clear & Effective Writing	8-10	15-20	under 1.6	under 10%

[36]

People do not understand it, because it is the word of God, and the word of God is not hard to understand; it is impossible to understand, without the guidance and enlightenment of the Holy Spirit. Spiritual things are spiritually discerned.[37] Rather than going to human sources to help us understand the Bible, we need to plead with God for that wisdom which he alone can impart.

"The King James Bible was published in the year Shakespeare began work on his last play, *The Tempest*. Both the play and the Bible are masterpieces of English, but there is one crucial difference between them. Whereas Shakespeare ransacked the lexicon, the King James Bible employs a bare 8000 words—God's teaching in homely English for everyman."[38]

---

[36] D.A. Waite, Jr., M.A., M.L.A., *The Comparative Readability of the Authorized Version* (1996), p. 11.

[37] 1 Corinthians 2:14

[38] Robert McCrum, William Cran, and Robert MacNeil, *The Story of English,* 3rd Rev. ed. (2002), p. 114.

"The English of the King James Version is not the English of the early 17th Century. To be exact, it is not a type of English that was ever spoken anywhere. It is Biblical English, which was not used on ordinary occasions even by the translators who produced the King James Version. As H. Wheeler Robinson (1940) pointed out, one need only compare the preface written by the translators with the text of their translation to feel the difference in style. And the observations of W.A. Irwin (1952) are to the same purport. The King James Version, he reminds us, owes its merit, not to 17th century English—which was very different—but to its faithful translation of the original. Its style is that of the Hebrew and of the New Testament Greek. Even in their use of thee and thou the translators were not following 17th-century English usage but biblical usage, for at the time these translators were doing their work, these singular forms had already been replaced by the plural you in polite conversation."[39]

The word of God declares, "The words of the LORD are pure words: as silver tried in a furnace of earth, purified seven times. Thou shalt keep them, O LORD, thou shalt preserve them from this generation for ever."[40] Why would the Words of God need to be purified unless they had become contaminated?

"I was shown a time when Satan especially triumphed.... At different periods there were but a very few copies of the Bible in existence, yet He would not suffer His Word to be lost, for in the last days copies of it were to be so multiplied that every family could possess it. I saw that when there were but few copies of the Bible, it was precious and comforting to the persecuted followers of Jesus. It was read in the most secret manner, and those who had this exalted privilege felt that they had had an interview with God, with His Son Jesus, and with His disciples. But this blessed privilege cost many of them their lives. If discovered, they were taken to the headsman's block, to the stake, or to the dungeon to die of starvation."[41]

God's Word had been contaminated and nearly destroyed during the Dark Ages. The papacy based their scriptures on a few corrupted manuscripts, but God had said that his Word would be purified in the

---

[39] Edward F. Hills, Th.D., *The King James Version Defended* (1984), p. 218.

[40] Psalm 12:6-7

[41] E. G. White, *Early Writings* (1882), p. 214.2.

furnace of the earth, seven times. As the reformation dawned at the end of the long dark night of papal tyranny, that purification process began:

1. William Tyndale, in 1525, published the New Testament. Genesis through 2 Chronicles and Jonah were translated, but published separately, not as a Bible. Tyndale translated as much as possible from the Greek and Hebrew rather than the Latin Vulgate as Wycliffe did.[42]

2. Myles Coverdale, in 1535, published the first complete English Bible. Coverdale built on Tyndale's work yet translated also from the German and Latin, but not completely from the original languages. Coverdale and Tyndale at times worked on this translation together.

3. John Rogers, in 1537, (using the pen name of Thomas Matthew) published the Matthew Bible, which combined the best of Tyndale's and Coverdale's work.

4. The Great Bible, of 1539, was completed by Myles Coverdale— and called great because of its large size. This Bible used Tyndale's unfinished Old Testament books which were translated from the Latin Vulgate and German translations rather than original Greek and Hebrew. The Great Bible was also called the Whitchurche Bible after its first English printer, the Cromwell Bible after the one who prepared it for publication, the Cranmer Bible after the preface by Cranmer, or the Chained Bible since it was chained in a convenient place for people to read in the churches.

---

[42] Wycliffe's translation was not a purification as it was translated from the corrupted Latin Vulgate. "Wycliffe's Bible had been translated from the Latin text, which contained many errors. It had never been printed, and the cost of manuscript copies was so great that few but wealthy men or nobles could procure it; and, furthermore, being strictly proscribed by the church, it had had a comparatively narrow circulation."
E. G. White, *The Great Controversy* (1911), p. 245.1.

Only two other bibles were common during this time and both were not purifications.
Tavener's 1539 bible was a minor revision of the Matthew's Bible, and had narrow circulation and little influence on subsequent translators. Tavener was a member of the "Inner Temple" which takes its name from Knights Templar, a Catholic order.
The 1582 Jesuit Douay-Rheims was a Catholic version based completely on the Latin Vulgate. Only the New Testament was done in 1582, the Old Testament did not appear until 1611.

5. The Geneva Bible, of 1560, was the first Bible to be translated completely from the original text. William Whittingham, Myles Coverdale, Christopher Goodman, Anthony Gilby, Thomas Sampson, William Cole, John Knox, and John Calvin participated. It was very popular because it was a study Bible with maps and cross references, and was small enough to be used for home study.

6. The Bishops' Bible, of 1568, was translated by Matthew Parker, Archbishop of Canterbury, and his fellow bishops. Because there was no supervisor, the translation practice varies greatly from book to book. They also removed the Calvinistic marginal notes of the Geneva Bible.

7. The King James Version of 1611, was the seventh purification—God's promise to preserve his pure Word.

The first six were the very texts that King James ordered to be used, along with the original languages, to prepare the seventh—the King James Bible, as seen in his rules of translation numbers 1 and 14:

"1. The ordinary Bible read in the church, commonly called the Bishops' Bible, to be followed, and as little altered as the truth of the original will permit.
"14. These translations to be used when they agree better with the text than the Bishops Bible, viz. Tindall's. Matthews'. Coverdale's. Whitchurch's. Geneva."[43]

"The words of the LORD are pure words: as silver tried in a furnace of earth, purified seven times. Thou shalt keep them, O LORD, thou shalt preserve them from this generation for ever."[44]

---

[43] Laurence Vance, Ph.D., *King James, His Bible, and Its Translators* (2009), p. 84.

[44] Psalms 12:6-7

11 The Bible's Built-in Dictionary

One of the most valuable characteristics of the King James Version of the Bible is its built-in dictionary. Not only did the translators preserve the Hebrew and Greek poetry and literary devices, not only did they give a transparent feel of the style and cadence of the original languages, but they preserved the repetition and redundancy that allows the Bible to interpret and define all its own words.

Professor Gerald Hammond of the University of Manchester reminds English Bible readers that this dictionary is available only in the King James Bible: "the context defines the word and gives it its specific meaning.... it constantly redefines and recontextualizes words. By ignoring this fact, translators frequently diminish the status of the text they translate.... A modern translator... perceives the word only as it appears in the lexicon....
"The literary loss is large. No readers of these modern versions can perceive, as they can easily in the Authorized Version [KJV], the narrative's economical linking... the Renaissance practice is more faithful to the original text... 'the repetition of key-words is so prominent in many biblical narratives that one can still follow it... especially if one uses the King James Version.'"[1]

By removing redundant wording and by defining the words only from the lexicon, rather than from the Bible itself, modern translations lose the most important key to understanding Scripture as God intended it to be understood. The NIV, for example, has over 60,000 less words than the King James Version of the Bible.[2]

Modern translators "now mask the techniques of repetition which are so basic to the literary effects of the Bible.... the Renaissance [i.e. KJV] translators' practice worked better. They were, for a start,

---

[1] Gerald Hammond, "English Translations of the Bible," in *The Literary Guide to the Bible,* ed. by Robert Alter, Ph.D., and Frank Kermode, FBA, (Cambridge, MA: Harvard University Press, 1987), p. 651-652.

[2] KJV: 788,280 (1769 edition of the 1611 King James Bible) – http://www.biblebelievers.com/believers-org/kjv-stats.html Retrieved: 1-27-2016.
KJV: 788,258 – Laurence Vance, Ph.D., *King James, His Bible, and Its Translators* (2009), p. 74.
Number of Words in NIV 727,969 – http://wiki.answers.com/Q/How_many_words_in_NIV_Bible Retrieved: 1-27-2016.
http://brandplucked.webs.com/nivmissing64000words.htm Retrieved: 1-27-2016.

shrewdly perceptive of the need to reproduce very close repetition, as, for instance, within a single verse....
"the reader of a modern version... can find no such pattern....
"Again, the modern versions do not allow their readers such an insight....
"Too often the contrast between old and new [versions] shows up not merely an imperviousness on the part of the modern versions toward the Bible's literary effects, but a real desire to suppress them."[3]

Understanding the Bible's built-in dictionary is a simple yet profound way to allow Scripture to be its own interpreter. When one encounters a word with which he is not familiar, or is not sure of the specific meaning, the Bible's own dictionary will define the words for him.

Example[4]: Chapmen

2 Chronicles 9:14 "Beside that which chapmen and merchants brought."

The repetition of the words in this verse define chapmen. We can see that the chapmen are probably merchants. Webster's definition: seller, a market-man. Because of this feature, most of the World's venerable English dictionaries actually obtained their original definitions from the King James Version of the Bible.

In the above example the definition was found in the verse itself, but this is not always the case; sometimes one must look further abroad.

Example: Adamant

Ezekiel 3:9 "As an adamant harder than flint have I made thy forehead...."

What does adamant mean? Searching for another instance of the word, we find the following verse:

---

[3] Gerald Hammond, "English Translations of the Bible," in *The Literary Guide to the Bible,* ed. by Robert Alter, Ph.D., and Frank Kermode, FBA, (1987), p. 654-655.

[4] For this, and the following examples, we are indebted to a presentation by Gail Riplinger, *The Language of the King James Bible.*

Zechariah 7:12 "they made their hearts as an adamant stone...."

Webster's definition: A very hard stone

By comparing the two verses, we discover in Ezekiel that the adamant is very hard, and in Zechariah that the adamant is a stone.

Example: Chambering

Romans 13:13 "chambering and wantonness..."

Webster's definition: "wanton"

The redundancy of the verse itself allows us to define chambering and wantonness. But, what if you do not know what wanton means? Repeat the process.

Example: Wantonness

2 Peter 2:18 "they allure through the lusts of the flesh, through much wantonness..."

Webster's definition: lewdness; promiscuousness

The text itself defines wantonness as the lusts of the flesh.

Example: Lasciviousness

2 Corinthians 12:21 "and have not repented of the uncleanness and fornication and lasciviousness which they have committed."

Webster's definition: Loose, wanton, lewd, lustful

This verse defines lasciviousness as uncleanness and fornication, very similar to the Webster's definition. What if you did not understand the word fornication? Find another instance of the word's usage.

Example: Fornication

2 Chronicles 21:11 "caused the inhabitants of Jerusalem to commit fornication...."

2 Chronicles 21:13 “made Judah and the inhabitants of Jerusalem to go a whoring....”

Webster’s definition: Lewdness, adultery, incest

Here is an example where the answer is not found in the same verse, but in very close proximity. Verse 13 defines fornication as going a whoring, once again very similar to the Webster’s definition.

When looking for the definition of a Bible word, the following sequence is helpful:

1. Look first at the words next to the word in question.
2. If the definition is not there, examine the rest of the words in the verse.
3. If the verse does not define the word in question search the preceding and subsequent verses.
4. If these verses contain no clues, the entire chapter containing the word should be read.
5. If the chapter does not define the word, find other instances of the word in the rest of the Bible.

With each definition, the Bible stated the thought in one way, then repeated the same idea in another. This manner of writing is comprised of literary devices used by the Bible writers to express their God-inspired thoughts, and is a very important feature of Holy Writ. Why did God place this repetition in his Word? To increase the likelihood that people would be familiar with one word or the other; to make certain the reader is not misunderstanding the text; to define words should they fall out of use; to compensate for regional variations; and to aid in memorization through:

a. Alliteration
b. Rhyme
c. Rhythm
d. Phonoasthesia.

Example: Alliteration

Alliteration is the occurrence of the same letter or sound at the beginning of adjacent or closely connected words.

Revelation 19:21 “fowls were filled with their flesh”

Job 30:18 "collar of my coat"

Revelation 3:18
appear / anoint
council / clothed
tried / fire
wretched /rich / raiment

Example: Rhyme

Revelation 3:18
I council thee
to buy of me
thou mayest be
thou mayest see

Example: Rhythm

Revelation 3:18
I /coun'/cil /thee'
to /buy' /of /me'
thou /may'/est /be'
thou /may'/est /see'

Example: Phonoasthesia

The KJV's plosives, like "d," sound more severe than other sounds.

Therefore, the use of "damnation" is sharper and more powerful (Hebrews 4:12) than the NKJV or NIV's "condemnation."

When modern bibles substitute words, even with the same meaning, these literary devices may be lost; the built-in dictionary is not preserved; the ability to memorize is reduced; and the Bible's ability to interpret itself is destroyed.

The following words, almost prophetic in nature, were penned more than 125 years ago: "Up to this day of the world's history, the Bible has not been seriously meddled with, but the time is coming when it will be; and when, in a sense which is not yet true, it will be true that much that will be in the Book will not be true. Just as soon as the wisdom of this world finds out that the only way to stop the onward progress of the Word of Truth, by which worldliness is condemned, will be by making an ally of the Bible, just as soon as it comes to be known that a statement in the Book settles things for a large class of people, then will it attempt to make the 'word of God,' as it will still be called, speak for it instead of for the truth. And, furthermore, as there shall be false Christs, so will there be errors that will pass for principles; and they may very easily creep through the printing press into the old Book itself.

"Lovers of the pure Word of God will be in great straits before the Lord comes, if they have not learned to know its flavour by the Spirit that is its life. But those who are in agreement with the Abiding Spirit will not be left to misunderstandings. They shall know and all things shall be brought to their remembrance just at the crisis when such knowledge and remembrance is needed. The Word can always utter itself over and over to the true-hearted, without the help of printers' ink, as well as in spite of it. Those, however, who have not the principles of God built into the character, will be 'at sea' in those days, and will be especially susceptible to any lies that may be printed in the form of the old Bible."[5]

---

[5] S.M.I. Henry, *The Abiding Spirit* (Battle Creek, MI: Review & Herald, 1899), p. 15-16.

12 Doctrine

The Bible says, "And I saw one of his heads as it were wounded to death; and his deadly wound was healed: and all the world wondered after the beast. And they worshipped the dragon which gave power unto the beast: and they worshipped the beast, saying, Who is like unto the beast? who is able to make war with him? And all that dwell upon the earth shall worship him, whose names are not written in the book of life of the Lamb slain from the foundation of the world."[1]

According to Scripture, the time is coming when the majority of the inhabitants of the earth will worship the beast and the dragon that gives the beast its power. Revelation 12:9[2] identifies the dragon as Satan himself. How is Satan able to deceive almost the entire planet? The word of God is our only defense against Satan's deceptions, and the means by which we are to live by every word;[3] therefore if he can rob the world of the pure doctrines of the word of God, Earth's inhabitants will accept his deceptions. If we do not have every Word that proceeds from the mouth of God, we cannot fully live.

Today it is popular to speak of doctrine as a bad word; something that is unimportant at best, or dangerous at worst. This idea directly contradicts the plainest statements of Scripture: "Take heed unto thyself, and **unto the doctrine**; continue in them: **for in doing this thou shalt both save thyself, and them that hear thee.**"[4] According to Scripture, doctrine has an important role to play in the salvation of humanity.

The Bible says the words of Christ are doctrine: "If any man teach otherwise, and consent not to wholesome words, even the words of our Lord Jesus Christ, and to the doctrine which is according to

---

[1] Revelation 13:3-4, 8

[2] Revelation 12:9 "And the great dragon was cast out, that old serpent, called the Devil, and Satan, which deceiveth the whole world: he was cast out into the earth, and his angels were cast out with him."

[3] Matthew 4:4 "But he answered and said, It is written, Man shall not live by bread alone, but by every word that proceedeth out of the mouth of God."

[4] 1 Timothy 4:16

godliness; He is proud, knowing nothing...."[5] The one that teaches contrary to the doctrine of Jesus is proud and knows nothing.

God promises that anyone who desires to do God's will, shall know what is true doctrine. "Jesus answered them, and said, My doctrine is not mine, but his that sent me. If any man will do his will, he shall know of the doctrine, whether it be of God, or whether I speak of myself."[6]

In this chapter we will look at specific doctrines that have been tampered with in a systematic manner. The list of verses changed for each doctrine is not intended to be comprehensive. Nor will every Bible doctrine be covered. There is much more that could be said.

The first Biblical doctrine we will examine, that has been undermined, is the divinity of Christ. This is the second most important doctrine of Scripture.[7]

The Divinity of Christ

In **KJV 1 Corinthians 15:47**, the Bible says, "The first man is of the earth, earthy. The second man is **the Lord** from heaven."

This is an obvious reference to the first man, or Adam, being made of the dust of the ground. The second man, Jesus Christ, is the Lord from heaven. Jesus was the second Adam.[8]

Many of the modern translations, including the NIV, NASB, ASV, CEV, DRB, ESV, GNB, ICB, RV, and the *New World Translation* (the Jehovah's Witness Bible—which has a vested interest in removing

---

[5] 1 Timothy 6:3-4

[6] John 7:16-17

[7] The single most important doctrine in the Bible is the doctrine of the infallible, inspired, preserved, true word of God. No other doctrine can be established without this doctrine. "for thou hast magnified thy word above all thy name." Psalm 138:2 If someone cannot agree to the preeminence and divine nature of Scripture, then there is no basis, or common ground for the establishment of any other truth. This is why Satan hates God's Word so much.

[8] See also 1 Corinthians 15:45.

the divinity of Christ) leave out the phrase, "the Lord." So, they say, "The first man is of the earth, earthy: the second man is of heaven."[9] The wording might be slightly different in each version, but they consistently leave out "the Lord." To some, this might not seem like a serious issue, since most Christians already believe that Jesus is divine. However, in order for Satan to command worship from the whole world, he must first convince them that Jesus is not divine.

Helena Petrovna Blavatsky, introduced earlier, demonstrates this point further.[10] Blavatsky uses this verse, as it is in modern versions, to try to prove the immortality of the soul.[11] She asserts that Paul "maintains that there is a psychical body which is sown in the corruptible, and a spiritual body that is raised in incorruptible substance. 'The first man is of the earth earthy, the second man from heaven.'"[12]

This perspective is highly revealing, for when you realize that the mother of modern occultism is saying the same thing as many modern Christians, then you begin to discern that there is not much distance between modern occultism and modern Christianity. This should not be surprising since God said that at the end of time nearly the whole world would worship Satan.[13]

Blavatsky is not applying the second man to Jesus Christ in any way. She is saying that the second man is a spiritual body that goes to

---

[9] *Revised Version* (1885), p. 133.

[10] Blavatsky is considered to be the mother of modern occultism and was a Luciferian, meaning that she believes that Lucifer is higher and older than Jehovah. To put it another way, she worshipped Satan. She greatly influenced Alice A. Bailey, who became probably the most prolific occult writer ever.
See Martin Klein, *Above all Thy Name*, Spiritualism in the Church.

[11] Scripture says that only God has immortality:
1 Timothy 6:15-16 "Which in his times he shall show, who is the blessed and only Potentate, the King of kings, and Lord of lords; Who only hath immortality, dwelling in the light which no man can approach unto; whom no man hath seen, nor can see: to whom be honour and power everlasting. Amen."
One day he will give us immortality, if we accept his gift, but the dead do not have an immortal soul. The teaching that they do, is Satan's deception of spiritualism, and his first lie in the garden of Eden: "ye shall not surely die."
The immortality of the soul is another doctrine that has been altered in modern bibles. This is discussed later in the chapter; but, for now, we will focus on the divinity of Christ.

[12] H. P. Blavatsky, *Isis Unveiled,* Vol. 2—Theology (1877), p. 281-282.

[13] Revelation 13:8

heaven when the individual dies. It suits the theological purposes of the mother of modern occultism for the phrase, "**the Lord**" to be left out of the verse. Should not Christians question aligning themselves with the mother of modern spiritualism, by choosing a modern version that contains this change?

In 1 Timothy 4:1-2, the Bible says, "Now the Spirit speaketh expressly, that in the latter times some shall depart from the faith, giving heed to seducing spirits, and doctrines of devils; Speaking lies in hypocrisy; having their conscience seared with a hot iron."

What Blavatsky is asserting is a doctrine of devils. People are departing from the faith, giving heed to seducing spirits and doctrines of devils. The issue at stake is whether we will accept the doctrines of Jesus Christ, or the doctrines of devils. There are only two choices.

In **KJV Ephesians 3:9**, Scripture states, "And to make all men see what is the fellowship of the mystery, which from the beginning of the world hath been hid in God, who created all things **by Jesus Christ**."

Here we have explicit reference to the fact that Jesus is the Creator. In verse 14, it tells us that God is the father of our Lord Jesus Christ. "For this cause I bow my knees unto the Father **of our Lord Jesus Christ**." In both cases, the bold part has been left out of many modern versions.[14]

Removed from Ephesians 3:9 is "**by Jesus Christ**," which eliminates the reference to his creatorship. In Ephesians 3:14 "**of our Lord Jesus Christ**," being left out, removes the connection that God the Father is the father of our Lord Jesus Christ. This alone does not prove a systematic attempt to remove the divinity of Jesus, but, these changes certainly make it easier to assert that he is not divine. If this just happened in one or two places, some might assert that nothing had materially changed in the doctrines of the Bible. But, once you see the pattern, and the vast amount of evidence pointing in this direction, you realize that these changes attack the power and majesty of Jesus Christ.

---

[14] NIV, ASV, CEV, DRB, ESV, GNB, ICB, NWT, RV, and many more.

KJV Revelation 1:6 "And he hath made us kings and priests unto **God and his Father**. To him be glory and dominion forever and ever. Amen."

Revelation 1:6 in modern bibles,[15] removes the divinity of Christ in a most subtle way. The changes can be ever so slight and yet make a huge difference in meaning. In this case, the words are the same, only the order of the words has been changed.

ASV Revelation 1:6 "and he made us to be a kingdom, to be priests unto **his God and Father**; to him be the glory and the dominion for ever and ever. Amen."[16]

Notice the King James Bible says "**God and his Father**." If you say "**God and his Father**," that means God is one person and his father is another person. So, the Father is the father of God. With this wording, the Bible is calling Jesus God, therefore Jesus is completely divine. But, in the modern versions, including the *New World Translation* (or Jehovah's Witness Bible), it says, "his God and Father." These are the very same words, in a slightly different order. "His God and Father" means that Jesus has a god and Jesus has a father. But, it is not calling Jesus God. The divinity of Christ has been removed from this verse by a simple change in word order. You may have to sit and think about this for some time to understand the implications, but this is a profound change.

Not only do modern bibles diminish the divinity of Christ, but they attack the three divine personalities of the Godhead. This they do, because the triune nature of the Godhead proves the divinity of Christ. The most notorious attack on God's Word is in the removal, in most modern versions, of the most explicit statement of the triune Godhead in all of Scripture: 1 John 5:7, and part of verse eight.

KJV 1 John 5:7-8 "For there are three that bear record in heaven, **the Father, the Word, and the Holy Ghost: and these three are**

---

[15] NIV, ASV, BBE, CEV, DRB, ESV, GNB, ICB, ISV, LITV, NWT, RV, etc.

[16] *American Standard Version* (1901), p. 236.
Also, the modern rendering causes the verse to contradict other Scriptures by saying that the Father will retain everlasting dominion, rather than Jesus. Daniel 7:13-14 makes it clear that everlasting dominion is given to Jesus.

one. And there are three that bear witness in earth, the Spirit, and the water, and the blood: and these three agree in one."

Although it varies from version to version, more or less of the bold portion is removed from most modern versions. The scholars refer to this statement as the Johannine Comma, with critical scholarship claiming that the verse was not added until the late fourth-century/early fifth-century Trinitarian controversies. "Unfortunately for the critics, these claims are either outright falsehoods, or else rest upon incomplete information. Worse, they continue to be propagated uncritically by naturalistic textual scholars like Bruce Metzger and Kurt and Barbara Aland, whose written works routinely perpetuate false information based upon a partial coverage of the evidence available."[17]

While it is true that the Comma is not found in the majority of the Greek manuscripts, it is found in a couple of the early lectionaries, some of the earliest translations (such as the old Latin and the Syriac), and the ancient Waldensian manuscripts, who preserved the word of God "unadulterated."[18] It is also quoted by numerous ancient sources, from Tertullian, Cyprian, and Priscillian, to Athanasius, Aurelius and Vigilius Tapensis, to name a few.

"The strongest evidence [for the authenticity of the Johannine Comma], however, is found in the Greek text itself. Looking at 1 John 5:8, there are three nouns which, in Greek, stand in the neuter (Spirit, water, and blood). However, they are followed by a participle that is masculine. The Greek phrase here is *oi marturountes* (who bare witness). Those who know the Greek language understand this to be poor grammar if left to stand on its own. Even more noticeable, verse six has the same participle but stands in the neuter (Gk.: *to marturoun*). Why are three neuter nouns supported with a masculine participle? The answer is found if we include verse seven. There we have two masculine nouns (Father and Son) follow by a neuter noun (Spirit). The verse also has the Greek masculine participle *oi marturountes*. With this clause introducing verse eight, it is very

---

[17] Timothy W. Dunkin, "A Defense of the Johannine Comma, Setting the Record Straight on 1 John 5:7-8" (Rev. 2010), p. 4.

[18] E. G. White, *The Great Controversy* (1911), p. 64.2-65.2.

proper for the participle in verse eight to be masculine because of the masculine nouns in verse seven. But if verse seven were not there it would become improper Greek grammar."[19] This was recognized by scholars as early as Gregory of Nazianzus (A.D. 390).

The Catholic *Dublin Review* makes the following scathing indictment against this excision: "On the 17th of May the English-speaking world awoke to find that its Revised Bible had banished the Heavenly Witnesses and put the devil in the Lord's Prayer. Protests loud and deep went forth against the insertion, against the omission none. It is well, then, that the Heavenly Witnesses should depart whence their testimony is no longer received. The Jews have a legend that shortly before the destruction of their Temple, the Shechinah departed from the Holy of Holies, and the Sacred Voices were heard saying, 'Let us go hence.' So perhaps it is to be with the English Bible, the Temple of Protestantism. The going forth of the Heavenly Witnesses is the sign of the beginning of the end."[20]

"God never asks us to believe, without giving sufficient evidence upon which to base our faith. His existence, His character, the truthfulness of His word, are all established by testimony that appeals to our reason; and this testimony is abundant. Yet God has never removed the possibility of doubt. Our faith must rest upon evidence, not demonstration. Those who wish to doubt will have opportunity; while those who really desire to know the truth will find plenty of evidence on which to rest their faith."[21]

Not only do modern versions tamper with the divinity of Christ, but they tamper with his humanity. The Bible teaches that Jesus, having the perfect divine nature of God, took on our sinful human nature[22] and became both human and divine—though he did not sin.

KJV Hebrews 2:16 "For verily he took not on him the nature of angels, but he took on him the seed of Abraham."

---

[19] Thomas Holland, Th.D., *Crowned With Glory* (2000), p. 163-168.

[20] *Dublin Review*, Third Series, Vol. 6, July—October (1881), p. 143.

[21] E. G. White, *Steps to Christ* (1892), p. 105.2.

[22] Romans 8:3 "For what the law could not do, in that it was weak through the flesh, God sending his own Son **in the likeness of sinful flesh**, and for sin, condemned sin in the flesh:"

Scripture assures us that Jesus did not take the nature of angels, but assumed the nature of humans, as a descendant of Abraham.
Once again modern bibles tamper with the evidence:
NIV Hebrews 2:16 "For surely it is not angels he helps, but Abraham's descendants."[23]

No longer a reference to the nature of Christ, which fits the context, it now becomes a claim that God does not help angels. Such a statement is false, and contradicts the testimony of Daniel 10:13,[24] which contains a very explicit example of Jesus coming to the help of an angel.

KJV Luke 2:33 "And Joseph and his mother marvelled at those things which were spoken of him."

"**Joseph and his mother**..." is a theologically correct statement, because the Bible tells us that Jesus was born of a virgin, and conceived by the Holy Spirit, making the Holy Spirit his father.[25] In the incarnation a fully divine being was his father, and a fully human being was his mother, making Jesus, on earth, fully human and fully divine. Therefore, Luke 2:33 refers to his earthly parents as "**Joseph and his mother**," indicating that although Joseph functioned as his adopted or earthly father, Joseph was not his biological father.

---

[23] *New International Version* (1978), p. 1289.

[24] That Michael is Christ is evident from Jude 1:9, which identifies Michael as the archangel, and 1 Thessalonians 4:16, which identifies the archangel as "the Lord himself." The name Michael means "who is what God is," or "who is like God." The word angel simply means messenger. See Exodus 3:2-4 where God appears to Moses in the burning bush, and is called an angel. See also Malachi 3:1 where the same word—malak—used for angel in Exodus 3:2 is used to specify a messenger. In Malachi, the same word is used to refer prophetically to John the Baptist (the messenger who prepares the way) and to Jesus as the "messenger of the covenant." Archangel simply means the messenger above all messengers. Arch means above, and should not be confused with the "ark" of the covenant. Christ is not one of the covering cherubs, rather the One who is covered. For further treatment of this subject, see Martin Klein, *Glimpses of the Open Gates of Heaven*, Daniel 10.

[25] See Matthew 1:20. This is not to say that the Holy Spirit is only the essence or presence of the Father, for Scripture portrays the one God—the Godhead—as three distinct personalities. Yet certain verses emphasize the unity of the Godhead and other verses emphasize their individuality. This verse simply demonstrates the unity of the Father and the Spirit.

In a subtle attack on the divinity of Christ, modern versions change "**Joseph and his mother**," to "His father and mother,"[26] which tends to reduce the connection with the fact that his father was divine. The same modification is performed on Luke 2:43. "Helvidius, the devoted scholar of Northern Italy (A.D. 400) who had the pure MSS, accused Jerome [the author of the Catholic Latin Vulgate] of using corrupt manuscripts on this very text.... Jerome did exactly what the American Revised and Jesuit Bibles did, that is, they gave Jesus a human father."[27]

In **KJV 1 John 3:16**, the Bible says, "Hereby perceive we the love of God, because he laid down his life for us: and we ought to lay down our lives for the brethren."

God laid down his life for us. Jesus is clearly being called God in this passage. Some might argue that the King James Version supplied the words "of God" and therefore the statement is not warranted. The context (going back to verse 9) demands that we are talking about God in verse 16.

The NIV changes this to: "This is how we know what love is: Jesus Christ laid down his life for us. And we ought to lay down our lives for our brothers."[28]

This is not a false statement, because it is true that Jesus laid down his life for us. However, the statement has removed reference to the divinity of Jesus, no longer calling him God. The proponents of the modern versions stand indicted for the very thing they accuse the King James Version of, by adding the words "Jesus Christ." Even the corrupted manuscripts do not contain these words. At least the KJV shows you which words are supplied, and supplies words faithful to the context. The NIV does not indicate that words have been

---

[26] *New American Standard Bible* (1977), p. 711.
Also, NIV, ASV, CEV, DRB, ESV, GNB, ICB, RV, NWT, etc. Notice that the Jehovah's Witness bible, the *New World Translation*, with a clear motive for removing the divinity of Christ, follows this pattern. The Spirit of Prophecy quotes only the KJV as Scripture.

[27] B.G. Wilkinson, Ph.D., *Our Authorized Bible, Answers to Objections* (Brushton, NY: Teach Services, Inc., 2008), p. 156.

[28] *New International Version* (1978), p. 1316.
NASB, NKJV, ASV, CEV, ERV, ESV, GNB, MSG, ICB, RSV, RV, etc.

supplied and by ignoring the context remove the infinite truth that it was the Sovereign of the Universe who laid down his life for us.

Despite the abundant evidence for a concerted effort to undermine the divinity of Christ, some might still find it hard to believe that these alterations are intentional, with a specific motive. Therefore, let us turn to the testimony of the translators themselves. Perhaps some of their beliefs help to explain how these changes occurred.

Vance Smith,[29] a member of the translation committee for the *Revised Version* of 1881 (the grandfather of all modern versions) claims the following, "It is well understood that the New Testament contains neither precept nor example which really sanctions the religious worship of Jesus Christ."[30]

Jesus told Satan, in the wilderness of temptation, "Thou shalt worship the Lord thy God, and him only shalt thou serve."[31] Therefore, by claiming that no precept or example in the New Testament sanctions the worship of Jesus, Smith is asserting that there is no evidence for the divinity of Christ.

Smith goes on to tell us, "The changes just enumerated are manifestly of great importance, and are they not wholly unfavorable to the popular theology? Many persons will deny this, but it is hard to see on what grounds they do so. Or, if it be true that the popular orthodoxy remains unaffected by such changes, the inference is unavoidable that popular orthodoxy must be very indifferent to the nature of the foundation on which it stands."[32]

Under the heading of "Doctrinal Changes," Smith writes, "Since the publication of the revised New Testament, it has been frequently said that the changes of the translation which the work contains are of little importance from a doctrinal point of view;—in other words that the great doctrines of popular theology remain unaffected, untouched

---

[29] Vance Smith denied the divinity or Christ.

[30] G. Vance Smith, Th.D., Ph.D., *Texts and Margins of the Revised New Testament* (London: Unitarian Association, 1881), p. 47.

[31] Matthew 4:10; Luke 4:8

[32] G. Vance Smith, Th.D., Ph.D., *Texts and Margins of the Revised New Testament* (1881), p. 47.

by the results of the revision.... To the writer any such statement appears to be in the most substantial sense contrary to the facts of the case."[33]

Here we have admission, from one of the translators, that the changes in the *Revised Version* are doctrinal in nature. In the face of such testimony, how can anyone argue that there are no changes affecting doctrine?

Is there similar evidence from the translators of other versions? It so happens that the chief editor of the *New International Version*, Edwin Palmer, echoes similar sentiments, regarding the divinity of Christ, in declaring that there are "few clear and decisive texts that declare Jesus is God."[34]

Further, he informs us that "forty-six times the KJV uses the term 'master' when for today's reader it should use the term 'teacher.'"[35] Now, why does today's reader need to hear "teacher" instead of "master"? Does today's reader not understand the word "master"? Is master an archaic word that has passed out of the English language? Master must be replaced with teacher in the *New International Version* because, in order to bring all religions together; the divinity of Jesus must be knocked down a little lower. Muslims, Unitarians, Jehovah's Witnesses, Hindus, occultists, and many others, do not accept the divinity of Christ.

Helena Petrovna Blavatsky, the mother of the new age and modern occultism, says exactly the same thing as these Bible translators: "there is not a word in the so-called sacred scriptures to show that Jesus was actually regarded as God by his disciples. Neither before nor after his death did they pay him divine honors."[36]

This statement, from a worshiper of Lucifer, is nothing but a doctrine of devils, for Scripture plainly states, "And Thomas answered and

---

[33] G. Vance Smith, Th.D., Ph.D., *Texts and Margins of the Revised New Testament* (1881), p. 45.

[34] Edwin Palmer, Th.D., *The NIV: The Making of a Contemporary Translation* (Oakland, CA: Academie Books, 1986), p. 143.

[35] *Ibid.*, p. 147.

[36] H.P. Blavatsky, *Isis Unveiled,* Vol. 2—Theology (1877), p. 192-193.

said unto him, my Lord and my God."[37] When bible translators presume to insert into Scripture, the doctrines of devils that the mother of occultism is promoting, and admit it with their own mouths, who can possibly continue to deny that there is a problem?

Following the same pattern many modern bibles remove the reference to worshipping Jesus, in Matthew 20:20.

KJV Matthew 20:20 "Then came to him the mother of Zebedee's children with her sons, **worshipping him**, and desiring a certain thing of him."

NKJV Matthew 20:20 "Then the mother of Zebedee's sons came to Him with her sons, kneeling down and asking something from Him."

The Bible tells us in **KJV Isaiah 7:14**, "Therefore the Lord himself shall give you a sign; Behold, a virgin shall conceive, and bear a son, and shall call his name Immanuel."

The foundation of the Biblical truth of Jesus' divinity is the fact that he was born of a virgin, for this was the sign that his father was divine. Yet, several modern versions remove the virgin birth. Notice how the *Good News Bible*[38] puts it: "Well then, the Lord himself will give you a sign. A young woman who is pregnant will have a son and will name him Immanuel."[39] How is a young woman being pregnant a sign? We must have millions of signs every day.

The Jewish religion does not accept the New Testament or believe that Jesus was the Messiah. They certainly do not accept that Jesus was divine. Therefore, a clear prediction in their Old Testament Scriptures for the virgin birth, fulfilled in the New Testament, is a problem for them, knowing that Christians appeal to this verse as evidence of the divinity and Messiahship of Jesus. As one might expect, the Jewish Publication Society does not like the verse, and also changed "virgin" to "young woman."

---

[37] John 20:28; See also Matthew 2:11; Matthew 8:2; Matthew 9:18; Matthew 14:33; Matthew 15:25; Matthew 28:9, 17; Mark 5:6; Mark 15:19; Luke 24:52; John 9:38.

[38] Right in the midst of the translations making these alterations is the *New World Translation*—the Jehovah's Witness bible—which also removes the virgin birth.

[39] *Good News Bible* (1976), p. 750.
Also, she names him Immanuel instead of God himself naming him Immanuel.

The *Revised Standard Version* does the same thing. As it turns out there was a Jewish scholar on the *Revised Standard Version* translation committee named H.M. Orlinsky, of the Jewish Institute of Religion in New York. It is quite probable that he lent his influence to the removal of the virgin birth in this version. Rabbi Balfour Brickner of the Temple Sinai in Washington, regarding this verse, declares, "I am delighted to know that at last this great error of translation has been finally corrected, and that at least some elements of the Christian world no longer maintain that Isaiah 7:14 is a prediction that Jesus would be born of the Virgin Mary."[40] Clearly he sees this change as denying the virgin birth.

In **KJV Revelation 11:17** the Bible says, "Saying, We give thee thanks, O Lord God Almighty, which art, and wast, **and art to come**; because thou hast taken to thee thy great power, and hast reigned."

This verse makes specific claims for the divinity of Jesus Christ. The twenty-four elders bow in worship to the Lord God Almighty. They are clearly worshipping the God of the universe "which art, and wast, and art to come." This can be none other than Jesus Christ himself, as he is the one that promised to come again. Therefore, the verse is presenting Jesus as the Lord God Almighty. This makes Jesus God. In order to avoid the conclusion that Jesus is the one specified in this text, modern bibles leave out the bold portion.[41]

Perhaps the *ExeGeses Companion Bible* demonstrates how far things have degenerated: ECB Revelation 11:17 "wording, We eucharistize you, O Yah Veh El Sabaoth, who is and who was and who is coming; for you are taking your mega dynamis and reign:"[42] Does this make any sense? Is this easier to read? The claim is continually made that modern versions are needed, because the old language cannot be comprehended. Notice the Catholic wording, "we eucharistize you." The Eucharist is the Catholic host or communion wafer, and is certainly not a Protestant word. Many Protestants lost their lives for their refusal to partake of the host.

---

[40] Les Garrett, *Which Bible Can We Trust?* (1982), p. 50.

[41] ASV, CEV, GNB, GS, ICB, SV, Moff, MSG, NASB, NIV, NWT, RSV, RV, etc.

[42] *ExeGeses Companion Bible* (e-Sword Bible Software), http://www.e-sword.net

"All the outward pomp and display of the Romish worship was brought to bear to confuse the mind and dazzle and captivate the imagination, and thus the liberty for which the fathers had toiled and bled was betrayed by the sons."[43]

In **KJV Revelation 16:5**, the Bible says, "And I heard the angel of the waters say, Thou art righteous, O Lord, which art, and wast, **and shalt be**, because thou hast judged thus."

Once again, following an intentional pattern, many modern versions leave out "**and shalt be**." "**Shalt be**" is a reference to the second coming and makes it clear that Jesus is Lord and judge.

---

[43] E. G. White, *The Great Controversy* (1911), p. 235.1.
Following is the context for the short statement quoted above: "Throughout Christendom, Protestantism was menaced by formidable foes. The first triumphs of the Reformation past, Rome summoned new forces, hoping to accomplish its destruction. At this time the order of the Jesuits was created, the most cruel, unscrupulous, and powerful of all the champions of popery. Cut off from earthly ties and human interests, dead to the claims of natural affection, reason and conscience wholly silenced, they knew no rule, no tie, but that of their order, and no duty but to extend its power. The gospel of Christ had enabled its adherents to meet danger and endure suffering, undismayed by cold, hunger, toil, and poverty, to uphold the banner of truth in face of the rack, the dungeon, and the stake. To combat these forces, Jesuitism inspired its followers with a fanaticism that enabled them to endure like dangers, and to oppose to the power of truth all the weapons of deception. There was no crime too great for them to commit, no deception too base for them to practice, no disguise too difficult for them to assume. Vowed to perpetual poverty and humility, it was their studied aim to secure wealth and power, to be devoted to the overthrow of Protestantism, and the re-establishment of the papal supremacy.
"When appearing as members of their order, they wore a garb of sanctity, visiting prisons and hospitals, ministering to the sick and the poor, professing to have renounced the world, and bearing the sacred name of Jesus, who went about doing good. But under this blameless exterior the most criminal and deadly purposes were often concealed. It was a fundamental principle of the order that the end justifies the means. By this code, lying, theft, perjury, assassination, were not only pardonable but commendable, when they served the interests of the church. Under various disguises the Jesuits worked their way into offices of state, climbing up to be the counselors of kings, and shaping the policy of nations. They became servants to act as spies upon their masters. They established colleges for the sons of princes and nobles, and schools for the common people; and the children of Protestant parents were drawn into an observance of popish rites. **All the outward pomp and display of the Romish worship was brought to bear to confuse the mind and dazzle and captivate the imagination, and thus the liberty for which the fathers had toiled and bled was betrayed by the sons.** The Jesuits rapidly spread themselves over Europe, and wherever they went, there followed a revival of popery."
Ibid., p. 234.2-235.1.

The Second Coming of Jesus

Regarding the second coming, as in the previous verse, modern versions tend to obscure the Biblical truth of a literal,[44] physical[45] return of Jesus at the end of the world.[46] Instead, they are more in line with the esoteric views of modern occultism, which spiritualize the coming into an individual, internal enlightenment, of the knowledge of one's own deity. This was Satan's original lie to Eve in the garden of Eden - "Ye shall be as gods..."[47]

KJV Matthew 24:3 "tell us, when shall these things be? and what shall be the sign of thy coming, and of the end of the world?"

RV (margin) Matthew 24:3 "Tell us, when shall these things be? and what *shall be* the sign of thy (*presence*), and of (*the consummation of the age*)?"[48]

Blavatsky, mother of modern occultism, says the following: "The sentences italicized are those which stand corrected in the New Testament after the recent revision in 1881 of the version of 1611; which version is full of errors, voluntary and involuntary. The word 'presence' for 'coming' and 'the consummation of the age' now standing for 'the end of the world,' have altered, of late, the whole meaning, even for the most sincere Christian, if we exempt the Adventists....

"Two things become evident to all in the above passages, now that their false rendering is corrected in the revision text: (a) 'the coming of Christ,' means *the presence of* CHRISTOS in a regenerated world, and not at all the actual coming in body of 'Christ' Jesus; (b) this Christ is to be sought neither in the wilderness nor 'in the inner chambers,' nor in the sanctuary of any temple or church built by man; for Christ—the true esoteric SAVIOR—is no man, but the DIVINE PRINCIPLE in every human being....

---

[44] John 14:2-3; Acts 1:11

[45] Revelation 1:7; 1 Corinthians 15:19-26; 1 Corinthians 15:51-58

[46] Matthew 13:49; Matthew 24:3

[47] Genesis 3:5

[48] *Revised Version* (1885), p. 20.

"Millenarians and Adventists of robust faith may go on saying that 'the coming of (the carnalized) Christ' is near at hand, and prepare themselves for 'the end of the world.' Theosophists—at any rate, some of them—who understand the hidden meaning of the universally expected Avatars, Messiahs, Sosioshes, and Christs—know that it is no 'end of the world,' but 'the consummation of the age,' i.e., the close of a cycle, which is now fast approaching."[49]

Blavatsky, once again, believes that the KJV version is full of errors and that these errors were corrected in the *Revised Version*, from which she claims that the coming of Jesus is not a literal coming of the physical Jesus Christ, but the inner discovery of one's own godhood. This should seriously concern any person who believes the Bible, or has reservations about occultism. Scripture says, "The heart is deceitful above all things, and desperately wicked: who can know it?"[50]

KJV Revelation 1:7 "Behold, he cometh with clouds. Every eye shall see him, and they also which pierced him. All the kindreds of the earth shall wail because of him."

Universalism is the theological name for the belief that everyone will be saved, no matter what they do. Some universalists actually go so far as to claim that the devil will be saved. In the King James Version this verse implies that people are crying because they realize that they are wrong and are lost. They are wailing because of him. There is clearly no universalism there. Notice how modern bibles alter the words to support universalism. The *Revised Version* says, "Behold, he cometh with clouds; and every eye shall see him, and they which pierced him; and all the tribes of the earth shall mourn over him. Even so, Amen."[51]

Wailing because of him and mourning over him are two totally different things. With this change the verse is no longer a reference to the fact that some are wailing because of their lost condition, instead they seem to be mourning his death, rather than rejoicing at

---

[49] H.P. Blavatsky, *Studies in Occultism,* No. V: The Esoteric Character of the Gospels (Point Loma, CA: The Aryan Theosophical Press, 1910), p. 1-4.

[50] Jeremiah 17:9

[51] *Revised Version* (1885), p. 182.

his coming. Some might claim that the original word can be translated mourn as well as wail. Perhaps. But, the context clearly does not support such a change. The statement does not even make sense.

Westcott tells us the reason for inserting this change into the text. He says, "all the tribes of the earth shall mourn over him in penitential sorrow, not as the Authorized Version,[52] shall wail because of him in the present expectation of terrible vengeance."[53]

Westcott understands very explicitly the theological implications of the two different renderings.[54] He understands the King James Version to mean that the kindreds of the earth are wailing because of Jesus, expecting terrible vengeance to come upon them because of their sins, since they have not repented. He says the change in his *Revised Version* shows that they mourn over him in penitential sorrow, implying that these people are giving penance, or coming to repentance at the second coming of Jesus, so that they can all be saved. Apparently, in Westcott's theology, Jesus forgives them and takes everyone to heaven, instead of vengeance falling on a certain group of people. He informs us of the very important difference in theology between the two versions. Two very different doctrines—one the doctrine of Jesus Christ, the other the doctrine of devils.[55]

---

[52] The "Authorized Version" is another name for the King James Version.

[53] B. F. Westcott, D.D., DC.L., *Some Lessons of the Revised Version of the New Testament* (London: Hodder and Stoughton, 1897), p. 196.

[54] "Perhaps there is something to Lewis Foster's advice regarding translations. He ought to know, since he was on the New International Version and New King James Version committees. 'Study the translators as well as their translations... A change may be better understood by knowing the position of the translator... whether they are based upon... a shift in the theological beliefs of the translator.'"
David Thiele, *Have the Faith of Jesus* (Ringgold, GA: Teach Services, 2014), Kindle ed., Kindle Locations 1012-1015.

[55] "No literal devil, and probation after the coming of Christ, are fast becoming popular fables. The Scriptures plainly declare that every person's destiny is forever fixed at the coming of the Lord. Revelation 22:11, 12: 'He that is unjust, let him be unjust still: and he which is filthy, let him be filthy still: and he that is righteous, let him be righteous still: and he that is holy, let him be holy still. And, behold, I come quickly; and My reward is with Me, to give every man according as his work shall be.'"
E. G. White, *Testimonies for the Church,* Vol. 1 (Nampa, ID: Pacific Press, 1855), p. 342.4.

KJV Titus 2:13 "Looking for that blessed hope, and the glorious appearing of the great God and our Saviour Jesus Christ;"

NASB Titus 2:13 "looking for the blessed hope and the appearing of the glory of our great God and Savior, Christ Jesus,"

"By changing the adjective 'glorious' to the noun 'glory,' the Revisers have removed the Second Coming of Christ from this text. In the King James Version, the object of our hope is the appearing of Christ, which is a personal and a future and an epochal event. In the Revised Version, the object of our hope is changed to be the appearing of the glory of Christ, which may be the manifestation among men, or in us, of abstract virtues, which may appear at any time and repeatedly in this present life."[56]

In case the reader might think that it is going too far to claim that the revisers intentionally removed the doctrine of the second coming, we shall quote one of the revisers himself, G. Vance Smith. This idea of the second coming, he says, "ought now to be passed by as a merely temporary incident of early Christian belief. Like many another error, it has answered a transitory purpose in the providential plan, and may well, at length, be left to rest in peace."[57]

But, the angels, at the ascension of Christ said, "this same Jesus, which is taken up from you into heaven, shall so come in like manner as ye have seen him go into heaven."[58]

Repentance and Salvation

Has the very foundational framework of the gospel and how we obtain salvation been modified in modern versions?

Scripture says that Jesus accomplished something for the sins of the entire world: 1 John 2:1-2 "My little children, these things write I unto you, that ye sin not. And if any man sin, we have an advocate with

---

[56] B.G. Wilkinson, Ph.D., *Our Authorized Bible Vindicated* (1930), p. 196.

[57] G. Vance Smith, Th.D., Ph.D., *The Bible and Its Theology as Popularly Taught* (London: Swan Sonnenschein & Co., 1892), p. 312.

[58] Acts 1:11

the Father, Jesus Christ the righteous: "And he is the propitiation for our sins: and not for ours only, but also for the sins of the whole world."

Jesus was reconciling the entire world to himself: "To wit, that God was in Christ, **reconciling the world** unto himself, not imputing their trespasses unto them..."[59] Surely the good will of God was being bestowed without measure on every human being, in the infinite gift of Jesus.[60] Therefore it would be perfectly consistent for the angels to announce over Bethlehem:

KJV Luke 2:14 "Glory to God in the highest, and on earth peace, **good will toward men**."

But the modern versions apparently cannot tolerate an inclusive gospel, therefore the peace is only announced for the special elite, favored class, or perhaps those with whom he is pleased:

NIV[61] Luke 2:14 "Glory to God in the highest, and on earth **peace to men on whom his favor rests**."[62]

RV Luke 2:14 "Glory to God in the highest, And on earth **peace among men in whom he is well pleased**."[63]

ICB Luke 2:14 "Give glory to God in heaven, and on earth **let there be peace to the people who please God**."[64]

By this, the entire plan of salvation is modified into a program where one must work to obtain God's favor before you can benefit from his gift. This is the Catholic doctrine of salvation by works.

---

[59] 2 Corinthians 5:19

[60] For further study on the infinite gift of reconciliation that God has bestowed on all men, see: Martin Klein, *The Most Precious Message*, Ch. 2: His Sacrifice for the Sins of the Whole World, www.savannahpictures.com

[61] NASB, ASV, CEV, DRB, ESV, GNB, NWT ("men of good will"), etc. The Spirit of Prophecy quotes this verse only from the KJV.

[62] *New International Version* (1978), p. 1100.

[63] *Revised Version* (1885), p. 43.

[64] *International Children's Bible: New Century Version* (Dallas: Word Publishing, 1988), p. 765.

Notice what Jesus says in **KJV Matthew 9:13**, "But go ye and learn what this meaneth. I will have mercy, and not sacrifice, for I am not come to call the righteous, but sinners **to repentance**." Jesus came to call us for a specific purpose. He is calling us to repentance. Repentance must precede forgiveness,[65] yet repentance is a gift from God just as forgiveness: "the goodness of God leadeth thee to repentance."[66] Repentance is needed, not to make God willing to forgive, but for us to admit our need, and make the choice to accept the gift of pardon. However, the modern bibles,[67] including the *New World Translation*, leave out "to repentance," as in, "For I have not come to call the righteous, but sinners."[68]

Call them to what? Call them to dinner? It no longer tells us what Jesus is calling us to. The important step of repentance is removed. Repentance does not go well with papal doctrine, because repentance implies a change of heart—a turning around, and a moving away from sin.

KJV Colossians 1:14 "In whom we have redemption **through his blood**, even the forgiveness of sins:"

NAB Colossians 1:14 "in whom we have redemption, the forgiveness of sins."[69]

---

[65] "Many are confused as to what constitutes the first steps in the work of salvation. Repentance is thought to be a work the sinner must do for himself in order that he may come to Christ. They think that the sinner must procure for himself a fitness in order to obtain the blessing of God's grace. But while it is true that repentance must precede forgiveness, for it is only the broken and contrite heart that is acceptable to God, yet the sinner cannot bring himself to repentance, or prepare himself to come to Christ. Except the sinner repent, he cannot be forgiven; but the question to be decided is as to whether repentance is the work of the sinner or the gift of Christ. Must the sinner wait until he is filled with remorse for his sin before he can come to Christ? The very first step to Christ is taken through the drawing of the Spirit of God; as man responds to this drawing, he advances toward Christ in order that he may repent."
E. G. White, *Selected Messages,* Vol. 1 (Nampa, ID: Pacific Press, 1958), p. 390.1.
See also Acts 5:31.

[66] Romans 2:4

[67] NIV, NASB, ASV, CEV, DRB, ESV, GNB, ICB, RV, WNT, NWT, etc.

[68] *New World Translation* (1984), p. 1226.
Repentance is also removed from Mark 2:17 in many modern versions.

[69] *Bible: New American Bible,* Rev. ed. (Washington, DC: Confraternity of Christian Doctrine, Inc., 2011), Kindle ed., Kindle Location 57814.

ASV Colossians 1:14 "In whom we have our redemption, the forgiveness of our sins."[70]

The phrase "through his blood" is missing from the Catholic *New American Bible* as well as the ASV. Origen denied that the body or soul of Jesus was offered for our salvation,[71] and was the originator of this omission. Jerome was a follower of Origen, and thus the phrase is missing from the Latin Vulgate. "This omission of the atonement through blood is in full accord with modern liberalism, and strikes at the very heart of the gospel."[72]

KJV John 6:47 "Verily, verily, I say unto you, He that believeth **on me** hath everlasting life."

What is the key to salvation? How do we attain salvation? On whom do we believe to gain everlasting life? Jesus Christ. Jesus Christ is the one name given among men, under heaven, whereby we must be saved. But, the NIV[73] changes this to: "I tell you the truth. He who believes has everlasting life."[74] Believes what? Removed is the one "name under heaven given among men, whereby we must be saved."[75]

If you want to have an ecumenical religion, for a One World Order, that pleases everyone, you cannot have one religion claiming that Jesus is the only way. That is not acceptable to Buddhists, Hindus, Muslims, and many others. Jesus must be reduced, on par with all the other religious leaders, which means his divinity must be denied, and his claim to be the only way to salvation must be removed. Modern versions are the ecumenical tools to unite all religions.

Eugene Nida, considered one of greatest modern linguists and Executive Secretary for Translations for the American Bible Society,

---

[70] *American Standard Version* (1901), p. 190.

[71] Isaiah 53:10, 12

[72] B.G. Wilkinson, Ph.D., *Our Authorized Bible Vindicated* (1930), p. 96.

[73] Also, NASB, ASV, ESV, GNB, ICB, RV, WNT, NWT, etc.

[74] *New International Version* (1978), p. 1145.

[75] Acts 4:12

recounts the following experience: "After completing a series of lectures at the Pontifical Biblical Institute in Rome, I chatted with a young Jesuit who expressed his appreciation for what I had said about putting the Scriptures into the every-day language of the people. He insisted that this was the most important development since the Reformation."[76] The goal of Rome has ever been world domination and control of all religions. Ever since the reformation they have bent every effort to reestablish their lost supremacy. If modern bibles are to the Jesuits the most important development since the reformation, then they are the most important tool to overthrow everything the reformation has done.

Speaking to the Parliament of World Religions, Philipp Schaff said, "There is a unity of Christian scholarship of all creeds... This unity has been strikingly illustrated in the Anglo-American Revision of the Authorized Version of the Scriptures."[77] Schaff credits the unity of all creeds at the parliament to the *American Standard Version* and *Revised Version* of the Bible.

KJV Revelation 21:24 "And the nations **of them which are saved** shall walk in the light of it: and the kings of the earth do bring their glory and honour into it."

Speaking of the New Jerusalem the King James Version tells us that the nations of those who are saved will walk in the light of it and bring into it their glory and honor. Only the nations of the saved will be there, according to the Bible. But, the universalist believes that everyone will be saved. So modern bibles have left that phrase out.

NIV[78] Revelation 21:24 "The nations will walk by its light, and the kings of the earth will bring their splendor into it."[79]

In this rendering, everyone is saved, not just the nations of them which are saved. A universalist approach is necessary to unite all

---

[76] David W. Daniels, M.Div., *Why They Changed The Bible: One World Bible For One World Religion* (2014), Kindle ed., Kindle Locations 1806–1809.

[77] John Wesley Hanson, D.D., *World's Congress of Religions: The addresses and papers delivered before the parliament* (1894), p. 616.

[78] NASB, ASV, CEV, DRB, ESV, GNB, ICB, RV, WNT, NWT, etc.

[79] *New International Version* (1978), p. 1340.

religions of the world—a religion universal enough for no religion to object to unification, but exclusive enough to categorize anyone who objects as not being among those upon whom God's favor rests.

KJV Mark 10:24 "And the disciples were astonished at his words. But Jesus answereth again, and saith unto them, Children, how hard is it **for them that trust in riches** to enter into the kingdom of God!"

NIV[80] Mark 10:24 "The disciples were amazed at his words. But Jesus said again, 'Children, how hard it is to enter the kingdom of God!'"[81]

The modern version also makes salvation very hard to obtain. The King James says that it is hard for them that trust in riches to enter the kingdom of God, but the NIV says "how hard it is to enter the kingdom of God!"

The lawyers in the Bible were the equivalent of today's theologians. The law of God was the foundation of the legal system of the Jewish nation. Therefore, when one studied law, he studied the Bible—God's law. Jesus warned them: "Woe unto you, lawyers! for ye have taken away the key of knowledge: ye entered not in yourselves, and them that were entering in ye hindered."[82] The modern theologians and bible translators have taken away the key of knowledge; they enter not into the kingdom of God themselves, and those that are trying to enter they hinder by their corrupt interpretation and modification of the word of God.

One of the saddest changes in relationship to repentance and salvation is where the Bible's ability to heal the brokenhearted has been removed. There are many brokenhearted people in this world. They want to go to the Bible to know that God understands them, to know that Jesus can heal their broken hearts and heal the wounds and pain they feel.

The Bible gives us that promise in **KJV Luke 4:18-19**. Jesus himself is speaking here: "The Spirit of the Lord is upon me, because he

---

[80] Bold missing: ASV, CEV, ESV, GNB, MSG, NASB, RSV, etc.

[81] *New International Version* (1978), p. 1086.

[82] Luke 11:52

hath anointed me to preach the gospel to the poor; **he hath sent me to heal the brokenhearted**, to preach deliverance to the captives, and recovering of sight to the blind, to set at liberty them that are bruised, To preach the acceptable year of the Lord."

Jesus wants to heal the brokenhearted. But in modern versions,[83] the phrase, "he hath sent me to heal the brokenhearted," is left out. They enumerate all the other things, but leave out the healing of the broken heart.[84]

Some might say that another verse in the Bible says he can heal the broken heart. It is true. In the Old Testament, in the book of Isaiah,[85] the modern versions do not remove the healing of the brokenhearted. Should not that be good enough? If someone is brokenhearted, and they are going to the Bible for hope and healing in the midst of heartbreak, are they more likely to go to the Old Testament or the New Testament? Are they more likely to read Isaiah or Luke? What if the only verse that they go to is missing the very comfort they need? Is this not an important truth that has been left out of God's Word? We must live by every word that proceeds from the mouth of God, even (and especially) if he repeats himself.

Prophecies Altered

KJV Daniel 8:14 "And he said unto me, Unto two thousand and three hundred days; then shall the sanctuary be cleansed."

NIV Daniel 8:14[86] "He said to me, 'It will take 2,300 evenings and mornings; then the sanctuary will be reconsecrated.[87]'"

---

[83] NIV, NASB, ASV, CEV, DRB, ESV, GNB, ICB, RV, WNT, NWT, NLT, etc.

[84] By leaving this phrase out they cause Jesus to misquote Isaiah, from which he was reading.

[85] Isaiah 61:1

[86] *New International Version* (1978), p. 959.

[87] Also, CEV, ESV, GNB, NASB ("properly restored"), RSV ("restored to its rightful state"), NWT ("brought to its rightful condition"). Spirit of Prophecy quotes only KJV as Scripture.

The sanctuary being reconsecrated is certainly not the same thing as the sanctuary being cleansed. This passage refers to the heavenly sanctuary, which, once consecrated is never reconsecrated. This alteration removes the focus from the heavenly sanctuary, placing it on the earthly, therefore lending to the popular notion that the Jerusalem temple will be rebuilt, and obscuring the Biblical message of the cleansing of the heavenly sanctuary during the investigative judgment before the second coming of Jesus.[88]

ICB Daniel 8:14 "The angel said to me, 'This will happen for 2,300 evenings and mornings.[89] Then the holy place will be repaired.'"[90]

Once again, repaired gives a very different meaning than cleansing. Additionally, this version refers to the "holy place" instead of the "sanctuary," also removing the investigative judgment.

The *Good News Bible* completely removes the 2,300-day prophecy by changing it to 1,150 days.

GNB Daniel 8:14 "I heard the other angel answer, 'It will continue for 1,150 days, during which evening and morning sacrifices will not be offered. Then the Temple will be restored."[91]

KJV Daniel 9:26 "And after threescore and two weeks shall Messiah be cut off, but not for himself...."

NIV[92] Daniel 9:26 "After the sixty-two 'sevens,' the Anointed One will be cut off and will have nothing...."[93]

---

[88] For further information on this subject, see Martin Klein, *Glimpses of the Open Gates of Heaven:* Daniel 8-9.
See also Hebrews 9.

[89] This version also contains a footnote stating: "2,300 evenings and mornings This could mean 1,150 days or 2,300 days."

[90] *International Children's Bible* (1988), p. 660-661.

[91] *Good News Bible* (1976), p. 971.

[92] NIV, ASV, CEV, ESV, GNB, RV, RSV, NASB (Messiah rather than Anointed One, but has "will have nothing,"), NWT ("Messiah the Leader" and "with nothing for himself"), ICB ("the appointed leader" and "will have nothing"). The Spirit of Prophecy quotes only KJV as Scripture.

[93] *New International Version* (1978), p. 959.

Daniel chapter nine outlines the most amazing Messianic prophecy in all Scripture, identifying the very year of the baptism of Jesus, the year of his death, and the year of the gospel going to the Gentiles. This prophecy is one of the ultimate evidences for the divine nature of Scripture, as no such human prediction could be fulfilled in such a precise manner. Yet modern bibles completely obscure the most powerful evidence for the Messiahship of Jesus.

The King James makes it very clear that the Messiah would be cut off, not for himself; but he would die for the sins of the world. The modern bibles simply say "anointed one" which could be any king, priest, or even Antiochus IV Epiphanes, as Jesuit preterism teaches. Even if one assumed that "the Anointed One" referred to Jesus, the next phrase says that he will be cut off and have nothing. Jesus most certainly did not have nothing as a result of his death on the cross. Instead, he gained everything.[94]

KJV Mark 13:14 "But when ye shall see the abomination of desolation, **spoken of by Daniel the prophet**, standing where it ought not, (let him that readeth understand,) then let them that be in Judaea flee to the mountains:"

NIV[95] Mark 13:14 "When you see 'the abomination that causes desolation' standing where it does not belong—let the reader understand—then let those who are in Judea flee to the mountains."[96]

In this verse, reference is removed to the fact that Jesus himself refers to the prophecy of the book of Daniel.

KJV Matthew 27:35 "And they crucified him, and parted his garments, casting lots: **that it might be fulfilled which was spoken**

---

94 Matthew 28:18 "And Jesus came and spake unto them, saying, All power is given unto me in heaven and in earth."
See also John 3:35; Daniel 7:13,14; Luke 1:33.

95 The bold portion is missing in the NIV, NASB, ASV, CEV, DRB, ESV, GNB, RV, RSV, NWT, etc.

96 *New International Version* (1978), p. 1091.

by the prophet, They parted my garments among them, and upon my vesture did they cast lots."[97]

Once again, the modern bibles remove a reference to the Old Testament prophecy by leaving out the bold words. The divine nature of prophecy is not appreciated by the higher critical skeptics that make up the modern revision committees.

The Bible's Message and its Morals

What about the Bible's message and its morals? Have these kinds of things been altered in modern bibles?

KJV Galatians 3:22 "But the scripture **hath concluded all under sin**, that the promise by faith of Jesus Christ might be given to them that believe."

ESV Galatians 3:22 "But the Scripture imprisoned everything under sin, so that the promise by faith in Jesus Christ might be given to those who believe."

The King James Version says that Scripture concludes that everyone is a sinner, which agrees with other Bible verses. However, the ESV says the Bible imprisoned everything under sin. It is the Bible's fault that we are sinners? Not much could be more preposterous.

In **KJV Acts 17:22**, it says, "Then Paul stood in the midst of Mars' hill, and said, 'Ye men of Athens, I perceive that in all things ye are **too superstitious**.'"

If someone tells you that you are too superstitious, is this a commendation or a reproof? Is this a compliment or is this something that needs to be changed? Paul is not giving a complement, but rather a reproof. However, in the *New King James Version* and other modern bibles, it says "Then Paul stood in the midst of the

---

[97] The bold portion is missing in the NASB, ASV, CEV, ESV, GNB, ICB, RV, NWT, etc. (This prophecy comes from Psalm 22:18).

Areopagus[98] and said, 'Men of Athens, I perceive that in all things you are **very religious**.'"[99]

In the King James Bible, Paul was giving a reproof; in the modern bible, he is giving a complement. It seems that the meaning and the theology has been changed.

Is the message of the Bible foolishness? How much faith could you put in a bible that called its own message foolishness? That would not make much sense, yet that is exactly what some of the modern bibles do.

KJV 1 Corinthians 1:21 "For after that in the wisdom of God the world by wisdom knew not God, it pleased God by the foolishness of preaching to save them that believe." What is foolish here, the message or the preaching? The preaching is foolish. In other words, it seems foolish to deliver the wisdom of God through preaching. Indeed, many modern evangelists seem to think that drama or movies, sports or coffee parlors, music or dancing—anything but preaching—is the way to take the gospel to the world.

Notice how the NASB[100] puts it: "For since in the wisdom of God the world through its wisdom did not come to know God, God was well-pleased through the foolishness of the message preached to save those who believe."[101] Is God going to save the world with a foolish message? Does this make any sense? The Moffatt Bible goes so far as to call it "the 'sheer folly' of the Christian message."[102]

KJV Mark 7:19 "Because it entereth not into his heart, but into the belly, and goeth out into the draught, purging all meats?"

---

98 Is "Areopagus" easier to read than "Mars' hill"?

99 *New King James Version* (1983), p. 1125.
NIV, NASB, ASV, CEV, ESV, GNB, ICB, etc.

100 CEV, ESV, GW ("God decided to use the nonsense of the Good News we speak"), NASB, NIV, NWT, RSV, etc. Spirit of Prophecy quotes only KJV as Scripture.

101 *New American Standard Bible* (1977), p. 796.

102 James Moffatt, D.D., D.Litt., M.A. (Oxon.), *The Bible: A New Translation* (1935), p. 205.

NIV[103] Mark 7:19 "'For it doesn't go into his heart but into his stomach, and then out of his body.' (In saying this, Jesus declared all foods 'clean.')"[104]

Apparently to align with current traditions, appetites, and passions, modern bibles inject the doctrine that meats God said were unfit for food are somehow made healthy in the New Testament.

What about morals? Are morals undermined in modern translations? This is a very serious issue; one of the most serious, perhaps, considering the moral degeneracy of our age.[105]

In **KJV Ecclesiastes 9:9**, the Bible says "Live joyfully with the wife whom thou lovest all the days of the life of thy vanity, which he hath given thee under the sun, all the days of thy vanity: for that is thy portion in this life, and in thy labour which thou takest under the sun."

The one you are supposed to live with joyfully, is your wife—the wife of your youth (or the first one). However, the REB says "Enjoy life with a woman you love."[106] This version leaves it as a woman, but not necessarily one that you are married to. Love seems to be the only essential ingredient. But, the *Good News Bible* says, "Enjoy life with the one you love..." Here marriage is not essential, nor is it essential that it be a woman. Just live with whoever you love "as long as you live this useless life that God has given you in this world. Enjoy every useless day of it, because it is all you will get for all your trouble."[107] Is our life useless? This wording occurs in no manuscript whatsoever, and certainly does not sound like good news.

---

[103] ASV, CEV, ERV, ESV, GNB, ISV, Moff, MSG, NASB, NIV, NWT, RV, RSV, etc.

[104] *New International Version* (1978), p. 1082.

[105] "One translator from the New International Version translation committee, Dr. Virginia Mollenkott, wrote three articles that give strong indication where her theology is headed: 'The Divine Feminine: The Biblical Imagery of God as Female;' 'Sensuous Spirituality: Out from Fundamentalism;' and 'Whore-ishly Implementing the Political Vision of the Christ-Sophia.'" David Thiele, *Have the Faith of Jesus* (Ringgold, GA: Teach Services, 2014), Kindle ed., Kindle Locations 1021-1023.

[106] *The Oxford Study Bible: Revised English Bible with Apocrypha* (Oxford: Oxford University Press, 1992), p. 690.

[107] *Good News Bible* (1976), p. 731.

The Theory of Evolution

In **Hebrews 11:3**, the Bible says, "Through faith we understand that **the worlds** were framed by the word of God, so that things which are seen were not made of things which do appear." The worlds were framed by the word of God. These are profound divine Words that tell us of his creative ability and power.

But the LITV says, "By faith we understand **the ages** to have been framed by the Word of God, so that the things seen should not come into being out of the things that appear."[108] This is actually an injection of the theory of evolution into Holy Writ.[109] According to this version, God's Word only framed the ages, and then the ages took care of themselves—according to the theory—allowing for evolution.

If God's Word framed the worlds, then it happened just as Genesis records—God spoke and it was so. However, having God's Word frame the ages gives the wiggle room to introduce theistic evolution. To have an ecumenical world where all religions become one, even the religion of evolution must be accommodated, so bibles must be created to provide room for all beliefs—doctrinal pluralism.

Some may say that too much is being read into this change. Let us see if other versions take this idea even further, and then investigate whether the translators actually intended such a meaning.

The *Amplified Bible* says, "By faith we understand that the worlds [during the successive ages][110] were framed—fashioned, put in order, and equipped for their intended purpose—by the word of God, so that what we see was not made out of things which are visible."[111]

In this version, God is not a creator, he just took what was there and put it in order, and equipped it for its intended purpose. "During the successive ages" is clearly intended to make room for the evolutionary theory. To demonstrate conclusively that this is what the

---

[108] Jay P. Green, Sr., *KJ3 Literal Translation of the Holy Bible* (Lafayette, IN: SGPBooks.com, Inc., 2010), p. 1130.

[109] Also, MKJV, RV (margin), YLT, etc.

[110] Brackets in original.

[111] *Amplified Bible*, 22nd ed. (Grand Rapids, MI: Zondervan Publishing House, 1958), p. 852.

translators had in mind, let us quote Westcott regarding this verse: "In this connection we can see the full meaning of the words used of creation in Heb. xi. 3: By faith we understand that the worlds (the ages, i.e. the universe under the aspect of time) have been formed by the Word of God.... The whole sequence of life in time, which we call 'the world,' has been 'fitted together' by God. His one creative word included the harmonious unfolding on one plan of the last issues of all that was made. **That which is in relation to Him 'one act at once' is in relation to us an evolution apprehended in orderly succession**."[112] This idea was incorporated into the margin of Westcott and Hort's Revised Version.[113]

Westcott boldly states that this change means that creation in relation to God seemed like an instant, but in relation to us, it was "**an evolution apprehended in orderly succession**." That he intended for this change to make provision for evolution is unambiguous. He tells us his sentiments on the subject explicitly: "No one now, I suppose, holds that the first three chapters of Genesis, for example, give a literal history—I could never understand how any one reading them with open eyes could think they did."[114]

Hort is of the same opinion: "But the book which has most engaged me is Darwin. Whatever may be thought of it, it is a book that one is proud to be contemporary with. I must work out and examine the argument more in detail, but at present my feeling is strong that the theory is unanswerable. If so, it opens up a new period."[115]

---

[112] B. F. Westcott, D.D., DC.L., *Some lessons of the Revised Version of the New Testament* (1897), p. 187.

[113] "Who was to imagine that an utterly untrustworthy new Greek Text, constructed on mistaken principles,—(say rather, on no principles at all,)—would be the fatal result? To speak more truly, who could have anticipated that the opportunity would have been adroitly seized to inflict upon the Church the text of Drs. Westcott and Hort, in all its essential features,—a text which, as will be found elsewhere largely explained, we hold to be the most vicious recension of the original Greek in existence.
"it was deliberately invented.
"Who will venture to predict the amount of mischief which must follow, if the New Greek Text which has been put forth by the men who were appointed to revise the English Authorized Version, should become used in our Schools and in our Colleges."
John William Burgon, B.D., *The Revision Revised* (1883), p. 114, 273, 345.

[114] Arthur Westcott, *The Life and Letters of Brooke Foss Westcott,* Vol. 2 (1903), p. 69.

[115] A. F. Hort, *Life & Letters of Fenton John Anthony Hort,* Vol. 1 (1896), p. 416.

This also demonstrates that changes inserted into the margin in early versions[116] are destined to appear within the text in later versions. Additionally, these changes are manifestly intentional, with theological implications.

How could any Bible believing Christian accept, as the basis of their faith, a modern version of the Bible that has as its basis the work and influence of these infidels?

The State of the Dead

What happens to people when they die is another important Biblical doctrine that has suffered theological manipulation in modern versions. This important doctrine is almost universally misunderstood because of the deceptions of Satan, and the doctrines of the anti-Christ power. Therefore, before we examine the systematic changes to modern versions in support of unbiblical theories, we must outline the teaching of Scripture on this subject, allowing the Bible to interpret itself.

The majority of the Christian world believes that at death the soul goes either to heaven or to hell. The prevailing belief about hell fire is that the unfortunate souls that end up there will be tortured throughout the ceaseless ages of eternity. These beliefs are held without respect to their origin, and without considering all the evidence of Scripture. This Catholic doctrine of hell has trickled into most Protestant churches of today. By portraying God as a sadistic tyrant, its horrific cruelty has caused many people to become atheists.

"The theory of the immortality of the soul was one of those false doctrines that Rome, borrowing from paganism, incorporated into the religion of Christendom. Martin Luther classed it with the 'monstrous fables that form part of the Roman dunghill of decretals.' Commenting on the words of Solomon in Ecclesiastes, that the dead know not anything, the Reformer says: 'Solomon judgeth that the dead are asleep, and feel nothing at all. For the dead lie there,

---

[116] (such as this change inserted by Westcott and Hort into the 1881 Revision Version).

accounting neither days nor years, but when they are awakened, they shall seem to have slept scarce one minute.'"[117]

"An eternally-burning hell preached from the pulpit, and kept before the people, does injustice to the benevolent character of God. It presents him as the veriest tyrant in the universe. This wide-spread dogma has turned thousands to Universalism, infidelity, and atheism.
"The word of God is plain. It is a straight chain of truth. It will prove an anchor to those who are willing to receive it, even if they have to sacrifice their cherished fables. It will save them from the terrible delusions of these perilous times.
"Satan has led the minds of the ministers of different churches to adhere as tenaciously to their popular errors, as he led the Jews in their blindness to cling to their sacrifices, and crucify Christ."[118]

Catholic paintings depict their idea of what happens in hell. In paintings, such as *Hortus Deliciarum*, you see people being tortured by flames, thrown into burning pots of oil, hung upside down and stabbed through and held over the flames by demons. Lucifer, himself chained in the fire, is torturing victims. There is a priest at the bottom left who is presiding over the whole thing. It is really quite a horrific picture.

This idea absolutely does not come from the Bible. The Bible teaches no such doctrine. It was dreamed up and brought into the Christian religion directly from pagan philosophy.

In Greek mythology, Tartarus was a prison of the Tartan gods. Tartarus was considered the place where the Tartan gods must suffer. Plato and Homer concocted these legendary myths. Plato wrote that souls were judged after death and those who received punishment were sent to Tartarus. Homer, in the *Iliad*, speaks of the underworld. The ghosts of the suitors who have died are herded there by Hermes. Then you have the Greek god Hades, oldest male child of Chronus and Rhea, with the brothers named Zeus and Poseidon. In fact, this Greek mythology so permeated the culture of Biblical times that the Greek word for hell is hades. The name of this Greek god became a common word to refer to a place of burning. It

---

[117] E. G. White, *The Faith I Live By* (Nampa, ID: Pacific Press, 1958), p. 175.2.

[118] E. G. White, *Spiritual Gifts,* Vol. 4b (Nampa, ID: Pacific Press, 1864), p. 104.2-4.

is Greek mythology which originated the idea of an eternally burning hell. This is the source of the popular Christian belief that somewhere hell fire is burning today. The hellfire of the Bible is totally different than the hellfire of Greek mythology.

In Revelation 20:9 the Bible tells us when hellfire burns: "And they went up on the breadth of the earth, and compassed the camp of the saints about, and the beloved city: and fire came down from God out of heaven, and devoured them."

Not until the saved have been taken to heaven for 1,000 years, to review the books of record, and the New Jerusalem has come down to the earth from God out of heaven, are the wicked resurrected to face their final punishment by fire. In one final demonstration to the universe that God's judgments were just, the wicked still try to kill God as they attack the city. Fire from God out of heaven devours them, putting a final end to sin and suffering and fulfilling the demands of justice.[119]

Therefore, hellfire is not burning somewhere today; it is the final destruction of sin and sinners—the final punishment that was only "prepared for the devil and his angels."[120] The question then arises as to how long hellfire burns. Two verses speak of "everlasting fire" and Revelation 20:10 says that the beast and false prophet are "tormented day and night for ever and ever." Therefore, some find it an easy matter to jump from these one or two verses to a belief in Greek mythology.

One principal of sound Biblical interpretation is that no doctrine may be built around a couple of verses.[121] In order to get a clear view of what the Bible says on a particular subject, one must examine all the evidence. If there are verses that seem to be contradictory, we must go with the weight of evidence and establish doctrine with the

---

[119] See Martin Klein, *Glimpses of the Open Gates of Heaven*, Revelation 20.

[120] Matthew 18:8; 25:41

[121] An extreme example of building a doctrine with just two texts would be to combine part of Matthew 27:5, [Judas] "departed, and went and hanged himself," with part of Luke 10:37 "Go, and do thou likewise," and claim that the Bible is teaching us to commit suicide. This, of course would be absolutely absurd. But, it illustrates the fact that single verses, or portions of verses, or even a few verses, taken out of context, without regard to the rest of the teachings of Scripture, can easily be misconstrued. Satan himself did this when quoting Scripture to Christ in the wilderness of temptation.

majority of texts on the subject rather than basing a doctrine on just one text. It is easy to twist or misunderstand one or two texts, but when you look at the whole overview, it is much more difficult to do so. The bulk of evidence can then give a framework for understanding the few verses that may at first seem contradictory.

When the Bible says the beast and false prophet are tormented forever and ever, must the phrase, by definition, always mean throughout the ceaseless ages of eternity? Turning to Jonah 2:6 we read the description of his experience of going down in the belly of the whale: "I went down to the bottoms of the mountains; the earth with her bars was about me **for ever**: yet hast thou brought up my life from corruption, O LORD my God." It certainly might have seemed to be "**for ever**," yet, the Bible tells us he was there only three days and three nights.[122]

In the same manner, the word that is used for forever in the New Testament means unto the age, or for a period of time. It is a word that can mean something a long way off in the future, or it can mean something relatively short, depending on the context. Therefore, it does not demand the meaning of 'through all ceaseless ages of eternity,' but can mean 'until it is out of sight,' or 'until it is forgotten.' So, in the case of Jonah going down in the whale, the idea of forever was not really for all eternity; rather what seemed like a long time for the situation.[123] We commonly do this in English; we might say that it took forever to get from one town to the next, and we certainly do not mean to say it took all eternity.

If it is true that God is a God of love, fairness, and justice, then it would not make sense for God to punish people for a short life of sin, of perhaps seventy years or even less, through the billions of years of eternity. This would not be a God of love. Heaven would not be a pleasant place for those righteous who had loved ones burning on through all eternity.

---

[122] Jonah 1:17

[123] This way of looking at these expressions of forever is, of course, dependent on additional Biblical evidence for a finite hell fire.

Let us examine the Scriptural evidence, and allow the Bible to interpret itself: Ezekiel 28:18-19, using the metaphor of the king of Tyre[124] to describe Satan, says, "Thou hast defiled thy sanctuaries by the multitude of thine iniquities, by the iniquity of thy traffic; therefore will I bring forth a fire from the midst of thee, it shall devour thee, and I will bring thee to ashes upon the earth in the sight of all them that behold thee. All they that know thee among the people shall be astonished at thee: thou shalt be a terror, and **never shalt thou be any more**."

According to Scripture, Satan himself will be consumed once and for all. He will not be in charge of hell, torturing people throughout eternity, but **never** will he be anymore.

Is there more evidence? Psalm 37:10: "For yet a little while, and the wicked shall not be: yea, thou shalt diligently consider his place, and it shall not be." The place of the wicked cannot even be discovered. Verse 20 says that the wicked "shall be as the fat of lambs: they shall consume; into smoke shall they consume away."

Psalm 9:5-6 says, "Thou hast rebuked the heathen, thou hast destroyed the wicked, thou hast put out their name for ever and ever. "O thou enemy, destructions are come to a perpetual end: and thou hast destroyed cities; their memorial is perished with them."

They are destroyed, their destructions are come to a perpetual end, and even their memory has perished—they cannot be remembered. Obviously, if they were being tortured in hell for all eternity, this would not be the case. You would be able to remember them. You would be able to find their name.

Malachi 4:3 speaks to this, "And ye shall tread down the wicked; for they shall be ashes under the soles of your feet in the day that I shall do this, saith the LORD of hosts." The Bible is telling us that we will actually walk on the ashes of those who have been completely consumed. This certainly does not sound like they are still writhing in

---

124 Some have claimed that this passage is only speaking of the literal king of Tyre. This is impossible because it says he was in Eden, the garden of God; that he was the anointed covering cherub; that he walked in the stones of fire; and was on the holy mountain of God. This is speaking of the heavenly throne room, and can only apply to Lucifer before his fall.

the flames of hell. This is not Greek mythology, but the Bible doctrine of what happens when hellfire burns.

Scripture tells us how hot the fire will be after it has completed its work of cleansing the earth. In Isaiah 47:14 it says, "Behold, they shall be as stubble; the fire shall burn them; they shall not deliver themselves from the power of the flame: there shall not be a coal to warm at, nor fire to sit before it."

Yes, it will be hot. Yes, it will burn the wicked. Yes, it will devour them. No one can deliver the wicked from the power of this fire. But, once it has completed its work, it will go out, so cold, that there will not even be a coal to warm at or a little campfire by which to sit.

Considering text after text of harmonious Bible doctrine allows us to see the true picture of hellfire, and gives a framework for interpreting the few texts that seem in contradiction.

Interestingly enough, there is someone who will live in eternal fire, but, it is not the wicked, as you may think. Isaiah 33:14-15: "The sinners in Zion are afraid; fearfulness hath surprised the hypocrites. Who among us shall dwell with the devouring fire? who among us shall dwell with everlasting burnings? He that walketh righteously, and speaketh uprightly; he that despiseth the gain of oppressions, that shaketh his hands from holding of bribes, that stoppeth his ears from hearing of blood, and shutteth his eyes from seeing evil."

The righteous will dwell in everlasting burnings, not the wicked. This is because the Bible tells us that our God is a consuming fire.[125] Sin cannot live in the presence of a God that is a consuming fire to sin. Thus, at the end of time, God will put an end to sin for all eternity, by destroying sin and sinners. He will destroy sin, and anyone who continues to hold onto their sins will be consumed with them. He has made abundant provision for us to have forgiveness and victory over our sin. That consuming fire of God's presence will not hurt the righteous. They will be able to live in the presence of that everlasting burning, just as Daniel's three friends walked with Jesus in the fiery furnace. The same eternal fire of God's presence, that is a comfort

[125] Hebrews 12:29

and honor for the righteous to walk in, destroys and consumes the wicked.

Linked with the idea of an eternally burning hellfire is the idea of what actually happens when people die. According to Greek mythology, and Catholic doctrine, as soon as someone dies, their spirit is separated from their body. The spirit is thought to be some kind of conscious living entity, which goes either to heaven or to hell. According to this idea there is consciousness for all eternity, in the hot place or in the good place.

This theory also does not come from the Bible. Ecclesiastes 9:5-6: "For the living know that they shall die: but the dead know not any thing, neither have they any more a reward; for the memory of them is forgotten. Also, their love, and their hatred, and their envy, is now perished; neither have they any more a portion for ever in any thing that is done under the sun."

God tells us that when we die, we do not know anything. The dead are not conscious living entities up in heaven or down in hell. They go to sleep and return to the dust of the earth. This is what the Bible teaches.

Jesus called death a sleep over and over again. When he went to resurrect Lazarus, he said, "Lazarus, come forth."[126] He did not tell him to come down. Think how ridiculous it would have been, if, at the point of death, Lazarus' spirit had gone to heaven and Jesus then called him back down to the earth. If he was up there enjoying the bliss of heaven, would it not be a rude trick to play on him, to call him back down into his body to continue his suffering on this sinful earth? Jesus told his disciples he was going to awaken Lazarus. Lazarus did not come out of the grave with any stories of heaven or of hell. He simply woke up.

The Bible tells us in Job 14:10-12, "But man dieth, and wasteth away: yea, man giveth up the ghost, and where is he? As the waters fail from the sea, and the flood decayeth and drieth up: So man lieth down, and riseth not: till the heavens be no more, they shall not awake, nor be raised out of their sleep."

---

[126] John 11:43

Job goes on to describe the resurrection in verse 13 and 14, "O that thou wouldest hide me in the grave, that thou wouldest keep me secret, until thy wrath be past, that thou wouldest appoint me a set time, and remember me! If a man die, shall he live again? all the days of my appointed time will I wait, till my change come." Job understood what happens to men when they die. They go into the grave, they become no more. They are hid there—kept secret. God remembers them. They do not know anything until the appointed time and their change comes. At the resurrection of the second coming, Jesus awakes those that are righteous from their dusty beds. He remembers where they were, who they were, and he makes them alive again. But, the dead are not some kind of conscious entity somewhere else outside their body.

"The dead praise not the LORD, neither any that go down into silence."[127] Surely, if some people went straight to heaven when they died, they would be praising God, would they not? If you were in heaven, would you not be praising God? But here the Bible tells us that the dead do not praise the Lord. They go down into silence, into the sleep of the grave.

"His breath goeth forth, he returneth to his earth; in that very day his thoughts perish."[128] It is the breath, or the power of God, that returns to the One who gave it. It is not some kind of conscious living entity, but just the power, the electricity, that keeps the light bulb going. When you turn off the light, what happens to the electricity? What happens to the light? The light is simply gone. Without the power from the electricity, the light is just not there. It is the same way with the breath of God. When he gives the breath of life, it gives life. When we die, that breath of life goes back to God. Our bodies go into the dust until God comes and resurrects us again at the second coming.

"For David is not ascended into the heavens: but he saith himself, The Lord said unto my Lord, Sit thou on my right hand, Until I make thy foes thy footstool."[129] The Bible calls David a man after God's

---

[127] Psalm 115:17

[128] Psalm 146:4

[129] Acts 2:34-35

own heart.[130] Surely, if people go to heaven as soon as they die, David would be in heaven. But the Bible assures us that he is not in heaven. That is because he is sleeping in the grave, awaiting the resurrection, just like everyone else. What a comfort it is to know that our loved ones who have died are not up there somehow suffering in heaven because they can see the pain and suffering we are still experiencing on this earth. Our loved ones are sleeping in the grave, awaiting the resurrection call. What sense would it make to have a resurrection if everyone is already in heaven or in hell? There would be no point of a judgment; all would already have their reward.

One of Satan's two original lies in the garden of Eden was that the dead do not really die: "Ye shall not surely die."[131] Maybe you will die, but you will not be completely dead. You will continue to live on. That original lie opened the whole realm of possibility of necromancy or speaking to 'the dead.' The Bible explicitly condemns this practice,[132] because if you speak to the dead, you are actually speaking to demons. You are not speaking to your dead loved one, because the Bible says your dead loved one knows nothing. "For such are false apostles, deceitful workers, transforming themselves into the apostles of Christ. And no marvel; for Satan himself is transformed into an angel of light."[133]

"They are dead, they shall not live; they are deceased, they shall not rise: therefore hast thou visited and destroyed them, and made all their memory to perish."[134] Again and again the Bible is consistent with this precious doctrine of what happens when you die.

---

[130] Acts 13:22

[131] Genesis 3:4

[132] Deuteronomy 18:10-12 "There shall not be found among you any one that maketh his son or his daughter to pass through the fire, or that useth divination, or an observer of times, or an enchanter, or a witch,
"Or a charmer, or a consulter with familiar spirits, or a wizard, or a necromancer.
"For all that do these things are an abomination unto the LORD: and because of these abominations the LORD thy God doth drive them out from before thee."

[133] 2 Corinthians 11:13-14

[134] Isaiah 26:14

"But I would not have you to be ignorant, brethren, **concerning them which are asleep**, that ye sorrow not, even as others which have no hope. For if we believe that Jesus died and rose again, even so **them also which sleep in Jesus** will God bring with him. For this we say unto you by the word of the Lord, that we which are alive and remain unto the coming of the Lord shall not prevent **them which are asleep.** For the Lord himself shall descend from heaven with a shout, with the voice of the archangel, and with the trump of God: and **the dead in Christ shall rise** first: Then we which are alive and remain shall be caught up together with them in the clouds, to meet the Lord in the air: and so shall we ever be with the Lord. Wherefore comfort one another with these words."[135] Once again, the Bible describes the dead as being asleep and rising from their graves. Comforting words, precious promise.

This brings us to the point of examining a few of the passages where the doctrine of what happens when you die, and the doctrine of hell, is tweaked in modern versions to support the doctrines of devils.

KJV 2 Peter 2:9 "The Lord knoweth how to deliver the godly out of temptations, and to reserve the unjust unto the day of judgment to be punished."

When, according to this verse, do the unjust get punished? At the day of judgment. This makes perfect sense, and sounds like a fair and just God who would wait till the day of judgment to punish the wicked. But, the BBE,[136] in the same verse, says, "keep evil-doers under punishment till the day of judging."[137]

Why would God need a day of judgment if he were already punishing people? This sounds like a despotic government. It is, in fact, an introduction of the theory of purgatory, which comes straight from the Roman church. Keeping them under punishment until the day of judgment? The NIV says, "if this is so, then the Lord knows how to

---

[135] 1 Thessalonians 4:13-18

[136] ASV, CEV, ESV, GNB, ICB (the Lord will hold evil people and punish them, while waiting for the Judgment Day.), NASB, NKJV, RV, RSV, NEB, etc. The Spirit of Prophecy quotes only the KJV.

[137] *Bible in Basic English* (Cambridge: University Press, 1956), p. 890.

rescue godly men from trials and to hold the unrighteous for the day of judgment, while continuing their punishment."[138]

The doctrine of the Bible has been exchanged for the doctrines of men. These words do not have the same meaning, and this change provides for the insertion of the Catholic doctrine of purgatory.

Job tells us that when he sees God, it will be in his flesh rather than as some kind of disembodied spirit.

KJV Job 19:26 "And though after my skin worms destroy this body, yet in my flesh shall I see God:"

When he resurrects me, he is going to breathe back that breath of life into my decayed body. He will remember exactly everything about me. He recreates my body. When I see God, I see him in my flesh. All those resurrected in Scripture (including Jesus) were resurrected in their bodies. When the disciples thought their resurrected Lord was a ghost, Jesus said, "Why are ye troubled? and why do thoughts arise in your hearts? Behold my hands and my feet, that it is I myself: handle me, and see; for a spirit hath not flesh and bones, as ye see me have."[139]

But, this Biblical doctrine does not fit well with the theory that when you die you go straight to heaven, and so the ASV[140] changed this verse to read, "And after my skin, even this body, is destroyed, Then **without my flesh** shall I see God;"[141] In other words, upon death, Job shows up in heaven as a spirit? These two versions are completely opposite in meaning and in doctrine. Simple rules of logic demand that both of these statements cannot be true. Therefore, one must be a lie—making it a doctrine of devils.

It is written: **KJV Psalm 146:4** "His breath goeth forth, he returneth to his earth; in that very day his thoughts perish." The day he dies,

---

[138] *New International Version* (1978), p. 1312.

[139] Luke 24:38-39

[140] Also, BBE, CJB, ERV, JPS, NASB ("Yet from my flesh"), NWT ("And after my skin, which they have skinned off, —this! Yet reduced in my flesh I shall behold God").

[141] *American Standard Version* (1901), p. 452.

his thoughts perish. All consciousness is gone in death, according to the Bible. This is clear testimony that there is not a spirit being that leaves the body at death.

NIV Psalm 146:4 "When their spirit departs, they return to the ground; on that very day their plans come to nothing."[142] The NIV changes "His breath goeth forth" to "their spirit departs." Clearly the King James Bible is in harmony with the rest of Scripture that the dead know not anything. The NIV[143] is supporting the Catholic doctrine of the immortality of the soul. Also changed is the phrase "his thoughts perish," to "their plans come to nothing." If one's thoughts perish there is no consciousness in death. If your plans come to nothing, you could be still conscious—only with a new set of plans.

Without a discussion of the meaning of the following verse, notice how modern bibles use its ambiguity to introduce pagan Greek philosophy:

KJV Job 26:5 "Dead things are formed from under the waters, and the inhabitants thereof."

The RSV Job 26:5 says, "The shades below tremble, the waters and their inhabitants."[144] Does this mean that there are window blinds shaking below? No. A quick look at Merriam Webster online dictionary reveals the following meaning for shade: 5.a: disembodied spirit, ghost.

To demonstrate that this is exactly the meaning the RSV translators intended, observe the rendering of this verse in the NIV "The dead are in deep anguish, those beneath the waters and all that live in them."[145] The *International Children's Bible*, containing a similar idea ought to have the children thoroughly confused: "The spirits of the

---

[142] *New International Version* (1978), p. 676.

[143] NKJV, ICB (changes last phrase), NASB (changes only first phrase), ESV (changes only second phrase), NWT (changes only first phrase).

[144] *Revised Standard Version* (New York: Oxford University Press, 1962), p. 637.

[145] *New International Version* (1978), p. 562.

dead beneath the waters shake. And so do those that live in the waters."[146]

"Satan has long been preparing for his final effort to deceive the world. The foundation of his work was laid by the assurance given to Eve in Eden: 'Ye shall not surely die... In the day ye eat thereof, then your eyes shall be opened, and ye shall be as gods, knowing good and evil.' Genesis 3:4, 5. Little by little he has prepared the way for his masterpiece of deception in the development of spiritualism. He has not yet reached the full accomplishment of his designs; but it will be reached in the last remnant of time."[147]

Philip Schaff, member of the 1881 *Revised Version* committee and President of the translation committee for the *American Standard Version* reveals the purpose of these modifications: "The changes made thus far and communicated by you in confidence are judicious and in the right direction... and should contain the germs of the new theology....

"Every age must produce its own theology....

"Such a theology will give new life to the church, and prepare the way for the reunion of Christendom."[148]

Clearly the changes are intentional, theological in nature, and for the purpose of reuniting Christendom. Preparing "the way for the reunion of Christendom," is a veiled way of stating the intention to bring all churches into subjection to Rome.

"God's word has given warning of the impending danger; let this be unheeded, and the Protestant world will learn what the purposes of Rome really are, only when it is too late to escape the snare. She is silently growing into power. Her doctrines are exerting their influence in legislative halls, in the churches, and in the hearts of men. She is piling up her lofty and massive structures in the secret recesses of which her former persecutions will be repeated. Stealthily and unsuspectedly she is strengthening her forces to further her own ends when the time shall come for her to strike. All that she desires

---

[146] *International Children's Bible* (1988), p. 383.

[147] E. G. White, *Darkness Before Dawn* (Nampa, ID: Pacific Press, 1997), p. 23.3.

[148] David Schley Schaff, Ph.D., *The Life of Philip Schaff* (1897), p. 427, 477-478.

is vantage ground, and this is already being given her. We shall soon see and shall feel what the purpose of the Roman element is. Whoever shall believe and obey the word of God will thereby incur reproach and persecution."[149]

KJV Psalm 55:15 "Let death seize upon them, and let them go down quick into hell: for wickedness is in their dwellings, and among them." While it is true that the word hell in the KJV can refer to the grave, rather than hellfire, the NIV has the enemies alive in the grave. This gives an impression of some kind of afterlife in the grave.

NIV Psalm 55:15 "Let death take my enemies by surprise; let them go down alive to the grave, for evil finds lodging among them."[150]

In a most profound prophecy of the resurrection of the wicked dead, at the end of the millennium, Isaiah describes the kings and mighty warriors that stir from their graves for the final battle of Gog and Magog.[151]

KJV Isaiah 14:9 "Hell from beneath is moved for thee to meet thee at thy coming: it stirreth up the dead for thee, even all the chief ones of the earth; it hath raised up from their thrones all the kings of the nations."

NIV[152] Isaiah 14:9 "The grave below is all astir to meet you at your coming; it rouses the spirits of the departed to greet you— all those who were leaders in the world; it makes them rise from their throne— all those who were kings over the nations."[153] The NIV turns a prophecy of the resurrection of the wicked for the final battle, into spirits that are astir to meet you and roused to greet you at your

---

[149] E. G. White, *The Great Controversy* (1911), p. 581.2.

[150] *New International Version* (1978), p. 614.

[151] See Martin Klein, *Glimpses of the Open Gates of Heaven*, Revelation 20.

[152] BBE ("the shades of the dead are awake before you"), CEV ("The world of the dead eagerly waits for you. With great excitement, the spirits of ancient rulers hear about your coming"), ERV, GNB ("The ghosts of those who were powerful on earth are stirring about. The ghosts of kings are rising from their thrones."), GW, ICB ("The place of the dead is excited to meet you when you come. It wakes the spirits of the dead to greet you"), JPS, MSG, NASB, RSV, TNIV, Darby and LITV turn the "chief ones of the earth," into "he-goats." etc.

[153] *New International Version* (1978), p. 748.

coming, all those who were (past tense) kings over nations (apparently in their previous life). This is perhaps one of the most blatant insertions of the papal doctrine of the immortality of the soul.

KJV Mark 9:43 "And if thy hand offend thee, cut it off: it is better for thee to enter into life maimed, than having two hands to go into hell, into the fire that never shall be quenched."

NIV[154] Mark 9:43 "If your hand causes you to sin, cut it off. It is better for you to enter life maimed than with two hands to go into hell, where the fire never goes out."[155]

Jesus speaks of the fire that cannot be quenched—a fire that no person can extinguish. This way of stating it does not demand that the fire never stops burning, but that it cannot be put out. It burns until its purpose is accomplished and there is nothing anyone can do to cause it to stop. The NIV changes "**fire that never shall be quenched**," to "where the fire never goes out." This is an obvious injection of the idea of eternally burning hellfire.

KJV Malachi 4:3 "And ye shall tread down the wicked; for they shall be ashes under the soles of your feet in the day that I shall do this, saith the LORD of hosts."

GNB[156] Malachi 4:3 "On the day when I act, you will overcome the wicked, and they will be like dust under your feet."[157]

The Bible informs us that after the final destruction of the wicked, the righteous will walk out onto ashes of the fire-cleansed earth. This would certainly be impossible if the fire were still burning. The fire must be out for this to be the case. The *Good News Bible*, in an apparent attempt to obscure the fact that the fire is now cold, changes "ashes" to "dust."

Some changes are so subtle that even when pointed out, some might not see the difference, yet notice the following, seemingly

---

[154] Also, BBE, CEV, ERV, ICB, GNB, MSG (in a furnace of eternal fire), TNIV, etc.

[155] *New International Version* (1988), p. 1148.

[156] Also, BBE.

[157] *Good News Bible* (1976), p. 1041.

insignificant change, and what a Catholic commentator says it means:

KJV Hebrews 9:27 "And as it is appointed unto men once to die, but after this **the judgment**:"

RV Hebrews 9:27 "And inasmuch as it is appointed unto men once to die, and after this **cometh judgment**;"[158]

The Catholic Dr. F.W. Farrar writes, "there is a positive certainty that it does not mean 'the judgment' in the sense in which that word is popularly understood. By abandoning the article which the King James translators here incorrectly inserted, the Revisers help, as they have done in so many other places, silently to remove deep-seated errors. At the death of each of us there follows 'a judgment,' as the sacred writer says: the judgment, the final judgment may not be for centuries to come. In the omission of that unauthorized little article from the A[uthorized] V[ersion] by the Revisers, lies no less a doctrine than that of the existence of an Intermediate State."[159]

Clearly this commentator sees the change as theological in nature believing that it silently removes "deep-seated errors," that he thinks are contained in the King James Version. He also informs us that the *Revised Version* has inserted the doctrine of an intermediate state, or purgatory.

The *International Children's Bible* makes the change even more bold:
ICB Hebrews 9:27 "Everyone must die once. After a person dies, he is judged."[160]

KJV Ezekiel 28:18 "Thou hast defiled thy sanctuaries by the multitude of thine iniquities, by the iniquity of thy traffic; therefore **will** I bring forth a fire from the midst of thee, it **shall** devour thee, and I

---

[158] *Revised Version* (1885), p. 167.

[159] F.W. Farrar, D.D., *Contemporary Review*, January - June, 1882, Vol. 41 (London: Strahan and Company, 1882), p. 368.

[160] *International Children's Bible* (1988), p. 909.

will bring thee to ashes upon the earth in the sight of all them that behold thee."

NKJV[161] Ezekiel 28:18 "You defiled your sanctuaries By the multitude of your iniquities, By the iniquity of your trading; Therefore I **brought** fire from your midst; It **devoured** you, And I **turned** you to ashes upon the earth In the sight of all who saw you."[162]

The one passage in Scripture that assures us that Satan himself will one day be burnt to ashes, devoured, never to be any more, has all been changed to past tense in the modern versions, so you could never get such an assurance. The prophecy is destroyed, for in the past tense it can no longer refer to Satan, since he is still alive and well today. Surely Satan laughs at this. Shall we accept the doctrines of Jesus Christ, or the doctrines of devils? Satan is about to deceive almost the entire planet.

The Sabbath

"And the ten horns out of this kingdom are ten kings that shall arise: and another {horn} shall rise after them; and he shall be diverse from the first, and he shall subdue three kings.
"And he shall speak great words against the most High, and shall wear out the saints of the most High, and **think to change times and laws**: and they shall be given into his hand until a time and times and the dividing of time."[163]

Catholics Speak

"The Church is above the Bible; and this transference of Sabbath observance from Saturday to Sunday is proof positive of that fact."[164]

---

[161] ASV, CEV, ERV, ESV, ICB, GNB, JPS, MKJV, MSG, NASB, NIV, NWT, RSV, RV, etc. The Spirit of Prophecy quotes only the KJV as Scripture.

[162] *New King James Version* (1983), p. 842.

[163] Daniel 7:24-25

[164] "Sabbath Observance," *The Catholic Record,* September 1, 1923, p. 4. http://biblelight.net/c-record.htm Retrieved: 02-09-2016.

"The Bible says, 'Remember that thou keep holy the Sabbath day.' The Catholic Church says: 'No! By my divine power I abolish the Sabbath day, and command you to keep holy the first day of the week.' And lo! the entire civilized world bows down in reverent obedience to the command of the holy Catholic Church."[165]

"Sunday is a Catholic institution, and its claims to observance can be defended only on Catholic principles... From the beginning to the end of Scripture there is not a single passage that warrants the transfer of weekly public worship from the last day of the week to the first."[166]

"If protestants would follow the Bible, they should worship God on the Sabbath day. In keeping the Sunday, they are following a law of the Catholic church."[167]

"Protestantism, in discarding the authority of the [Roman Catholic] Church, has no good reason for its Sunday theory, and ought, logically, to keep Saturday as the Sabbath."[168]

"Since the [Catholic] Church has probably influenced Constantine to make the day Sunday a holiday, it can claim the honor of having granted man a rest from his labors every seven days."[169]

"Reason and common sense demand the acceptance of one or the other of these alternatives: either Protestantism and the keeping holy

---

[165] Father Enright, CSS. R. to E.E. Franke, January 11, 1892, in "An Adventist Minister on Sunday Laws," *American Sentinel,* June 1, 1893, p. 173.

[166] M. Long, "Rampant Sabbaterianism," *Catholic Press,* August 25, 1900, p. 22, biblelight.net/Catholic Press.jpg Retrieved: 01-31-2016.

[167] Albert Smith, Chancellor of Archdiocese of Baltimore, replying for the Cardinal in a letter dated February 10, 1920.

[168] John Gilmary Shea, L.L.D., *American Catholic Quarterly Review*, Vol. 8—January, 1883—No. 29 (Philadelphia: Hardy & Mahony, Publishers and Proprietors, 1883), p. 152.

[169] C. S. Mosna, S.C.J., *Storia della Domenica Dalle Origini Fino Agli Inizi del v Secolo [History of Sunday From its Origins to the Early Fifth Century]* (1969), p. 366.
Italian: "Avendo la Chiesa influito probabilmente su Constantino per rendere la domenica giorno <<festivo>>, Essa può rivendicarsi l'onore di aver voluto concedere all'uomo una pausa alle sue fatiche ogni sette giorni."

of Saturday, or Catholicity and the keeping holy of Sunday. Compromise is impossible."[170]

Methodists Speak

"But the moral law contained in the ten commandments, and enforced by the prophets, he [Christ] did not take away. It was not the design of his coming to revoke any part of this. This is a law which never can be broken.... Every part of this law must remain in force upon all mankind, and in all ages; as not depending either on time or place, or any other circumstances liable to change, but on the nature of God and the nature of man, and their unchangeable relation to each other."[171]

"Take the matter of Sunday. There are indications in the New Testament as to how the church came to keep the first day of the week as its day of worship, but there is no passage telling Christians to keep that day, or to transfer the Jewish Sabbath to that day."[172]

Presbyterians Speak

"The Sabbath is a part of the decalogue—the Ten Commandments. This alone forever settles the question as to the perpetuity of the institution.... Until, therefore, it can be shown that the whole moral law has been repealed, the Sabbath will stand.... The teaching of Christ confirms the perpetuity of the Sabbath."[173]

---

[170] "The Christian Sabbath," *The Catholic Mirror*, December 23, 1893, p. 8-9.

[171] John Emory, *The Works of the Reverend John Wesley*, Vol. 1 (New York: J. Collord, 1831), p. 221-222.

[172] Harris Franklin Rall, Ph.D., D.D., *Christian Advocate*, July 2, 1942, p. 26.

[173] T.C. Blake, D.D., *Theology Condensed* (Cumberland Presbyterian Publishing House, 1882), p. 474, 475.

Dwight L. Moody

"The sabbath was binding in Eden, and it has been in force ever since. This fourth commandment begins with the word 'remember,' showing that the sabbath already existed when God wrote the law on the tables of stone at Sinai. How can men claim that this one commandment has been done away with when they will admit that the other nine are still binding?"[174]

Anglicans/Episcopalians Speak

"And where are we told in Scripture that we are to keep the first day at all? We are commanded to keep the seventh; but we are nowhere commanded to keep the first day.... The reason why we keep the first day of the week holy instead of the seventh is for the same reason that we observe many other things, not because the Bible, but because the [Roman] church has enjoined it."[175]

"There is no word, no hint, in the New Testament about abstaining from work on Sunday... Into the rest of Sunday no divine law enters... The observance of Ash Wednesday or Lent stands on exactly the same footing as the observance of Sunday."[176]

Congregationalists Speak

"It is quite clear that however rigidly or devoutly we may spend Sunday, we are not keeping the Sabbath.... The Sabbath was founded on a specific Divine command. We can plead no such command for the obligation to observe Sunday.... There is not a single sentence in the New Testament to suggest that we incur any penalty by violating the supposed sanctity of Sunday."[177]

---

[174] D. L. Moody, *Weighed and Wanting: Addresses on the Ten Commandments* (Chicago: Fleming H. Revell Company, 1898), p. 31.

[175] Isaac Williams, B.D., *Plain Sermons on the Catechism*, Vol. 1 (London: Rivingtons, 1882), p. 334-336.

[176] Canon Eyton, *The Ten Commandments* (London: Trubner & Co., 1894), p. 62, 63, 65.

[177] Robert William Dale, LL.D., D.D., *The Ten Commandments,* 5th ed. (London: Hodder and Stoughton, 1885), p. 100-101.

Disciples of Christ Speak

"'But,' say some, 'it was *changed* from the seventh to the first day.' Where? when? and by whom? No man can tell. No, it never was changed, nor could it be, unless creation was to be gone through again: for the reason assigned must be changed before the observance, or respect to the reason, can be changed! It is all old wives' fables to talk of the change of the sabbath from the seventh to the first day. If it be changed, it was that august personage changed it who changes times and laws *ex officio*—I think his name is DOCTOR ANTICHRIST."[178]

Baptists Speak

"There was and is a command to keep holy the Sabbath day, but that Sabbath day was not Sunday. It will however be readily said, and with some show of triumph, that the Sabbath was transferred from the Seventh to the First day of the week, with all its duties, privileges and sanctions. Earnestly desiring information on the subject, which I have studied for many years, I ask, where can the record of such a transaction be found? Not in the New Testament—absolutely not. There is no scriptural evidence of the change of the Sabbath institution from the Seventh to the First day of the week...

"I wish to say that this Sabbath question, in this aspect of it, is the gravest and most perplexing question connected with Christian institutions which at present claims attention from Christian people; and the only reason that it is not a more disturbing element in Christian thought and in religious discussion is because the Christian world has settled down content on the conviction that somehow a transference has taken place at the beginning of Christian history.

"To me it seems unaccountable that Jesus, during three years' discussion with His disciples, often conversing with them upon the Sabbath question, discussing it in some of its various aspects, freeing it from its false [Jewish traditional] glosses, never alluded to any transference of the day; also, that during forty days of His resurrection life, no such thing was intimated. Nor, so far as we know, did the Spirit, which was given to bring to their remembrance

---

178 Alexander Campbell, "Address to the Readers of the Christian Baptist, No. 3," *The Christian Baptist,* Vol. 1-7, ed. Alexander Campbell, rev. from 2nd ed. by D.S. Burnet (Cincinnati: D.S. Burnet, 1835), p. 44.

all things whatsoever that He had said unto them, deal with this question. Nor yet did the inspired apostles, in preaching the gospel, founding churches, counseling and instructing those founded, discuss or approach the subject.

"Of course I quite well know that Sunday did come into use in early Christian history as a religious day, as we learn from the Christian Fathers and other sources. But what a pity that it comes branded with the mark of Paganism, and christened with the name of the sun-god, then adopted and sanctified by the Papal apostasy, and bequeathed as a sacred legacy to Protestantism."[179]

Lutherans Speak

"The festival of Sunday, like all other festivals, was always only a human ordinance, and it was far from the intentions of the apostles to establish a Divine command in this respect, far from them, and from the early apostolic Church, to transfer the laws of the Sabbath to Sunday."[180]

"They [Roman Catholics] allege the Sabbath changed into the Sunday, the Lord's day, contrary to the Decalogue, as it appears; neither is there any example more boasted of than the changing of the Sabbath day. Great, say they, is the power and authority of the Church, since it dispensed with one of the ten commandments."[181]

"But they err in teaching that Sunday has taken the place of the Old Testament Sabbath and therefore must be kept as the seventh day had to be kept by the children of Israel.... These churches err in their teaching, for Scripture has in no way ordained the first day of the

---

[179] Edward T. Hiscox, D.D., [Author of the Baptist Manual], before a New York ministers conference, November 13, 1893, *New York Examiner*, November 16, 1893, as cited in Gary Hullquist, M.D., *Sabbath Diagnosis* (Brushton, NY: Teach Services, 2004), p. 173.

[180] Augustus Neander, D.D., *The History of the Christian Religion and Church,* trans. Henry John Rose (New York: Stanford and Swords, 1848), p. 186.

[181] Martin Luther, Th.D., & Philip Melancthon, Th.B., *The Unaltered Augsburg Confession, as the Same was Read Before and Delivered to the Emporor Charles V, of Germany, June 25, 1530,* trans. Christian Heinrich Schott (New York: H. Ludwig & Co., 1848), p. 171.

week in place of the Sabbath. There is simply no law in the New Testament to that effect."[182]

Not only do individuals of great authority and learning from most major churches tell us the same thing, regarding the Sabbath day and its supposed change to Sunday, but this truth was printed by those faithful to God's Word above the traditions of men, as far back as 1657.

"The first Royal Law that ever Jehovah instituted, and for our Example celebrated, (namely his blessed Seventh-day Sabbath,) is in these very last days become the last great controversy between the Saints and the Man of sin, The Changer of Times and Laws....
"Therefore rouse up yourselves, ye spirited Citizens of Zion; shake off the dust and trash of beastly Babylon; and whiles that imperious Harlot shames not to assert that Ignorance is the Mother of Devotion, let heavenly wisdom be your sole design, with raised expectations of his faithful performance; who has promised, That the earth shall be filled with the knowledge of the glory of the Lord, as the waters cover the Sea.
"You are assured Christians the Horn has changed the Laws, and he cannot be that Horn unless he change your Times also; will you therefore wisely weigh that he had no Times to change, save the Lord's Sabbath time, and the Lord's Supper time, and these he and none but he changed."[183]

"But further how dreadful is it to father that change of the Sabbath upon the precious Son of God, which is the detestable design of the little horn. The changer of times and Laws, what! charge that upon Christ which is the proper presumption of Antichrist! Is not this the whores mark, to change the Saints times? the Saints Sabbath time, and the Saints supper time.... Whore she has most impudently changed the fourth lively oracle....
"It is the faithful promise of the Sabbath's Lord to make a rich return for all the reproofs, sorrows and sufferings of Christian Sabbath-

---

182 John Theodore Mueller, "Sabbath or Sunday" Tract No. 152 (St. Louis, MO: Concordia Publishing House, 1948) p. 15, 16.

183 Thomas Tillam, *The Seventh Day Sabbath Sought Out and Celebrated* (London: printed for the author, 1657), p. 1-5.

keepers, and we may rest upon it, for it is a gracious Gospel-promise."[184]

Is it possible that the papacy's change from the Bible Sabbath to the veneration of the day of the Sun, has been foisted upon modern Protestantism, at least partially, by tampering with the divine Oracles? Now we shall examine the evidence to that question.

KJV Exodus 20:10 "But the seventh day is **the** sabbath of the LORD thy God: in it thou shalt not do any work, thou, nor thy son, nor thy daughter, thy manservant, nor thy maidservant, nor thy cattle, nor thy stranger that is within thy gates:"

NIV[185] Exodus 20:10 "but the seventh day is **a** Sabbath to the LORD your God. On it you shall not do any work, neither you, nor your son or daughter, nor your manservant or maidservant, nor your animals, nor the alien within your gates."[186]

A seemingly insignificant, yet very serious change has been made in modern versions to the fourth commandment. There is nothing in the original text to warrant such a change from the definite article "the" to the indefinite "a."[187] This change in modern versions supports Sunday as the papal sabbath, by making God's Holy Sabbath into only one of several sabbaths, instead of **the** Sabbath—the only Sabbath. The same, prophetically predicted change of "times and laws," is performed in modern versions in the second copy of the ten commandments in Deuteronomy, as well as in Jesus' Matthew

---

[184] Thomas Tillam, *The Seventh Day Sabbath Sought Out and Celebrated* (1657), p. 124–125, 173.

[185] NASB, ASV, CEV (leaves out Sabbath), ESV, GNB (leaves out Sabbath), ICB ("is a day of rest to honor the Lord your God"), RV, RSV, NWT, etc.
Spirit of Prophecy quotes only KJV.

[186] *New International Version* (1978), p. 81.

[187] In the Hebrew language, when a noun has already been used with the definite article, there is no need to continue using that article with the same noun. It is expected that the next identical noun without the article would refer to the previous noun with the article. In Exodus 20:8 the noun Sabbath appears with the definite article in the phrase "the Sabbath day." When in Exodus 20:10 we find the expression "sabbath of the LORD," we know that the noun Sabbath of this verse is referring to the phrase "the Sabbath day" of Exodus 20:8.

reference to keeping the Sabbath holy when Jerusalem would be destroyed some forty years in the future.[188]

NIV[189] Deuteronomy 5:14 "But the seventh day is **a** Sabbath to the LORD your God. On it you shall not do any work, neither you, nor your son or daughter, nor your manservant or maidservant, nor your ox, your donkey or any of your animals, nor the alien within your gates, so that your manservant and maidservant may rest, as you do."[190]

KJV Matthew 24:20 "But pray ye that your flight be not in the winter, neither on **the** sabbath day:"

ASV[191] Matthew 24:20 "And pray ye that your flight be not in the winter, neither on **a** sabbath:"[192]

Removal of evidence of the Sabbath being kept in the New Testament is systematic in modern versions as seen in Acts 17:2.

KJV Acts 17:2 "And Paul, as his manner was, went in unto them, and **three sabbath days** reasoned with them out of the scriptures,"

RSV Acts 17:2 "And Paul went in, as was his custom, and for **three weeks** he argued with them from the scriptures,"[193]

Regarding the theological changes that were being introduced into the Revised Version Westcott writes: "But the value of the Revision is most clearly seen when the student considers together a considerable group of passages, which bear upon some article of the Faith. The accumulation of small details then produces its full effect.

---

188 Matthew 24:15-20.

189 NASB, ASV, CEV (leaves out Sabbath), ESV, GNB (leaves out Sabbath), ICB ("is a day of rest to honor the Lord your God"), RV, RSV, NWT, etc.

190 *New International Version* (1978), p. 193.

191 Also, CEV, ERV, ESV, GNB, ICB, ISV, MSG, NASB, RV, RSV, etc. The Spirit of Prophecy quotes only KJV as Scripture.

192 *American Standard Version* (1901), p. 25.

193 *Revised Standard Version* (1962), p. 1341.

Points on which it might have seemed pedantic to insist in a single passage become impressive by repetition."[194]

KJV Acts 13:42 "And when the **Jews** were gone out of the synagogue, the Gentiles besought that these words might be preached to them the next sabbath."[195]

In this passage it is clear that both Jews and Gentiles are meeting for sacred services on the seventh-day sabbath, well after the resurrection. To obscure this embarrassing fact, that shatters the idea that the day of worship was changed, modern bibles change "Jews" to "they" or to "Paul and Barnabas." That way it is not so obvious that it was the Jewish day of worship that the post-ascension apostles were keeping holy, while preaching to both the Jews and the Gentiles. In the King James Version, the Jewish sabbath is the Christian sabbath. Using the modern versions, one could argue that the sabbath the Gentiles referred to was different than the Jewish sabbath. "The accumulation of small details" have produced their effect.

KJV Hebrews 4:4-11 "For he spake in a certain place of the seventh day on this wise, And God did rest the seventh day from all his works. And in this place again, If they shall enter into my rest. Seeing therefore it remaineth that some must enter therein, and they to whom it was first preached entered not in because of unbelief: "Again, he limiteth a certain day, saying in David, To day, after so long a time; as it is said, To day if ye will hear his voice, harden not your hearts. For if **Jesus** had given them rest, then would he not afterward have spoken of another day. There remaineth therefore a rest to the people of God. For he that is entered into his rest, he also hath ceased from his own works, as God did from his. Let us labour therefore to enter into that rest, lest any man fall after the same example of unbelief."

Here the Bible expressly tells us, in the New Testament, after the ascension, that if Jesus had given a new day of rest, he would have

---

[194] B. F. Westcott, D.D., DC.L., *Some lessons of the Revised Version of the New Testament* (1897), p. 184, 185.

[195] The bold is changed in NASB, NIV, ASV, CEV, DRB, ESV, GNB, ICB, RV, RSV, NWT, NEB, etc. (some say "they" and some say "Paul and Barnabas"). The Spirit of Prophecy quotes only KJV.

spoken of that other day, but since he did not speak of any such change, there remains a rest to the people of God—the same seventh-day rest that God rested on at the end of his creation. Jesus, reinforcing the original seventh-day sabbath rest to his people in the New Testament, would clearly be a threat to the papal sabbath, therefore the verse has been modified in modern versions, to say Joshua instead of Jesus. That way the verse can be dismissed as an Old Testament rite that has been done away with in the New Testament. The problem is, Joshua did not give the sabbath to the Israelites, God did. Joshua was not even the leader of the Israelites until the death of Moses, forty years later. Even before the ten commandments were given to Moses on Sinai, God showed the sacredness of the sabbath by providing a miracle to preserve the Friday manna for the sabbath.[196]

NIV[197] Hebrews 4:8 "For if **Joshua** had given them rest, God would not have spoken later about another day."[198]

Some will doubtless argue that the Hebrew word for Jesus is yehôshûa or the same word used for Joshua. This argument is dependent upon the ignorance of the hearer, for while it sounds very conclusive and scholarly, it contains a complete falsification. The Hebrew word yehôshûa is indeed the name Joshua, but the name Jesus is never used in the Old Testament. Not only that, the word that is used in Hebrews 4:8 is not the Hebrew word yehôshûa, because the New Testament was not written in Hebrew, it was written in Greek. The word used is the Greek word Iēsous, which is never translated as Joshua in the KJV, and only here, and Acts 7:45 in the modern versions, when it serves their theological purposes. Why do not the modern versions become confused with their translation of this word and have baby Joshua in the manger, or Joshua on the cross? Some will appeal to the lexicon which most likely will say that Iēsous can be Joshua. Remember, that the same scholars that made the changes in the modern bibles, also wrote the lexicons. Therefore, when an unwarranted change is initiated in their translation, the lexicon can be updated to support the change in question.

---

[196] See Exodus 16

[197] NKJV, NASB, ASV, CEV, ESV, GNB, RV, NWT, etc.

[198] *New International Version* (1978), p. 1290.

The progression of the modification of this verse in the *International Children's Bible* demonstrates that this is certainly the intention for such a change. The ICB translation "team included men with translation experience on such accepted versions as the *New International Version*, the *New American Standard Bible* and the *New King James Version*."[199]

This is how they boldly modify the verse making it say the exact opposite of the King James Version:
ICB Hebrews 4:8 "We know that Joshua did not lead the people into that rest. We know this because **God spoke later about another day**."[200]

The popular use of the term "Lord's day," to refer to Sunday is yet another attempt to legitimize the papal sabbath. Although most modern versions were not bold enough to go as far as this, one can clearly see where the changes are leading when contemplating what *The Message* bible does:

KJV Revelation 1:10 "I was in the Spirit on the Lord's day, and heard behind me a great voice, as of a trumpet."

MSG Revelation 1:10 "**It was Sunday and I was in the Spirit**, praying. I heard a loud voice behind me, trumpet-clear and piercing."[201]

Scripture is clear which day is the Lord's day: "Therefore the Son of man is Lord also of the sabbath."[202] "If thou turn away thy foot from the sabbath, from doing thy pleasure on my holy day; and **call the sabbath a delight, the holy of the LORD**, honourable; and shalt honour him, not doing thine own ways, nor finding thine own pleasure, nor speaking thine own words: Then shalt thou delight thyself in the LORD; and I will cause thee to ride upon the high

---

[199] The publisher's preface to the *International Children's Bible* (Dallas, TX: Word Publishing, 1988).

[200] *International Children's Bible* (1988), p. 906.

[201] Eugene H. Peterson, M.A., *The Message* (2002), p. 2237.

[202] Mark 2:28

places of the earth, and feed thee with the heritage of Jacob thy father: for the mouth of the LORD hath spoken it."[203]

"You will see ere long that there will be those who will become weary of hearing repeated the things that they ought to do but do not desire to do, and they will change the wording of the Bible. We know what the Lord says in Revelation about those who do that."[204]

KJV Galatians 3:1 "O foolish Galatians, who hath bewitched you, **that ye should not obey the truth**, before whose eyes Jesus Christ hath been evidently set forth, crucified among you?"

NASB[205] Galatians 3:1 "You foolish Galatians, who has bewitched you, before whose eyes Jesus Christ was publicly portrayed as crucified?"[206]

The bold portion is removed. The entire Christian world has been bewitched that they should not obey the truth. And, it is not in the best interests of the power that has changed God's times, laws, and Word, for you to know that you should obey the truth. So, they removed that part from this verse.

By the modification of the divine law, Satan achieves almost universal worship from the world: "all the world wondered after the beast. And they worshipped the dragon which gave power unto the beast: and they worshipped the beast...."[207]

"Great peace have they which love thy law: and nothing shall offend them."[208]

---

[203] Isaiah 58:13-14

[204] E. G. White, *Manuscript 146-1906*, par. 28.

[205] Bold missing: ASV, CEV, ERV, ESV, GNB, ICB, ISV, MSG, NIV, RSV, RV, etc.

[206] *New American Standard Bible* (1977), p. 814.

[207] Revelation 13:3-4

[208] Psalm 119:165

13 The NKJV, and The Message

Most of the changes in modern versions follow predictable lines, and are very similar between multiple modern renderings. Most of these versions follow Westcott and Hort's Revised Version,[1] or their new Greek text, or take things a step further than Westcott and Hort could in their day. One version that stands out from the other modern versions is the 1982 *New King James Version*. Because of its title, the fact that it seems to use much of the familiar wording of the King James, and its claim to be translated from the Textus Receptus, or the same manuscripts as the King James, many have accepted it as their primary study bible, who would have otherwise been unwilling to be induced to change versions. It is true that the most blatant changes, such as the missing verses, are absent in the *New King James Version*. However, despite its claim to following the manuscripts of the King James Version, it frequently deviates to include renderings from the corrupted Alexandrian manuscripts. Not a few of these changes lean distinctly toward Catholic doctrine. For example:

KJV Revelation 19:8 "And to her was granted that she should be arrayed in fine linen, clean and white: for **the fine linen is the righteousness of saints.**"

NKJV[2] Revelation 19:8 "And to her it was granted to be arrayed in fine linen, clean and bright, for **the fine linen is the righteous acts of the saints.**"[3]

As discussed in the chapter 6: "Fingerprints of the Anti-Christ," "**the fine linen is the righteousness of saints**," gets changed to "the fine linen is the righteous acts of the saints." This expressly contradicts the Bible doctrine that "all our righteousnesses are as

---

[1] Today the most commonly published Greek text, designated NU/UB for Nestle-Aland/United Bible Society, currently in its 28th edition, was heavily influenced by Westcott and Hort's new Greek text, and follows, almost exclusively, the Alexandrian manuscripts.

[2] ASV, CEV, ESV, GNB, ICB, ISV, NASB, NIV, RV, etc. Spirit of Prophecy quotes only KJV as Scripture.

[3] *New King James Version* (1983), p. 1315.

filthy rags."[4] In the King James Bible, the righteousness is owned by the saints because it was given to them by Christ, but it does not come from their own works. In the modern versions it is their own works or acts that form their righteousness. This is the Catholic doctrine of salvation by works, a rendering which comes from the corrupted Alexandrian manuscripts that practically all modern versions follow.[5]

KJV John 5:39 "Search the scriptures; for in them ye think ye have eternal life: and they are they which testify of me."

NKJV John 5:39 "You search the Scriptures, for in them you think you have eternal life; and these are they which testify of Me."

This modification changes a command of Jesus for us to search the Scriptures, into a simple observation that the Jews searched the Scriptures. The *Dublin Review*, a Catholic periodical, noted the following regarding the 1881 R.V., which the NKJV followed here: "But perhaps the most surprising change of all is John [5]:39. It is no longer 'Search the Scriptures,' but 'Ye search' and thus Protestantism has lost the very cause of its being."

"The following significant paragraph is from the *Watchman and Reflector*, the leading organ of the Baptist denomination: — 'Dr. Guthrie, speaking of the exit of the Presbyterian church from Rome, says, 'Three hundred years ago, our church, with an open Bible on her banner, and this motto, Search the Scriptures, on her scroll, marched out from the gates of Rome.' Then he significantly asks, 'Did they come clean out of Babylon?'"[6]

---

[4] Isaiah 64:6.

[5] There are only two modern versions which seem to have no problematic renderings. The UKJV, available on e-Sword, and the 21st Century King James Version available in print with a very nice leather binding option. Both these versions claim to have updated only archaic spelling, and the few words (such as prevent) whose meanings have completely changed. Still, the 21st Century KJV has claimed a copyright because of the different fonts and bolding that they use to tell you which parts are important, and which parts are not so important. Is it a good thing for a human to tell you which parts of the Bible are important? But, for those who really think they must have something modern for their child to understand, the 21st Century KJV might be a good gift option that sounds very up-to-date.

[6] *Collection of Facts for the Times, Consisting of Valuable Extracts from Eminent Authors,* 2nd Rev. ed. (Battle Creek, MI: Steam Press, 1875), p. 70.

KJV 2 Peter 2:9 "The Lord knoweth how to deliver the godly out of temptations, and to reserve the unjust unto the day of judgment to be punished:"

NKJV[7] 2 Peter 2:9 "then the Lord knows how to deliver the godly out of temptations and to reserve the unjust under punishment for the day of judgment,"[8] Reserving the unjust under punishment for the day of judgment is the Catholic doctrine of purgatory, and this modification comes from the Alexandrian texts, which the NKJV supposedly does not follow.

KJV Acts 3:13 "The God of Abraham, and of Isaac, and of Jacob, the God of our fathers, hath glorified **his Son Jesus**; whom ye delivered up, and denied him in the presence of Pilate, when he was determined to let him go."

NKJV[9] Acts 3:13 "The God of Abraham, Isaac, and Jacob, the God of our fathers, glorified **His Servant Jesus**, whom you delivered up and denied in the presence of Pilate, when he was determined to let Him go."[10]

The NKJV, in multiple places, following most other modern versions, downgrades Jesus from Son to Servant. It is true that Jesus humbled himself to be a servant, but these changes remove references to his divinity. "Therefore the Jews sought the more to kill him, because he... said also that God was his Father, making himself equal with God."[11]

KJV Acts 3:26 "Unto you first God, having raised up **his Son Jesus**, sent him to bless you, in turning away every one of you from his iniquities."

---

[7] ASV, CEV, ESV, GNB, ICB, NASB, NIV (while continuing their punishment), RV, RSV, NEB, etc. The Spirit of Prophecy quotes only KJV as Scripture.

[8] *New King James Version* (1983), p. 1277.

[9] ASV, CEV, ESV, GNB, ICB, ISV, NIV, RV, etc. The Spirit of Prophecy quotes only KJV as Scripture.

[10] *New King James Version* (1983), p. 1108.

[11] John 5:18

NKJV[12] Acts 3:26 “To you first, God, having raised up **His Servant Jesus**, sent Him to bless you, in turning away every one of you from your iniquities.”[13]

KJV Acts 4:27, 30 “For of a truth against thy **holy child Jesus**, whom thou hast anointed, both Herod, and Pontius Pilate, with the Gentiles, and the people of Israel, were gathered together,
“By stretching forth thine hand to heal; and that signs and wonders may be done by the name of thy **holy child Jesus**.”

NKJV[14] Acts 4:27, 30 “For truly against Your **holy Servant Jesus**, whom You anointed, both Herod and Pontius Pilate, with the Gentiles and the people of Israel, were gathered together
“by stretching out Your hand to heal, and that signs and wonders may be done through the name of Your **holy Servant Jesus**.”[15]

Like most other modern versions following the Alexandrian manuscripts, the *New King James Version* makes its own message into foolishness.

KJV 1 Corinthians 1:21 “For after that in the wisdom of God the world by wisdom knew not God, it pleased God by **the foolishness of preaching** to save them that believe.”

NKJV[16] 1 Corinthians 1:21 “For since, in the wisdom of God, the world through wisdom did not know God, it pleased God through **the foolishness of the message preached** to save those who believe.”[17]

KJV Acts 2:47 “Praising God, and having favour with all the people. And the Lord added to the church daily **such as should be saved**.”

---

[12] ASV, ESV, GNB, ICB, ISV, NIV, RV, etc. Spirit of Prophecy quotes only KJV as Scripture.

[13] *New King James Version* (1983), p. 1108.

[14] ASV, CEV, ESV, GNB, ICB, ISV, NIV, RV, etc. Spirit of Prophecy quotes only KJV as Scripture.

[15] *New King James Version* (1983), p. 1109.

[16] NIV, NASB, CEV, ESV, Moff (“the ‘sheer folly’ of the Christian message”), NWT, etc. Spirit of Prophecy quotes only KJV as Scripture.

[17] *New King James Version* (1983), p. 1159.

NKJV[18] Acts 2:47 "praising God and having favor with all the people. And the Lord added to the church daily **those who were being saved**."[19]

The NKJV changes the salvation that God grants in a moment, into a process. This makes room for the things we do to have a part in that process—the Catholic doctrine of salvation by works. "The grace of Christ is freely to justify the sinner without merit or claim on his part. Justification is a full, complete pardon of sin. **The moment a sinner accepts Christ by faith, that moment he is pardoned.** The righteousness of Christ is imputed to him, and he is no more to doubt God's forgiving grace."[20]

KJV Hebrews 4:8 "For if **Jesus** had given them rest, then would he not afterward have spoken of another day."

NKJV[21] Hebrews 4:8 "For if **Joshua** had given them rest, then He would not afterward have spoken of another day."[22]

Following most other modern bibles, the NKJV substitutes Joshua for Jesus, to avoid the binding nature of the Bible sabbath.[23]

KJV 2 Corinthians 2:17 "For we are not as many, which **corrupt**[24] **the word of God**: but as of sincerity, but as of God, in the sight of God speak we in Christ."

NKJV[25] 2 Corinthians 2:17 "For we are not, as so many, **peddling the word of God**; but as of sincerity, but as from God, we speak in the sight of God in Christ."[26]

---

[18] CEV, ESV, GNB, ISV, NIV, RV, etc.

[19] *New King James Version* (1983), p. 1107.

[20] E. G. White, *The Faith I Live By* (1958), p. 107.2.

[21] ASV, CEV, ESV, GNB, ICB, NASB, NIV, RV, NWT, etc.

[22] *New King James Version* (1983), p. 1250.

[23] See Martin Klein, *Above All Thy Name*, Doctrine: The Sabbath, Hebrews 4:4-11.

[24] Tyndale: "chop and change".

[25] NIV, NASB, CEV, ESV, GNB, ICB, NWT, etc.

[26] *New King James Version* (1983), p. 1177.

Corrupting the word of God and peddling the word of God are most certainly not the same thing. Here the NKJV is hiding the fact that Scripture predicted that people would corrupt God's Word by saying that it is wrong to sell God's Word. Of course, the NKJV publishers sell bibles and thus are condemned by their own revision.

KJV Acts 17:22 "Then Paul stood in the midst of Mars' hill, and said, Ye men of Athens, I perceive that in all things ye are **too superstitious**."

NKJV[27] Acts 17:22 "Then Paul stood in the midst of the Areopagus and said, 'Men of Athens, I perceive that in all things you are **very religious**.'"[28]

Imitating many other modern versions, the NKJV departs, once again, from the text used by the KJV, calling the men of Athens "very religious," rather than "**too superstitious**."

KJV Titus 3:10 "A man that is **an heretick** after the first and second admonition reject;"

NKJV[29] Titus 3:10 "Reject **a divisive man** after the first and second admonition,"[30]

This verse in Titus is one of the most dangerous changes in NKJV and in all other modern versions making a similar change. In the KJV the man that is an heretick is the one to be rejected. A heretick is one not following Bible doctrine, therefore the Bible is the criteria for rejecting someone. In modern bibles, people are given license to reject someone on the basis of their being divisive, even if they are presenting the truth. When has truth ever not been divisive? Jesus himself said: "I am come to set a man at variance against his father, and the daughter against her mother, and the daughter in law

[27] NIV, NASB, ASV, CEV, ESV, GNB, ICB, etc.

[28] *New King James Version* (1983), p. 1125.

[29] NIV, NASB, ASV, CEV, ESV, GNB, ICB ("someone causes arguments"), etc.

[30] *New King James Version* (1983), p. 1240.

against her mother in law. And a man's foes shall be they of his own household."[31]

Therefore, the modern versions give license to reject Jesus himself, for his teachings were divisive. This is a change that suits Rome very well. Indeed, the BBE goes so far as to say, "A man whose opinions are not those of the church, after a first and second protest, is to be kept out of your society."[32] This is papal dogma. "But God will have a people upon the earth to maintain the Bible, and the Bible only, as the standard of all doctrines and the basis of all reforms. The opinions of learned men, the deductions of science, the creeds or decisions of ecclesiastical councils, as numerous and discordant as are the churches which they represent, the voice of the majority–not one nor all of these should be regarded as evidence for or against any point of religious faith. Before accepting any doctrine or precept, we should demand a plain 'Thus saith the Lord' in its support."[33]

KJV Revelation 1:6 "And hath made us kings and priests unto **God and his Father**; to him be glory and dominion for ever and ever. Amen."

NKJV[34] Revelation 1:6 "and has made us kings and priests to **His God and Father**, to Him be glory and dominion forever and ever. Amen."[35] As in most of the other modern versions, the divinity of Christ is here removed from the NKJV.[36]

The King James Bible says "**God and his Father**." If you say "**God and his Father**," that means God is one person and his father is another person. So, the Father is the father of God. With this wording, the Bible is calling Jesus God, therefore Jesus is completely divine. But, in many modern versions, it says, "his God and Father." These are the very same words, in a slightly different order. "His God and Father" means that Jesus has a god and Jesus

---

[31] Matthew 10:36

[32] *Bible in Basic English* (University of MI: University Press, 1949), p. 874.

[33] E. G. White, *The Great Controversy* (1911), p. 595.1.

[34] ASV, ESV, GNB, ICB, NIV, RV, etc. Spirit of Prophecy quotes only KJV as Scripture.

[35] *New King James Version* (1983), p. 1302.

[36] See Martin Klein, *Above All Thy Name*, Doctrine: The Divinity of Christ, Revelation 1:6.

has a father. But, it is not calling Jesus God. The divinity of Christ has been removed from this verse by a simple change in word order.

How would Alexandrian corruptions and papal dogmas find their way into the text of the NKJV? Executive Editor of the *New King James Version*, Dr. Farstad, during a debate on the John Ankerberg Show gives us a clue by indicating that he uses the Catholic Latin Vulgate for his personal devotions. Dr. Gipp, who participated in the same debate shares this experience in his book: "Dr. Farstad's greatest testimony of the value of the New King James Version came during our round table discussion on the John Ancherberg [sic] Show when he admitted that he didn't even think it was worth using for his personal devotions. During this broadcast, the Editor-in-Chief of the New King James Version admitted that he preferred to use the Latin in his daily devotions rather than the very translation that he had helped to create! Are you going to use a 'bible' that its chief editor rejects?"[37]

Message Problems

The Message bible is another version that is quite different than most of the rest of the modern bibles. Although many people realize that it is a paraphrase rather than a translation, yet it seems to be quite popular, especially as a gift for children. Since it is so different from the rest, we will show a few problems (there are many more) unique to this version.

MSG Romans 15:13 "Oh! May the God of green hope fill you up with joy, fill you up with peace, so that your believing lives, filled with the life-giving energy of the Holy Spirit, will brim over with hope!"[38]

Do you worship the god of green hope? This is occult language masquerading as a Bible—doctrines of devils. To further demonstrate the occult nature of this version, let us have a look at how the rose of Sharon has been transplanted with an occult symbol:

---

[37] Samuel Gipp, Th.D., *Gipp's Understandable History of the Bible* (Miamitown, OH: DayStar Publishing, 1987), p. 341.

[38] Eugene H. Peterson, M.A., *The Message* (2002), p. 2060.

MSG Song of Solomon 2:1-2 "I'm just a wildflower picked from the plains of Sharon, **a lotus blossom** from the valley pools. A lotus blossoming in a swamp of weeds—that's my dear friend among the girls in the village."[39]

The lotus flower is a very common symbol in New Age and occult literature, as well as pagan and Eastern religions. A short quote from Blavatsky demonstrates this connection: "In chapter lxxxi. of the Ritual (Book of the Dead), called 'Transformation into the Lotus,' a head emerging from this flower, the god exclaims: 'I am the pure lotus, emerging from the Luminous one.... I carry the messages of Horus. I am the pure lotus which comes from the Solar Fields'"[40] This is pure Satanism, and has been planted into something that some people call a Bible.

The King James Version, although very matter-of-fact, without glossing over sin, presents sensitive matters in a discreet manner – not so in *The Message*.

KJV Jeremiah 2:24 "A wild ass used to the wilderness, that snuffeth up the wind at her pleasure; in her occasion who can turn her away? all they that seek her will not weary themselves; in her month they shall find her."

MSG Jeremiah 2:24 "tracks of a wild donkey in rut, Sniffing the wind for the slightest scent of sex. Who could possibly corral her! On the hunt for sex, sex, and more sex– insatiable, indiscriminate, promiscuous."[41]

Is this obscene language appropriate in a bible used as a gift for children? Besides its obsession with sex, *The Message* has Peter swearing at Simon Magus.

---

[39] Eugene H. Peterson, M.A., *The Message* (2002), p. 1184.

[40] H. P. Blavatsky, *The Secret Doctrine,* Vol. 1—Cosmogenesis (1888), p. 380.

[41] Eugene H. Peterson, M.A., *The Message* (2002), p. 1347.

Act 8:20 KJV "But Peter said unto him, **Thy money perish with thee**, because thou hast thought that the gift of God may be purchased with money."

MSG Act 8:20 "Peter said, '**To hell with your money**! And you along with it. Why, that's unthinkable– trying to buy God's gift!'"[42]

Just as unthinkable as it was for Simon Magus to try to buy the gift of the Holy Spirit, is it for this bible to mutilate in such a manner the gift of the Words of the Holy Spirit. It is putting no difference between the holy and the profane.

The Bible has strong words for such Satanic work: "**There is a conspiracy of her prophets in the midst thereof,** like a roaring lion ravening the prey; they have devoured souls; they have taken the treasure and precious things; they have made her many widows in the midst thereof. **Her priests have violated my law, and have profaned mine holy things: they have put no difference between the holy and profane**, neither have they showed difference between the unclean and the clean, and have hid their eyes from my sabbaths, and **I am profaned among them**."[43]

---

[42] Eugene H. Peterson, M.A., *The Message* (2002), p. 1983.

[43] Ezekiel 22:25-26

14 Messages from Outer Space

For nearly a half century science has been listening to outer space in search of extraterrestrial intelligence. As stated in Newsweek, "the real hope is not just to intercept an alien weather report, but to hear a message intended for earth, or for the universe at large."[1] U.S. News and World Report published the statement, "If anyone is trying to get in touch with us, we're ready to listen."[2] Wikipedia describes the Square Kilometer Array (SKA); a global multi-radio telescope project with twelve member countries participating. The project aims at distributing 50' wide radio telescopes with a combined collecting surface area of approximately one square kilometer, arranged in a spiral, extending 3000 kilometers from the central core. The array will be able to survey the sky ten-thousand times faster than before, requiring more data bandwidth than the combined global internet traffic. Construction is scheduled to begin in 2018, with initial observations scheduled for 2020. Among the SKA's missions: finding an answer to the question are we alone?

The apostle Paul writes, "For I think that God hath set forth us the apostles last, as it were appointed to death: for we are made a spectacle unto the world, and to angels, and to men."[3] There are extraterrestrial beings out in space somewhere, but they are not the kind of intelligence that modern science wants to recognize. They are beings that communicate with human beings, but much of their communication has been disrupted.

At one time the communication with these extraterrestrial intelligences was face to face. God walked and talked in the cool of the garden with Adam and Eve. Heavenly angels conversed openly with our first parents. But, something sad and dramatic occurred that drew down the veil between their dimension and ours, and disrupted the transmission of messages: Adam and Eve "heard the voice of the LORD God walking in the garden in the cool of the day: and

---

[1] Newsweek, January 31, 1983.

[2] US News & World Report, May 2, 1983.

[3] 1 Corinthians 4:9

Adam and his wife hid themselves from the presence of the LORD God amongst the trees of the garden."[4] Disobedience to the command of God brought sin, suffering, and death into the perfect paradise. By this act, Adam transferred his divinely ordained dominion of planet Earth to the devil.[5] Sin disrupted direct communication with heavenly intelligences: "But your iniquities have separated between you and your God, and your sins have hid his face from you, that he will not hear."[6] Yet, God could not forget the love he had for his created beings on Earth. "Can a woman forget her sucking child, that she should not have compassion on the son of her womb? yea, they may forget, yet will I not forget thee. Behold, I have graven thee upon the palms of my hands; thy walls are continually before me."[7] God unveiled the plan of salvation to rescue man from the tyranny of Satan, and instituted an emergency method of communication: "Surely the Lord GOD will do nothing, but he revealeth his secret unto his servants the prophets."[8] God ordained that he would communicate his will, directly through special revelation, to faulty and frail human beings of his own choosing, called prophets. These individuals were commissioned by God himself to bear messages of Divine revelation to the rest of humankind.

The prophet did not sign up, or volunteer, or even train for the position. The commission and their message did not come from the prophet's will or decision, but by the will of God almighty: "For the prophecy came not in old time by the will of man: but holy men of God spake as they were moved by the Holy Ghost."[9] The power of the Holy Spirit moved upon these consecrated human servants of God, to give an infallible Divine message. The writers of Scripture were human; the author was Divine. This was the same miraculous combination of human and Divine as the Divine Son of God becoming a man. Not only did God choose his messengers, but God

---

[4] Genesis 3:8

[5] John 14:30

[6] Isaiah 59:2

[7] Isaiah 49:15,16

[8] Amos 3:7

[9] 2 Peter 1:21

chose the method of delivery for the message. God said, "Hear now my words: If there be a prophet among you, I the LORD will make myself known unto him in a vision, and will speak unto him in a dream."[10]

Believing in God is only the foundation; if we would prosper, we must believe his prophets: "...Believe in the LORD your God, so shall ye be established; believe his prophets, so shall ye prosper."[11] Yet, just as Satan has created corrupted copies of Scripture, so the father of lies has created corrupted prophetic messengers, called false prophets. Jesus himself warned us that all the way to the end of time these deceivers would arise. "For there shall arise false Christs, and false prophets, and shall show great signs and wonders; insomuch that, if it were possible, they shall deceive the very elect."[12]

If God has given genuine prophetic messages, through divinely chosen messengers, but has warned us to beware of the deceptions of false Christs and false prophets, surely, he has provided the means for discerning the difference. There are at least eight infallible marks of a true prophet:

1. **A true prophet's message must be in harmony with the word of God and the law of God:** "To the law and to the testimony: if they speak not according to this word, it is because there is no light in them."[13] "Her gates are sunk into the ground; he hath destroyed and broken her bars: her king and her princes are among the Gentiles: the law is no more; her prophets also find no vision from the LORD."[14]
2. **A true prophet will have Dreams and Visions:** "And he said, Hear now my words: If there be a prophet among you, the LORD will make myself known unto him in a vision, and will speak unto him in a dream."[15]

---

[10] Numbers 12:6

[11] 2 Chronicles 20:20

[12] Matthew 24:24

[13] Isaiah 8:20

[14] Lamentations 2:9

[15] Numbers 12:6

3. **A true prophet's predictions must come true:** "When a prophet speaketh in the name of the LORD, if the thing follow not, nor come to pass, that is the thing which the LORD hath not spoken, but the prophet hath spoken it presumptuously: thou shalt not be afraid of him."[16]
4. **A true prophet edifies God's people:** "But he that prophesieth speaketh unto men to edification, and exhortation, and comfort. He that speaketh in an unknown tongue edifieth himself; but he that prophesieth edifieth the church."[17]
5. **A true prophet exalts Christ as the Son of God:** "Whosoever shall confess that Jesus is the Son of God, God dwelleth in him, and he in God."[18] "And beginning at Moses and all the prophets, he expounded unto them in all the scriptures the things concerning himself."[19]
6. **A true prophet speaks with authority:** "For he taught them as one having authority, and not as the scribes."[20]
7. **A true prophet will bear good fruit:** "Wherefore by their fruits ye shall know them."[21]
8. **A true prophet will exhibit certain physical signs when in vision:**
    a. The prophet's eyes are open during the vision: "He hath said, which heard the words of God, which saw the vision of the Almighty, falling into a trance, but having his eyes open."[22]
    b. A true prophet first falls down and has no strength, is then strengthened, but has no breath (even when speaking) while in vision: "And I Daniel alone saw the vision: for the men that were with me saw not the vision; but a great quaking fell upon them, so that they fled to hide themselves. Therefore I

---

16 Deuteronomy 18:22

17 1 Corinthian 14:3, 4

18 1 John 4:15

19 Luke 24:27
This verse refers to Jesus himself first turning to the writings of the prophets to prove his divinity and messiahship, before he appealed to the evidence of his resurrection.

20 Matthew 7:29
This verse refers to Jesus teaching with authority, but it also applies to his prophets, as the Bible refers to Jesus as a prophet. See Deuteronomy 18:15.

21 Matthew 7:20

22 Numbers 24:4

> was left alone, and saw this great vision, and there remained no strength in me: for my comeliness was turned in me into corruption, and I retained no strength. Yet heard I the voice of his words: and when I heard the voice of his words, then was I in a deep sleep on my face, and my face toward the ground. And, behold, an hand touched me, which set me upon my knees and upon the palms of my hands... And when he had spoken this word unto me, I stood trembling... And, behold, one like the similitude of the sons of men touched my lips: then I opened my mouth, and spake, and said unto him that stood before me, O my lord, by the vision my sorrows are turned upon me, and I have retained no strength. For how can the servant of this my lord talk with this my lord? for as for me, straightway there remained no strength in me, **neither is there breath left in me.**"[23] Daniel's burning question to Jesus is, how can I talk to you when I have no strength and I am not breathing? Daniel was wondering at the supernatural manifestation of God in sustaining him in vision without oxygen. God breathed into Adam "the breath of life; and man became a living soul."[24] As the all-powerful creator of the universe, if God chooses to sustain the life of his prophets without breath as unmistakable evidence of the divine origin of the message—evidence that cannot be counterfeited by Satan—divinity has that prerogative.

When Christ ascended he gave the gifts of the Spirit, "Wherefore he saith, When he ascended up on high, he led captivity captive, and gave gifts unto men... And he gave some, apostles; and **some, prophets**; and some, evangelists; and some, pastors and teachers; For the perfecting of the saints, for the work of the ministry, for the edifying of the body of Christ: Till we all come in the unity of the faith, and of the knowledge of the Son of God, unto a perfect man, unto the measure of the stature of the fulness of Christ."

One of the gifts of the Spirit is that some would be prophets, and these gifts would be poured out on the body of Christ until we come "unto the measure of the stature of the fulness of Christ." It is true

---

[23] Daniel 10:7-18

[24] Genesis 2:7

that the Scriptures were written by prophets of God under the inspiration of the Holy Spirit, but it is also true that those same Scriptures testify that God will continue to bestow the gift of prophecy at his will until he comes the second time: "And it shall come to pass afterward pour out my spirit upon all flesh; and your sons and your daughters shall prophecy, your young men shall see visions and your old men shall dream dreams."[25] Though the prophets were the writers of Scripture, their work was not confined to the writing of the Holy Oracles. The Bible itself records many true prophets, both men and women, who never contributed a word to Scripture: Gad,[26] Nathan,[27] Huldah,[28] and Deborah[29] are examples in the Old Testament. John the Baptist, whom Jesus said was the greatest prophet,[30] never wrote a word of Scripture. New Testament examples include Simeon, Anna, Agabus, Barnabus, and Phillip's four daughters. In fact, we are commanded in Scripture not to despise prophesyings, but the hold fast to what is good.[31] The very fact that the Bible warns against false prophets, implies that there are true. If there were never again to be another prophet after the completion of the canon of Scripture, God would have told us never to listen to another prophet. Instead he says, "Beloved, believe not every spirit, but try the spirits whether they are of God: because many false prophets are gone out into the world."[32] We are to try the spirits, whether they are of God. This means that some prophets will not be false. And, just as with Israel of old, to reject a true prophetic message from the Lord would be at the peril of our souls.

Is it possible that God has sent a prophetic message of vital importance in these last days? Just after the prophetic period of the 2300 years of Daniel 8:14 had closed, in December of 1844, Ellen G.

---

[25] Joel 2:28

[26] 1 Samuel 22:5

[27] 2 Samuel 7:2

[28] 2 Kings 22:14

[29] Judges 4:4

[30] Luke 7:28

[31] 1 Thessalonians 5:20,21

[32] 1 John 4:1

Harmon (later White),[33] at age 17, had her first vision. Do the messages she received fulfill the Biblical criteria for the prophetic gift?

1. Did she exalt Word of God and the Law of God?
"The Holy Scriptures are to be accepted as an authoritative, infallible revelation of His will. They are the standard of character, the revealer of doctrines, and the test of experience."[34]

"Brethren, cling to your Bible, as it reads, and stop your criticisms in regard to its validity, and obey the Word, and not one of you will be lost."[35] "The Bible, and the Bible alone, is to be our creed, the sole bond of union; ...God's Word is infallible.... lift up the banner on which is inscribed, The Bible our rule of faith and discipline."[36]

"The Lord designs to warn you, to reprove, to counsel, through the testimonies given, and to impress your minds with the importance of the truth of His word. The written testimonies are not to give new light, but to impress vividly upon the heart the truths of inspiration already revealed. Man's duty to God and to his fellow man has been distinctly specified in God's word, yet but few of you are obedient to the light given. Additional truth is not brought out; but God has through the Testimonies simplified the great truths already given and in His own chosen way brought them before the people to awaken and impress the mind with them, that all may be left without excuse."[37]

"Then present to them the prophecies; show them the purity and binding claims of the law of God. Not one jot or tittle of this law is to lose its force, but hold its binding claims upon every soul to the end of time."[38]

---

[33] On August 30, 1846 Ellen Harmon was united in marriage to James White, becoming Ellen G. White.

[34] E. G. White, *The Great Controversy*, p. vii.1.

[35] E. G. White, *Selected Messages*, Vol. 1, p. 18.

[36] *Ibid.*, p. 416.

[37] E. G. White, *Testimonies to the Church*, Vol. 5 p. 665.

[38] E. G. White, *Manuscript Releases*, Vol. 15 p. 351.

2. Did she receive vision & dreams?
Over the course of 70 years she received over 2000 visions[39] ranging in length from less than a minute to over four hours.

3. Did her predictions come true?
"Ellen White's Civil War visions were perhaps the most stunning of her many predictions.... Her first Civil War vision, lasting twenty minutes, occurred during an afternoon church service in Parkville, Michigan... on January 12, 1861."[40]

"The Parkville vision occurred three months before the guns fired on Fort Sumter, April 12, 1861. At that time many people believed that there would be no war, but should war begin, it would be short and the North would win in a brief fight."[41]

"In mid-February 1861 Thomas R. R. Cobb, Georgia secessionist and committee member preparing the Confederate constitution, wrote: 'The almost universal belief here [Montgomery] is that we shall not have war.'
"Two days before his Inaugural Address of March 4, 1861, Lincoln declared in Philadelphia: 'I have felt all the while justified in concluding that the crisis, the panic, the anxiety of the country at this time is artificial.' Cited in *Harper's Weekly*, March 2, 1861, p. 135"[42]

At the close of the vision, she stood and related to the congregation what she had seen. "Her words made a lasting impression (as reported by J. N. Loughborough, an eye-witness): 'Men are making light of the secession ordinance that has been passed by South Carolina [Dec. 20, 1860]. They have little idea of the trouble that is coming on our land. No one in this house has even dreamed of the trouble that is coming. I have just been shown in vision that a number of States are going to join South Carolina in this secession, and a terrible war will be the result. In the vision I saw large armies raised by both the North and the South. I was shown the battle

---

[39] Ellen G. White Estate, *Advent Pioneers Biographical Sketches and Pictures*, p. 22.5.

[40] Herbert Edgar Douglass, *Dramatic Prophecies of Ellen White* (Nampa, ID: Pacific Press, 2007), p. 13.

[41] Herbert Edgar Douglass, *Messenger of the Lord* (Nampa, ID: Pacific Press, 1998), p. 159.

[42] *Ibid.*, p. 167.

raging.'"[43] "There is not a person in this house who has even dreamed of the trouble that is coming upon this land. People are making sport of the secession ordinance of South Carolina, but I have just been shown that a large number of states are going to join that state, and there will be a most terrible war.
"In this vision I have seen large armies of both sides gathered on the field of battle. I heard the booming of the cannon, and saw the dead and dying on every hand. Then I saw them rushing up engaged in hand-to-hand fighting [bayoneting one another].
"'Then I saw the field after battle, all covered with the dead and dying. Then I was carried to prisons, and saw the sufferings of those in want, who were wasting away. Then I was taken to the homes of those who had lost husbands, sons, or brothers in the war. I saw their distress and anguish.' Then, surveying her audience, Ellen slowly added a foreboding note: 'There are those in this house who will lose sons in that war.'"[44] Two men in the congregation, Judge Osborne, and Mr. Shellhouse looked at Elder Loughborough and shook their heads, disbelieving what Ellen White had predicted. One year later they again sat together in the same church as Elder Loughborough preached about the gift of prophecy, using the civil war vision as an example. Tears streamed down the faces of both men. One had lost his only son, the other had lost a son on a different battlefield, with a second son in a Southern prison. The local elder stated he could probably count ten families from their congregation who had lost sons in the war.

From things she was shown in vision, Ellen White predicted the San Francisco earthquake of April 18, 1906;[45] both World Wars;[46] and the events of 9/11 in New York City.[47]

In 1903, from things she saw in vision she stated, "In the world gigantic monopolies will be formed. Men will bind themselves

---

[43] Herbert Edgar Douglass, *Messenger of the Lord* (1998), p. 158.

[44] Roger W. Coon, *The Great Visions of Ellen G. White* (Washington D.C.: Review and Herald Publishing Association), p. 80.

[45] E. G. White, *Evangelism* (1946), p. 403.4; E. G. White, *Life Sketches* (1915), p. 407-409.

[46] E. G. White, *Testimonies for the Church*, Vol. 1 (1871), p. 268.

[47] E. G. White, *Testimonies for the Church*, Vol. 9 (1909), p. 11-14;
E. G. White, *Manuscript Releases*, Vol. 11 (1990), p. 361.1.

together in unions that will wrap them in the folds of the enemy. A few men will combine to grasp all the means to be obtained in certain lines of business. Trades unions will be formed, and those who refuse to join these unions will be marked men."[48] How could she possibly have predicted this 115 years ago, without divine enlightenment? On February 20, 2014, CNBC (itself a mega-merger) published an article titled "Why 2014 could be the year of the mega-merger." Following are a list of some recent mega-merger monopolies that have been formed:[49]

Delta and Northwest, 2008.
Continental and United, 2010-2012.
Microsoft—Hotmail, Skype, NBC, 157 others.
VW and Porsche, 2012, plus Audi, Seat, Bugatti, Bentley.
Facebook and WhatsApp, 2014 - $16.5B 5th largest tech deal ever.
Comcast and Time Warner Cable, 2014 - $69.3B.
Forest Laboratories and Actavis - $25B.
Chrysler and Fiat, 2014 - $3.6B.
Nest Labs and Google - $3.2B.

Against the prevailing opinions of her time, in a day when physicians were prescribing smoking for lung disease, Ellen White predicted, in 1864, "Tobacco is a poison of the most deceitful and **malignant** kind, having an exciting, then a paralyzing influence upon the nerves of the body. It is all the more dangerous because its effects upon the system are so slow, and at first scarcely perceivable. Multitudes have fallen victims to its poisonous influence."[50]

It was not until 1957 (almost 100 years later) that a committee of scientists appointed by the American Cancer Society and the American Heart Association concluded that smoking was a causative factor in lung cancer.

---

[48] E. G. White, *Manuscript Releases*, Vol. 4 (1990), p. 75.1.

[49] Patti Domm, "Why 2014 could be the year of the megamerger" February 20, 2014, http://www.cnbc.com/id/101432520, retrieved January 18, 2017.

[50] E. G. White, *Spiritual Gifts*, Vol. 4, (1864) p. 128.

4. Did she edify the church?

"Ellen White received messages for individuals and groups that covered a broad array of subjects. Men and women received admonition, encouragement, and reproof regarding their personal lives and their Christian influence. Individuals and groups received insights, caution, and direction in general ideas, including education, health, administrative policy, evangelistic and publishing principles, and church finance."[51]

"Her messages to the church were far-reaching. On one hand, she covered the whole range of the salvation story; on the other, she dealt with civil government, the home, and questions of race relations, health, and education. The striking point is that all this instruction was creative: whenever followed faithfully, schools and hospitals, publishing houses and ministerial institutes, temperance and welfare societies sprang up worldwide. Even more striking is that this woman, without a church office and without formal training in any one of the many areas of her profound instruction, was the leading inspiration in molding all these various interests into a united organization."[52]

"Every test which can be brought to bear upon such manifestations, proves these genuine. The evidence which supports them, internal and external, is conclusive. They agree with the word of God, and with themselves. They are given, unless those best qualified to judge are invariably deceived, when the Spirit of God is especially present. They are free from the disgusting contortions and grimaces which attend the counterfeit manifestations of Spiritualism. Calm, dignified, impressive, they commend themselves to every beholder, as the very opposite of that which is false or fanatical....

"Further, their fruit is such as to show that the source from which they spring is the opposite of evil.

"They tend to the purest morality. They discountenance every vice, and exhort to the practice of every virtue. They point out the perils through which we are to pass to the kingdom. They reveal the devices of Satan. They warn us against his snares. They have nipped in the bud scheme after scheme of fanaticism which the enemy has tried to foist into our midst. They have exposed hidden

---

[51] Herbert Edgar Douglass, *Messenger of the Lord* (1998), p. 138.

[52] *Ibid.*, p. 183.

iniquity, brought to light concealed wrongs, and laid bare the evil motives of the false-hearted. They have warded off dangers from the cause of truth upon every hand. They have aroused and re-aroused us to greater consecration to God, moved zealous efforts for holiness of heart, and greater diligence in the cause and service of our Master.

"They lead us to Christ. Like the Bible, they set him forth as the only hope and only Saviour of mankind. They portray before us in living characters his holy life and his godly example, and with irresistible appeals they urge us to follow in his steps.

"They lead us to the Bible. They set forth that book as the inspired and unalterable word of God. They exhort us to take that word as the man of our counsel, and the rule of our faith and practice. And with a compelling power, they entreat us to study long and diligently its pages, and become familiar with its teaching, for it is to judge us in the last day.

"They have brought comfort and consolation to many hearts. They have strengthened the weak, encouraged the feeble, raised up the despondent. They have brought order out of confusion, made crooked places straight, and thrown light on what was dark and obscure. And no person, with an unprejudiced mind, can read their stirring appeals for a pure and lofty morality, their exaltation of God and the Saviour, their denunciations of every evil, and their exhortations to everything that is holy and of good report, without being compelled to say, 'These are not the words of him that hath a devil.'"[53]

5. Did she exalt Christ as the Son of God and our Savior?

"The world's Redeemer was treated as we deserve to be treated, in order that we might be treated as he deserved to be treated. He came to our world and took our sins upon his own divine soul, that we might receive his imputed righteousness. He was condemned for our sins, in which he had no share, that we might be justified by his righteousness, in which we had no share. The world's Redeemer gave himself for us. Who was he?—The Majesty of heaven, pouring out his blood upon the altar of justice for the sins of guilty man. We should know our relationship to Christ and his relationship to us."[54]

---

[53] Uriah Smith, *The Visions of Mrs. E. G. White* (Battle Creek, MI: Seventh-day Adventist Publishing Association, 1868), p. 5.2-7.2.

[54] E. G. White, *The Review and Herald*, March 21, 1893 par. 6.

6. Did she speak with authority?
"I am instructed to say to those who endeavor to tear down the foundation that has made us Seventh-day Adventists: We are God's commandment keeping people. For the past fifty years every phase of heresy has been brought to bear upon us, to becloud our minds regarding the teaching of the Word—especially concerning the ministration of Christ in the heavenly sanctuary, and the message of heaven for these last days, as given by the angels of the fourteenth chapter of Revelation. Messages of every order and kind have been urged upon Seventh-day Adventists, to take the place of the truth which, point by point, has been sought out by prayerful study and testified to by the miracle-working power of the Lord. But the waymarks which have made us what we are, are to be preserved, and they will be preserved, as God has signified through His word and the testimonies of His Spirit. He calls upon us to hold firmly with the grip of faith, to the fundamental principles that are based upon unquestionable authority."[55]

7. Did she bear good fruit?
Everywhere she went she raised up churches, hospitals, and universities. Her messages on health have impacted the entire world and saved millions of lives.

On June 6, 1863, in Otsego, Michigan, Ellen White had her famous health vision, revealing the true principles of health. On the basis of the information she received in this vision she helped to found a sanitarium (or health retreat) called the Western Health Reform Institute. During its first ten years, from 1866 to 1876, the Institute served two thousand patients. Of these, ten died: an average of one a year. So unusual was this record that the new institution was soon projected to national prominence. This record was set during the ten years before Koch and Pasteur first demonstrated (in 1876) that the anthrax microbe produced the disease anthrax.

Despite their meager funds, Ellen and her husband James White helped to finance a young student through medical school named

[55] E. G. White, *Manuscript Releases*, Vol. 4, p. 246.1.

John Harvey Kellogg, eventually of Kellogg's cornflakes fame. Using the principles of health that God showed Ellen White, Kellogg built up the Institute (renamed Battle Creek Sanitarium) so that by 1885, it had become the largest institution, in the world, of its kind.[56]

---

[56] In 1926 it had a service staff of eighteen hundred and in 1927, accommodations for over fifteen hundred patients. Its giant furnaces and boilers burned fifty-five tons of coal a day. By 1938 the Sanitarium facilities included thirty-two buildings on 27.5 acres of land and a dining room for eight hundred guests. The sanitarium attracted the attention of many famous guests and patients. President William Howard Taft was patient number 100,000. President Warren G. Harding was also a patient. Other notable guests and patients included:
Industrialists: Henry Ford; James Buick; Harvey Firestone; John D. Rockefeller, Jr.; Alfred du Pont; Edgar Welch, grape juice producer; A. E. McKinstry, president of International Harvester; E. H. Little, president of Colgate-Palmolive Company; and General David Sarnoff, president of Radio Corporation of America.
Businessmen: J. C. Penney; Montgomery Ward; R. H. and A.H. Kress; and S. S. Kresge.
Writers, editors, and publishers: Dr. Morris Fishbein, editor of Journal of the American Medical Association; George Bernard Shaw, Dale Carnegie, author of How to Win Friends and Influence People;
Sportsmen: Bill Tilden, tennis champion; Gene Sarazen, golfer; Johnny Weissmuller, champion swimmer.
Politicians: W. A. Julian, treasurer of the United States; George W. Wickersham, attorney general; William Jennings Bryan, secretary of state; Frank Knox, secretary of the navy; James J. Davis, secretary of labor; plus, governors, congressmen, and senators. (Footnote cont. on next page.)

Even though most Seventh-day Adventists do not fully avail themselves of the scientific heritage that God has entrusted them through the gift of prophecy, they have still become famous for better health and greater longevity than the rest of the world.

Dan Buettner in his *National Geographic* cover article states, "From 1976 to 1988 the National Institutes of Health funded a study of 34,000 California Adventists to see whether their health-oriented lifestyle affected their life expectancy and risk of heart disease and cancer. The study found that the Adventists' habit of consuming beans, soy milk, tomatoes, and other fruits lowered their risk of developing certain cancers. It also suggested that eating whole wheat bread, drinking five glasses of water a day, and, most surprisingly, consuming four servings of nuts a week reduced their risk of heart disease. And it found that not eating red meat had been helpful to avoid both cancer and heart disease.
"In the end the study reached a stunning conclusion, says Gary Fraser of Loma Linda University: The average Adventist lived four to ten years longer than the average Californian. That makes the Adventists one of the nation's most convincing cultures of longevity."[57]

One of the most notable nutrition researchers in the world, Dr. T. Colin Campbell, director of the famous China Study, the most comprehensive nutritional study ever conducted, in an interview with

---

Scientists: Ivan Pavlov, Nobel prize-winning Russian physiologist; Sir Frederick Grant Banting, discoverer of insulin and also a Nobel prize winner; Drs. Charles and William Mayo of the Mayo Clinic; Dr. William M. Scholl, manufacturer of foot appliances and remedies.
Inventor Thomas Edison; explorer Admiral Richard Byrd; oil men Harry F. Sinclair and L. E. Phillips.
Educator Booker T. Washington; Red Cross founder Clara Barton; evangelist Billy Sunday; pilot Amelia Earhart.
Amelia Earhart took Kellogg for an airplane ride over Battle Creek. Admiral Byrd counseled with Kellogg about diet before making his two major expeditions to explore the North and South Poles. Johnny Weissmuller, Olympic champion swimmer, after following a vegetarian diet prescribed by Kellogg, broke his previous record, swimming 300 meters in 3 minutes, 33.6 seconds, a record he had tried to break for several years. Weissmuller had broken fifty-four world records.
Unfortunately, Kellogg did not follow all the advice given to him from God, through the prophetic gift, including not to make the Sanitariums so large. Twice, God's warning hand touched the huge Sanitarium, and twice it burned to the ground. These warnings were tempered with the mercy that not a single person died in either fire. God also sent warnings and reproofs regarding the spiritualism that Kellogg eventually embraced, causing him to apostatize completely from the truths he once believed.

[57] Dan Buettner, "The Secrets of Long Life," *National Geographic Magazine*, November, 2005.

Don Mackintosh on February 24, 2005, said, “I am not aware of anyone who was more on point than Ellen White. Given her background she was truly an amazing woman. I am convinced that almost 100% of her statements are now substantially supported by the scientific evidence that has been developed in the last two to three decades. What I have come to realize, to even deeply worry about, is why it is that this message of Ellen and others has been so mislaid on shelves out of sight. It is now abundantly clear to me that now is the time to bring this forward in whatever way that each of us are able to do.”[58] The scientific evidence is only now catching up, in the last two to three decades, with the things she wrote a hundred and fifty years ago.

8. Did she exhibit the physical signs?

She received many of her visions in public often in front of hundreds of witnesses. “In passing into vision, she gives three enrapturing shouts of ‘Glory!’ which echo and re-echo, the second, and especially the third, fainter but more thrilling than the first, the voice resembling that of one quite a distance from you, and just going out of hearing. For about four or five seconds she seems to drop down like a person in a swoon, or one having lost his strength; she then seems to be instantly filled with superhuman strength, sometimes rising at once to her feet and walking about the room.

“There are frequent movements of the hands and arms, pointing to the right or left as her head turns. All these movements are made in a most graceful manner. In whatever position the hand or arm may be placed, it is impossible for anyone to move it. Her eyes are always open, but she does not wink; her head is raised, and she is looking upward, not with a vacant stare, but with a pleasant expression, only differing from the normal in that she appears to be looking intently at some distant object.”[59]

Nellie Starr, an eyewitness of the June 12, 1868 vision gives the account as follows:

“She walked back and forth and talked to us, and as she walked, she fell right down. She fell down gently. She went down as if an angel’s hands were under her....

---

[58] *What’s the Connection* directed by Jim Doss, with Don Mackintosh (Three Angel’s Media Ministry, 2005), Disk 1, 00:09:55-00:11:30.

[59] Arthur L. White, *Ellen G. White*: The Early Years, Vol. 1 (Hagerstown, MD: Review and Herald Publishing Association, 1985), p. 122.5.

"Sister White lay perfectly quiet and unconscious....
"Her eyes were open, with a pleasant expression on her face. Nothing unnatural or unusual.
"Brother White said to these large men, 'Take her hands apart. You have two hands to her one. Just pull her hands apart.' So they tried. They pulled and pulled till some of us got anxious that they would hurt her.
"Brother White said, 'Don't be anxious; she is safe in God's keeping, and you can pull until you are perfectly satisfied.' They said, 'We are satisfied now. We don't need to pull anymore.'
"He said, 'Take up one finger at a time.' That was impossible. They could not do so much as move a finger. It seemed like a block of granite....
"Brother White said to these men, 'Now hold her.' I think they thought they could. They grasped her by the wrists, but they could not retard the motion. It looked like any child could hold her, but she went on just the same.
"Elder White said, 'Now we are satisfied with that. Now we must see if her eyelids will close.' There was a large Rochester [kerosene] lamp close by on the stand. He removed the shade and put this light right in front of her eyes. We thought she would move her eyes to protect them. She didn't. She was perfectly unconscious.
"'Now,' Brother White said, 'we must see if there is any breath in her body.' There didn't seem to be any. Everything looked all right, only there was no breath. Brother White said, 'Now we will send out and get a mirror, and we will test it.' So someone went to the next door and got a mirror, and it was held close to her face, but no moisture gathered. So there was no breathing."[60]

David H. Lamson of Hillsdale, MI was present on June 26, 1854, when a medical examination was conducted of Mrs. White's physical condition while in vision: "Two physicians came in, an old man and a young man. Brother White was anxious that they should examine Sister White closely, which they did. A looking glass was brought, and one of them held it over her mouth while she talked; but very soon they gave this up, and said, 'She doesn't breathe.' Then they closely examined her sides as she spoke, to find some evidence of deep breathing, but they did not find it.

---

[60] Arthur L. White, *Ellen G. White*: The Progressive Years, Vol. 2 (1985), p. 233-234.

"As they closed this part of the examination, she arose to her feet, still in vision, holding a Bible high up, turning from passage to passage, quoting correctly, although the eyes were looking upward and away from the Book."[61]

Mrs. Drusilla Lamson, wife of David Lamson's cousin was also present and gave the following testimony. "I remember the meeting when the trial was made, namely, to test what Brother White had frequently said, that Sister White did not breathe while in vision, but I cannot recall the name of the doctor who was present.... It must have been Dr. Fleming, as he was the doctor called sometimes for counsel. He is, however, now dead. I can say this much, that the test was made, and no sign of breath was visible on the looking glass."

David Seeley, of Fayette, Iowa, wrote, "This is to certify that I have read the above testimonials of David Lamson and Mrs. Drusilla Lamson, concerning the physician's statement when examining Mrs. E. G. White while she was in vision, June 26, 1854.
"I was present at that meeting, and witnessed the examination. I agree with what is stated by Brother and Sister Lamson, and would say further that it was Doctor Fleming and another younger physician who made the examination. After Mrs. White rose to her feet, as they have stated, quoting the texts of Scripture, Doctor Fleming called for a lighted candle. He held this candle as near her lips as possible without burning, and in direct line with her breath in case she breathed. There was not the slightest flicker of the blaze. The doctor then said, with emphasis, 'That settles it forever; there is no breath in her body.'"[62]

Paul Harvey, in his noontime ABC radio-broadcast of September 27, 1997, reported: "Women have been honored on American postage stamps for more than 100 years, starting with one woman who was not an American, Queen Isabella, in 1893. Since then, 86 women have been honored, ranging from Martha Washington to Marilyn Monroe. Also, many women authors like Louisa May Alcott, Emily Dickinson, Willa Cather, and Rachel Carson.
"But I can name an American woman author who has never been honored thus, though her writings have been translated into 148

---

[61] Arthur L. White, *Ellen G. White*: The Early Years, Vol. 1 (1985), p. 302.

[62] Arthur L. White, *Ellen G. White*: The Early Years, Vol. 1, (1985) p. 303.

languages. More than Marx or Tolstoy, more than Agatha Christie, more than William Shakespeare. Only now is the world coming to appreciate her recommended prescription for optimum spiritual and physical health: Ellen White. Ellen White! You don't know her? Get to know her."

"Ellen White is thought to be the third [and possibly the second] most translated author in history and the most translated American author, male or female. So far as we know, she wrote and published more books, and in more languages, which circulate to a greater extent than the written works of any other woman in history. By the close of her seventy-year[s of prophetic] ministry, her literary productions totaled approximately 100,000 pages, or the equivalent of 25 million words, including letters, diaries, periodical articles, pamphlets, and books"[63]

"Where there is no vision, the people perish."[64]

---

[63] Herbert E. Douglass, *Messenger of the Lord* (1998), p. 108, 121.

[64] Proverbs 29:18

15 The Spirit of Prophecy

"The Bible, and the Bible alone, is to be our creed, the sole bond of union; all who bow to this Holy Word will be in harmony. Our own views and ideas must not control our efforts. Man is fallible, but God's Word is infallible.[1] Instead of wrangling with one another, let men exalt the Lord. Let us meet all opposition as did our Master, saying, 'It is written.' Let us lift up the banner on which is inscribed, The Bible our rule of faith and discipline."[2]

"In His Word, God has committed to men the knowledge necessary for salvation. The Holy Scriptures are to be accepted as an authoritative, infallible revelation of His will. They are the standard of character, the revealer of doctrines, and the test of experience."[3]

"Men act as though they had been given special liberty to cancel the decisions of God. The higher critics put themselves in the place of God, and review the Word of God, **revising** or endorsing it. **In this way, all nations are induced to drink the wine of the fornication of Babylon**. These higher critics have fixed things to suit the popular heresies of these last days. If they cannot subvert and misapply the Word of God, if they cannot bend it to human practices, they break it."[4]

"Brethren, cling to your Bible, as it reads, and stop your criticisms in regard to its validity, and obey the Word, and not one of you will be lost. The ingenuity of men has been exercised for ages to measure the Word of God by their finite minds and limited comprehension. If the Lord, the Author of the living oracles, would throw back the curtain and reveal His wisdom and His glory before them, they would

---

[1] These statements of the infallibility of God's Word are in direct contradiction with the views of the translators of the *Revised Version*: "I reject the word infallibility—of Holy Scripture overwhelming." Arthur Westcott, *The Life and Letters of Brooke Foss Westcott, Vol. 1* (1897), p. 207.
"If you make a decided conviction of the absolute infallibility of the New Testament... I fear I could not join you."
A. F. Hort, *Life and Letters of Fenton John Anthony Hort,* Vol. 1 (1896), p. 420.

[2] E. G. White, "A Missionary Appeal," *Review and Herald*, December 15, 1885, p. 770.

[3] E. G. White, *The Faith I Live By* (1958), p. 13.2.

[4] E. G. White, *The Upward Look* (1982), p. 35.5.

shrink into nothingness and exclaim as did Isaiah, 'I am a man of unclean lips, and I dwell in the midst of people of unclean lips' (Isaiah 6:5)."[5] "The work of higher criticism, in dissecting, conjecturing, reconstructing, is destroying faith in the Bible as a divine revelation. It is robbing God's word of power to control, uplift, and inspire human lives."[6]

"I take the Bible just as it is, as the Inspired Word. I believe its utterances in an entire Bible. Men arise who think they find something to criticize in God's Word. They lay it bare before others as evidence of superior wisdom. These men are, many of them, smart men, learned men, they have eloquence and talent, the whole lifework [of whom] is to unsettle minds in regard to the inspiration of the Scriptures. They influence many to see as they do. And the same work is passed on from one to another, just as Satan designed it should be, until we may see the full meaning of the words of Christ, 'When the Son of man cometh, shall he find faith on the earth?'"[7]

"When a message is presented to God's people, they should not rise up in opposition to it; they should go to the Bible, comparing it with the law and the testimony, and if it does not bear this test, it is not true. God wants our minds to expand. He desires to put His grace upon us. We may have a feast of good things every day, for God can open the whole treasure of heaven to us."[8]

Ellen White's Use of Modern Translations:

"According to the index, there are listed 15,117 Scripture references in the 25 volumes that are listed. 95% of these references are from the King James Version (KJV) and 5% from all other versions. The Revised Version came out in 1881. Since 1881 more than three quarters of Sister White's writings have been produced. Therefore, several of the revised versions were available during most of Sister

[5] E. G. White, *Selected Messages,* Vol. 1 (1958), p. 18.1.

[6] E. G. White, *The Acts of the Apostles* (1911), p. 474.1.

[7] E. G. White, *Selected Messages*, Vol. 1 (1958), p. 17.

[8] E. G. White, *Maranatha* (Nampa, ID: Pacific Press, 1976), p. 23.

White's writing years."[9]

"The proportion of Revised Version and marginal rendering of texts is very small when we consider that there are more than 850 scriptures quoted in *The Great Controversy*, or an average of a little more than one scripture text to a page, whereas there is approximately one Revised Version rendering and one marginal rendering for each one hundred pages."[10]

"In the Conflict of the Ages series, she used the revised versions only 96 times out of a total of 4,511 Bible references. With her crowded schedule, it took twenty-seven years of laborious writing to give us those five books. That figures out to only 3.55 references per year from the revised versions."[11] (97.9% KJV; 2.1% from all others)

"She used the KJV almost 99% of the time in *The Great Controversy*, the book which defines our doctrines more than any other book she wrote."[12] This is only nine Scripture references, out of 857, from other versions.

Ellen White used only the KJV in preaching, and used the *Revised Version* less and less over time. In *Testimonies,* Volume 9, the last volume of the testimonies, and one of the last books she wrote, she never once quotes from any version other than the King James.

More than two dozen Bible translations were available during some part of her writing years.[13]

She stated, "Unless the whole Bible is given to the people just as it reads, it would be better for them not to have it at all."[14]

---

[9] George Burnside, *The New International or the King James Version (*Payson, AZ: Leaves of Autumn Books, 1988), p. 48.

[10] Arthur L. White, D.D., "The E. G. White Counsel on Versions of the Bible" (Washington D.C.: Ellen G. White Estate, December 9, 1953), Ch. 6.

[11] Ted Schultz, *Assault on the Remnant: The Advent Movement The Spirit of Prophecy and Rome's Trojan Horse* (2013), Kindle ed., Kindle Locations 1916-1918.

[12] *Ibid.,* Kindle Locations 1988-1989.

[13] i.e.: Noyes', Leeser's, and Rotherham's which she quotes from about a dozen times in all her published material.

[14] E. G. White, *The Spirit of Prophecy*, Vol. 4 (1884), p. 344.1.

It seems that her son, Willie, and some of her secretaries had a burden for her to use the *Revised Version*: "When the first revision was published, I purchased a good copy and gave it to Mother. She referred to it occasionally, but **never used it in her preaching**. Later on, as manuscripts were prepared for her new books and for revised editions of books already in print, Sister White's attention was called from time to time by myself and Sister Marian Davis, to the fact that she was using texts which were much more clearly translated in the Revised Version. Sister White studied each one carefully, and in some cases she instructed us to use the Revised Version. In other cases she instructed us to adhere to the Authorized Version.

"When *Testimonies for the Church,* Vol. 8, was printed and it seemed desirable to make some lengthy quotations from the Psalms, it was pointed out to Sister White that the Revised Version of these Psalms was preferable, and that by using the form of blank verse the passages were more readable. Sister White gave the matter deliberate consideration, and instructed us to use the Revised Version. When you study these passages you will find that in a number of places where the Revised Version is largely used, the Authorized Version is used where translation seems to be better.

"We cannot find in any of Sister White's writings, nor do I find in my memory, any condemnation of the American Revised Version of the Holy Scriptures. Sister White's reasons for not using the A.R.V. in the pulpit are as follows:

"'There are many persons in the congregation who remember the words of the texts we might use as they are presented in the Authorized Version, and to read from the Revised Version would introduce perplexing questions in their minds as to why the wording of the text had been changed by the revisers and as to why it was being used by the speaker.'

"She did not advise me in a positive way not to use the A.R.V., but she intimated to me quite clearly that it would be better not to do so, as the use of the different wording brought perplexity to the older members of the congregation."[15]

Some claim that this statement should be a reason to use modern versions since it was the older members to which it brought perplexity. Her quoted words are "many persons in the

---

[15] W.C. White, as quoted in "The E. G. White Counsel on Versions of the Bible" (Washington D.C.: Ellen G. White Estate, December 9, 1953), Ch. 6.

congregation." However, Willie takes that to mean the older members. Further, he is making this statement some thirty years after her death, and with a clearly favorable disposition towards the *Revised Version*. He is also rationalizing, because he first says, "She did not advise me in a positive way not to use the A.R.V," and then states, "but she intimated to me quite clearly that it would be better not to do so." It seems that intimating "quite clearly that it would be better not to" use the *Revised Version* is advising "in a positive way not to use" it.

Further, there are explicit statements that she was directly opposed to her workers replacing the Scriptures used in her writings with revised versions:

"There are plans laid in every way to change the sentiments of the Bible, that it shall not be so forbidding, they say, so forbidding. And I write my works, I write as I am talking to you. I am up hours before any one moves in my house. I am up writing page after page, page after page, and it is coming out to the people. But it is because I am unable to sleep as I consider the peril of souls in various places, and they seem to be dead asleep. They have got the Word.
"They come to me, those that are copying my writings, and say, 'Now here is the better revised words, and I think I will put that in.' Don't you change one word, not a word. The revised edition we do not need at all. We have got the word that Christ has spoken Himself and given us. And don't you in my writings change a word for any revised edition. There will be revised editions, plenty of them, just before the close of this earth's history, and I want all my workers to understand, and I have got quite a number of them. I want them to understand that they are never to take the revised word, and put it in the place of the plain, simple words just as they are. They think they are improving them, but how do they know but that they may switch off on an idea, and give it less importance than Christ means them to have."[16]

---

[16] E. G. White, *Manuscript 188-1907*, par. 25-26.

Additionally, there are many examples that could be cited where the modern version explicitly contradicts the "Testimony of Jesus."[17] Following are a few such examples.

Keep the Commandments or Wash Robes?

Revelation 22:14 "Blessed are they that do his commandments, that they may have right to the tree of life, and may enter in through the gates into the city."

NASB Revelation 22:14 "**Blessed are those who wash their robes**..."

While it is true that Scripture teaches that the saints wash their robes in the blood of the lamb (Revelation 7:14), inserting "wash their robes" here removes important evidence that God requires obedience to his law.[18] Further, this change does not include the specification of Revelation 7:14 for the agent of cleansing. Will we have a right to the tree of life if we do our laundry?

"Says the Saviour, '**Blessed are they that do his commandments, that they may have right to the tree of life, and may enter in through the gates into the city.**' These are the words of God; they are not my words. Keep the commandments of God, and you will have a right to the tree of life."[19]

Joshua or Jesus providing them rest?

KJV Hebrews 4:8 "For if **Jesus** had given them rest"

RV Hebrews 4:8 "For if **Joshua** had given them rest"

---

17 Revelation 19:10 "And I fell at his feet to worship him. And he said unto me, See thou do it not: I am thy fellowservant, and of thy brethren that have the testimony of Jesus: worship God: for **the testimony of Jesus is the spirit of prophecy**."

18 See Matthew 19:17; John 14:15; 1 John 2:3; Revelation 14:12.

19 E. G. White, "We Should Glorify God," *The Review and Herald,* April 30, 1889, par. 13

"Israel fell short of the high ideal which had been set before her. Another than Joshua must guide His people to the true rest of faith."[20]

Marcus the Cousin of Barnabas?

In **Colossians 4:10** Modern Bibles call Marcus the cousin of Barnabas. The Spirit of Prophecy and the KJV, say that Marcus is the nephew of Barnabas.[21]

Eclipse at the Crucifixion?

"With amazement angels witnessed the Saviour's despairing agony. The hosts of heaven veiled their faces from the fearful sight. Inanimate nature expressed sympathy with its insulted and dying Author. The sun refused to look upon the awful scene. Its full, bright rays were illuminating the earth at midday, when suddenly it seemed to be blotted out. Complete darkness, like a funeral pall, enveloped the cross. 'There was darkness over all the land unto the ninth hour.' **There was no eclipse or other natural cause for this darkness**, which was as deep as midnight without moon or stars. It was a miraculous testimony given by God that the faith of after generations might be confirmed."[22] The darkness was in fulfillment of the Old Testament prophecy: "And it shall come to pass in that day, saith the Lord GOD, that I will cause the sun to go down at noon, and I will darken the earth in the clear day: And I will turn your feasts into mourning, and all your songs into lamentation; and I will bring up sackcloth upon all loins, and baldness upon every head; and I will make it as the mourning of an only son, and the end thereof as a bitter day."[23]

---

[20] E. G. White, *Thoughts from the Mount of Blessing* (1896), p. 1.1.

[21] E. G. White, *The Spirit of Prophecy,* Vol. 3 (Nampa, ID: Pacific Press, 1878), p. 353.2.

[22] E. G. White, *The Desire of Ages* (1898), p. 753.3.

[23] Amos 8:9-10

NAB[24] Luke 23:44-45 "It was now about noon and darkness came over the whole land until three in the afternoon because of an eclipse of the sun. Then the veil of the temple was torn down the middle."[25]

The NAB rendering is quite preposterous, as the crucifixion occurred at the time of the passover during the full moon. It is impossible to have a solar eclipse at the time of a full moon.

The reason for this rendering is that the Greek on which almost all modern versions are based contains the word ekleipontos, which can only be translated eclipse. However, the Greek on which the King James Version is based uses a different word—skotizō. Thus, the underlying manuscripts on which the modern versions are based are untrustworthy. The modern versions which do not include this ridiculous statement (most of them) are being inconsistent with themselves by discarding their own "oldest and best" manuscripts as unreliable on this verse—their own testimony indicting them.

Although *The Clear Word* does not make the darkness at the crucifixion an eclipse, it does contradict the Testimony of Jesus by making it a natural cause—dark clouds.

TCW Luke 23:44 "By this time it was noon; Jesus had been hanging on the cross for about three hours. Then some dark clouds appeared and soon Jerusalem and the entire surrounding area was covered with a dense, eerie darkness which lasted until three o'clock in the afternoon."[26]

Slave or Servant?

"God does not force the will or judgment of any. He takes no pleasure in a slavish obedience."[27]

Modern Bibles frequently change servant to slave.

---

[24] GS, NAB, NRSV—margin, Moff, etc.

[25] *Bible: New American Bible*, Rev. ed. (2011), Kindle ed., Kindle Location 52683.

[26] Jack Blanco, Th.D., *The Clear Word* (US: Jack Blanco, 2000), p. 1382.

[27] E. G. White, *The Great Controversy* (1911), p. 541.3.

NASB[28] 1 Corinthians 7:22 "For he who was called in the Lord while a slave, is the Lord's freedman; likewise he who was called while free, is Christ's slave."[29]

The Devil in the Lord's Prayer?[30]

KJV Matthew 6:9 "After this manner therefore pray ye: Our Father which art in heaven, Hallowed be thy name."
KJV Matthew 6:13 "And lead us not into temptation, but **deliver us from evil**: For thine is the kingdom, and the power, and the glory, for ever. Amen."

NIV Matthew 6:13 "And lead us not into temptation, but **deliver us from the evil one.**"[31]

In the closing of the Lord's Prayer, not only does the NIV and other modern versions remove the reference to God's kingdom and power and glory, but it also substitutes the evil one, instead of asking for deliverance from temptation. This makes the prayer end with the Devil.

The Spirit of Prophesy states, "The last like the first sentence of the Lord's Prayer, points to our Father as above all power and authority and every name that is named."[32]

---

[28] TCW, ASV, CEV, DRB, ICB, MSG, NIV, NKJV, RSV, RV, etc.

[29] *New American Standard Bible* (1977), p. 799.

[30] The Catholics made note of the "devil in the Lord's Prayer," (and the removal of the 1 John 5:7): "On the 17th of May the English-speaking world awoke to find that its Revised Bible had banished the Heavenly Witnesses and put the devil in the Lord's Prayer. Protests loud and deep went forth against the insertion, against the omission none. It is well, then, that the Heavenly Witnesses should depart whence their testimony is no longer received. The Jews have a legend that shortly before the destruction of their Temple, the Shechinah departed from the Holy of Holies, and the Sacred Voices were heard saying, 'Let us go hence.' So perhaps it is to be with the English Bible, the Temple of Protestantism. The going forth of the Heavenly Witnesses is the sign of the beginning of the end... the New Version will be the death-knell of Protestantism."
Dublin Review, Third Series, Vol. 6, July—October (1881), p. 143.

[31] *New International Version* (1978), p. 1041.

[32] E. G. White, *Thoughts from the Mount of Blessings* (Nampa, ID: Pacific Press, 1896), 120.1.

God was Manifest in the Flesh

"The union of the divine with the human nature is one of the most precious and most mysterious truths of the plan of redemption. It is this of which Paul speaks when he says: 'Without controversy great is the mystery of godliness: **God was manifest in the flesh**.'"[33]

This statement uses 1 Timothy 3:16 to prove the most mysterious truth of the plan of redemption—the union of the human and divine natures. Modern versions remove this truth from this verse by saying "he appeared in a body." No longer is "he"—Jesus—called God.

KJV 1 Timothy 3:16 "And without controversy great is the mystery of godliness: **God was manifest in the flesh**, justified in the Spirit, seen of angels, preached unto the Gentiles, believed on in the world, received up into glory."

NIV[34] 1 Timothy 3:16 "Beyond all question, the mystery of godliness is great: **He appeared in a body**, was vindicated by the Spirit, was seen by angels, was preached among the nations, was believed on in the world, was taken up in glory."[35]

Judgment Given to the Saints

"Daniel declares that when the Ancient of Days came, 'judgment was given to the saints of the Most High.' Daniel 7:22.... It is at this time that, as foretold by Paul, 'the saints shall judge the world.' In union with Christ they judge the wicked, comparing their acts with the statute book, the Bible, and deciding every case according to the deeds done in the body. Then the portion which the wicked must suffer is meted out, according to their works; and it is recorded against their names in the book of death."[36]

---

[33] E. G. White, *Testimonies,* Vol. 5 (Nampa, ID: Pacific Press, 1882), p. 746.2.

[34] NASB, ASV, CEV, ESV, GNB, ICB, RV, RSV, NWT, etc. (Change God to He, the flesh is varied). The Spirit of Prophecy quotes only KJV as Scripture.

[35] *New International Version* (1978), p. 1275-1276.

[36] E. G. White, *The Great Controversy* (1911), p. 660.4.

Many modern versions directly contradict this theological position by changing Daniel 7:22 into "pronounced judgment in favor of the saints."[37]

Lord Remember Me

"Remember the story of the thief on the cross. Well, according to the Sinaiticus and Vaticanus manuscripts (and thus all the modern New Testament translations based largely on these manuscripts), the thief did not call Jesus 'Lord.' Vaticanus, and Sinaiticus record that the thief simply said, 'Jesus, remember me....' However, in my research I came across this extended statement in that classic volume on the life of Christ, *The Desire of Ages*.... Here is what Ellen White says: 'Hope is mingled with anguish in his voice as the helpless, dying soul casts himself upon a dying Saviour. 'Lord, remember me,' he cries, 'when Thou comest into Thy kingdom.' How grateful then to the Saviour was the utterance of faith and love from the dying thief! While the leading Jews deny Him, and even the disciples doubt His divinity, the poor thief, upon the brink of eternity, calls Jesus Lord.... Many were ready to call Him Lord when He wrought miracles, and after He had risen from the grave; but none acknowledged Him as He hung dying upon the cross save the penitent thief who was saved at the eleventh hour. The bystanders caught the words as the thief called Jesus Lord.'

"Ellen White wrote *The Desire of Ages*, which was published 13 years after the publication of the Revised Version (which was based largely on the manuscripts that had been relatively recently discovered). And more significantly, Ellen White had that Revised Version available to her at this point in time. How do we know? She actually quoted passages from the Revised Version or its marginal readings about two dozen times right there in *The Desire of Ages*. Yet, even though she was fully aware of that bible translation and quoted from it repeatedly, she never used it when it came to the passage in Luke 23:42."[38]

---

[37] TCW, CEB, GNB, ICB, MSG, NASB, NIV, NKJV, etc.

[38] Ron du Preez, "No Fear for the Future*:* The Babble Over the Bible," American Christian Ministries, 2005, MP3, http://americanchristianministries.org/index.php/no-fear-for-the-future-mp3s.html Retrieved 3-28-16.

Woman Taken in Adultery

"The woman had stood before Jesus, cowering with fear. His words, 'He that is without sin among you, let him first cast a stone,' had come to her as a death sentence. She dared not lift her eyes to the Saviour's face, but silently awaited her doom. In astonishment she saw her accusers depart speechless and confounded; then those words of hope fell upon her ear, 'Neither do I condemn thee: go, and sin no more.' Her heart was melted, and she cast herself at the feet of Jesus, sobbing out her grateful love, and with bitter tears confessing her sins.

"This was to her the beginning of a new life, a life of purity and peace, devoted to the service of God. In the uplifting of this fallen soul, Jesus performed a greater miracle than in healing the most grievous physical disease; He cured the spiritual malady which is unto death everlasting. This penitent woman became one of His most steadfast followers. With self-sacrificing love and devotion she repaid His forgiving mercy."[39] Under the inspiration of the Holy Spirit this amazing story of grace and forgiveness is repeated here. Yet, the Sinaitic manuscript omits the entire story, and on that basis the New English Bible leaves out twelve whole verses.[40] Most modern versions question the authenticity of the story by italics or brackets and a footnote that says, "not found in the oldest and best manuscripts."

"If any man shall add unto these things, God shall add unto him the plagues that are written in this book: And if any man shall take away from the words of the book of this prophecy, God shall take away his part out of the book of life, and out of the holy city..."[41]

---

[39] E. G. White, *The Desire of Ages* (1898), p. 462.1-2.

[40] John 7:53-8:11

[41] Revelation 22:18-19

16 The Sanctuary and Its Services

"And the LORD spake unto Moses, saying... let them make me a sanctuary; that I may dwell among them."[1]

As the word of God was the message of salvation in written form, so the wilderness tabernacle was the message of salvation in symbolic form. This fact is not well understood today, although vestiges of this knowledge are almost universally accepted throughout Christendom. For example, if someone speaks of the Lamb of God, Christians everywhere know that the lamb symbolizes Jesus Christ. The remaining symbolism in the sanctuary and its services has been lost sight of, to a great degree. As always, Scripture defines its own symbols. The many layers of meaning depicted in these God-given services provide glimpses into the infinite wisdom of the God who could maintain both justice and mercy while rescuing a race in rebellion.

This plan of salvation was instituted before the world was created for Jesus is called "the Lamb slain from the foundation of the world."[2] The plan was, in fact, instituted in heaven itself. This becomes plain as we realize that the earthly sanctuary was actually a small scale replica, patterned after something infinitely greater.[3] "Now of the things which we have spoken this is the sum: We have such an high priest, who is set on the right hand of the throne of the Majesty in the heavens; A minister of the sanctuary, and of the true tabernacle, which the Lord pitched, and not man."[4]

The true tabernacle is the heavenly sanctuary, which God himself erected—the very throne room of the Majesty of Heaven. "Thy way, O God, is in the sanctuary: who is so great a God as our God?"[5] This is the edifice after which the earthy tabernacle was patterned.

---

[1] Exodus 25:1, 8

[2] Revelation 13:8

[3] To glimpse how much greater, see Martin Klein, *Full Disclosure: The Coming New World Order*, (Savannah Pictures, 2012), www.savannahpictures.com

[4] Hebrews 8:1-2

[5] Psalms 77:13

"It was therefore necessary that the patterns of things in the heavens should be purified with these {the blood of calves and goats[6]}; but the heavenly things themselves with better sacrifices than these {the blood of Christ}."[7] "Who serve unto the example and shadow of heavenly things, as Moses was admonished of God when he was about to make the tabernacle: for, See, saith he, that thou make all things according to the pattern showed to thee in the mount."[8]

Thus, the eternal throne room of God himself is a depiction of the plan of salvation—each item representing different aspects of the design to rescue the fallen race.

The door represents Jesus, for he said, "I am the door: by me if any man enter in, he shall be saved..."[9] "Verily, verily, I say unto you, He that entereth not by the door into the sheepfold, but climbeth up some other way, the same is a thief and a robber."[10]

The lamb, as we have already seen, represents Jesus.[11]

---

[6] Words in {brackets} supplied.

[7] Hebrews 9:24

[8] Hebrews 8:5

[9] John 10:9

[10] John 10:1

[11] John 1:29

The altar of burnt offering represented the sacrifice of Jesus on the cross in our behalf. "Christ... hath given himself for us an offering and a sacrifice..."[12] The altar's position in the outer court shows that the event symbolized would occur on the earth.

The outer court contained furniture made only from brass. According to Revelation 11, the outer court represents the earth.[13] Therefore, all the literal events which were represented symbolically in the outer court would occur in reality on the earth. The holy and most holy places of the earthly tabernacle represented the heavenly throne room; therefore, every piece of furniture was made from pure gold, with the boards of the walls even overlaid with gold. All the literal events symbolized by the items in the holy and most holy places would occur in reality in heaven.

The laver contained water with which the priests were to wash. "Christ also loved the church, and gave himself for it; That he might sanctify and cleanse it with the washing of water by the word."[14] Thus, the water of the laver represents the word of God. However, in John 1:1, 14 we are told, "In the beginning was the Word, and the Word was with God, and the Word was God. And the Word was made flesh, and dwelt among us..." Therefore, the water represents Jesus. "Jesus stood and cried, saying, If any man thirst, let him come unto me, and drink."[15]

Jesus came from heaven and the first thing he did as he entered his earthly ministry, at age thirty, was to be washed at his baptism. Baptism represents death, burial, and resurrection to new life. The next event outlined in the sanctuary was his death on the cross, at the altar of sacrifice. After, his death he was buried and resurrected to new life—back at the laver. He still walked on the earth for a short time (forty days) after his resurrection, before returning to heaven—

---

[12] Ephesians 5:2

[13] Revelation 11:2 "But the court which is without the temple leave out, and measure it not; for it is given unto the Gentiles: and the holy city shall they tread under foot forty and two months."
In order for the court to be given unto the Gentiles for the specified time period, it must be on this earth, as the Gentile could not tread heaven under foot.

[14] Ephesians 5:25-26

[15] John 7:37

entering the holy place. "For Christ is not entered into the holy places made with hands, which are the figures of the true; but into heaven itself, now to appear in the presence of God for us:"[16]

The table of shewbread held two stacks of six loaves each, of unleavened bread. Jesus said, "I am the living bread which came down from heaven..."[17] Thus the showbread represents Jesus.

The smoke from the altar of incense ascends "with the prayers of the saints."[18] The smoke represents Jesus whose righteousness makes the prayers of the saints acceptable before the throne of God.[19] "Christ also hath loved us, and hath given himself for us an offering and a sacrifice to God for a sweetsmelling savour."[20]

Jesus said, "I am the light of the world..."[21] The light of the seven-branched candlestick represents Jesus. The oil used to burn the lamps also represents the Holy Spirit.[22] The oil was to be pure olive oil made by beating the olives,[23] representing the fact that Jesus was "bruised for our iniquities."[24]

A veil, or curtain separated the holy from the most holy place. What does the veil represent? Jesus. "By a new and living way, which he hath consecrated for us, through the veil, that is to say, his flesh."[25] He veiled his divinity in the flesh of humanity, so that we could behold him. When Christ died, the veil between the holy and most holy place was rent showing that his death was the ultimate

---

[16] Hebrews 9:24

[17] John 6:51

[18] Revelation 8:4

[19] Many have identified the smoke as the prayers of the saints but notice that the Bible says the smoke ascends "with the prayers of the saints," therefore, the smoke cannot be the prayers of the saints.

[20] Ephesians 5:2

[21] John 8:12

[22] 1 Samuel 16:13

[23] Leviticus 24:2

[24] Isaiah 53:5

[25] Hebrews 10:20

revelation of divinity—the flesh of God being rent for us—the glory of the Almighty blazing forth from the most holy place, now exposed to our sight.

Inside the veil was the most holy place containing the ark of the covenant. Covering the ark was the mercy seat, or throne of God. "Being justified freely by his grace through the redemption that is in Christ Jesus: Whom God hath set forth to be a propitiation through faith in his blood..."[26] God has set forth Jesus as a propitiation. The Greek word[27] translated propitiation means mercy seat. God has set forth Jesus as our mercy seat. The mercy seat therefore represents Christ. Underneath the mercy seat are the ten commandments, indicating that God's mercy, the death of Christ, shields us from the condemnation of his law. On either side of the ark are two cherubim, or angels, representing the real heavenly beings that guard the throne of God in heaven.

---

[26] Romans 3:24-25

[27] Greek—hilastērion; see Hebrews 9:5

The Jewish ceremonial year[28] was also an outline of the plan of salvation. The year began in the spring and the first symbolic feast was the passover. The passover was commemorative of the exodus from Egypt, when the destroying angel passed over the houses of the Israelites on whose doors he found the blood of the lamb. The passover also pointed forward to Jesus who would be sacrificed for

---

[28] When Jesus died, the curtain separating the holy place from the most holy place in the temple was torn from top to bottom (Matthew 27:51) indicating that Jesus—the reality of these symbols—had arrived, and that the ceremonies were ended and our attention was to be on the reality rather than the symbols. The Bible predicted this change. An Old Testament prophecy begins to unlock the mystery: "I will also cause all her mirth to cease, her feast days, her new moons, and her sabbaths, and all her solemn feasts." Hosea 2:11 Here the Bible explicitly foretells a time when God would cause Israel's feast days, her new moons, and her sabbaths to cease. The New Testament records the fulfillment of this prophecy: "Blotting out the handwriting of ordinances that was against us, which was contrary to us, and took it out of the way, nailing it to his cross....Let no man therefore judge you in meat, or in drink, or in respect of an holyday, or of the new moon, or of the sabbath days: Which are a shadow of things to come; but the body is of Christ." Colossians 2:14-17

Notice that the same components (feast/holydays, new moons, and sabbaths/solemn feasts) are mentioned in the identical order in both passages. Paul, in Colossians, is quoting from Hosea. Paul repeats Colossians 2:14 in Ephesians 2:15: "Having abolished in his flesh the enmity, even the law of commandments contained in ordinances; for to make in himself of twain one new man, so making peace." Here the Bible speaks of a law that has been done away with. Some assume that this is the Ten Commandments, but a careful study of Scriptures indicates that it is the ceremonial law that was abolished at the death of Jesus.

Jesus himself said, "Think not that I am come to destroy the law, or the prophets: I am not come to destroy, but to fulfill. For verily I say unto you, Till heaven and earth pass, one jot or one tittle shall in no wise pass from the law, till all be fulfilled." Matthew 5:17, 18. Thus, the sabbath days of Colossians 2:16 are ceremonial sabbaths, not the weekly Sabbath (because the weekly Sabbath is part of the Ten Commandments). The Scripture teaches of two different laws. The Bible says clearly that the Ten Commandments were written on stone with the finger of God and placed inside the ark. "And I will write on the tables the words that were in the first tables which thou brakest, and thou shalt put them in the ark..." Deuteronomy 10:1-5. The Bible also specifies that Moses wrote words in a book, which was placed in the side of the ark to be there as a witness against the people. "When Moses had made an end of writing the words of this law in a book, until they were finished, That Moses commanded the Levites... saying, take this book of the law, and put it in the side of the ark of the covenant of the LORD your God, that it may be there for a witness against thee." Deuteronomy 31:24-26. This is almost identical wording to the phrase in Colossians 2:14, "handwriting of ordinances that was against us." The Bible tells us that there are sabbaths besides the weekly Sabbath of the Lord from the Ten Commandments: "These are the feasts of the LORD, which ye shall proclaim to be holy convocations, to offer an offering made by fire unto the LORD, a burnt offering, and a meat offering, a sacrifice, and drink offerings, every thing upon his day: **Beside the sabbaths of the LORD**, and beside your gifts, and beside all your vows, and beside all your freewill offerings, which ye give unto the LORD." Leviticus 23:37, 38.

One cannot deny that the Bible says that Christ did away with a law. And, the Bible calls the law which Christ did away with, the "handwriting of" or "the commandments contained in" ordinances. It also defines these laws as "shadows of things to come." This means that it was the ceremonial laws of types and shadows that were nailed to the cross—not the Ten Commandments, not the entire five books of Moses, not the health laws, not the principles that expanded and enlarged on the moral law (i.e. the prohibition of a man lying with a beast or another man is clearly an expansion of the commandment to not commit adultery); but the ceremonial laws of types and shadows.

So, from the death of Jesus, the focus changed from keeping these ceremonies, to understanding their heavenly reality. Despite the fact that these ceremonies have been done away with, they still portray amazing truths that affect our reality today.

our sins as the passover lamb. "For even Christ our passover is sacrificed for us."[29] Jesus was crucified on Friday afternoon, on the very day of passover—at the very time of day when the passover lamb would have been killed.

Next was the feast of unleavened bread, the seven days immediately following passover. All leaven (representing sin—1 Corinthians 5:8) was to be removed from their dwelling places during this time. The bread eaten was to be made without leaven. The second day of the feast of unleavened bread was the day of the wavesheaf offering—an offering of grain waved before the Lord. This pointed forward to Christ's resurrection as the first-fruits of the dead, and was the guarantee of the harvest of resurrected righteous at the end of the world. "But now is Christ risen from the dead, and become the firstfruits of them that slept. But every man in his own order: Christ the firstfruits; afterward they that are Christ's at his coming."[30] Jesus rose from the grave on Sunday morning, on the very day when the wavesheaf was to be presented to the Lord.

Pentecost was fifty days from the wavesheaf offering and pointed forward to Jesus' anointing as our high priest in the heavenly sanctuary. "We have such an high priest, who is set on the right hand of the throne of the Majesty in the heavens; A minister of the sanctuary, and of the true tabernacle, which the Lord pitched, and not man."[31] Jesus said "Nevertheless I tell you the truth; It is expedient for you that I go away: for if I go not away, the Comforter will not come unto you; but if I depart, I will send him unto you."[32] Jesus had to be anointed in heaven in order that the Holy Spirit could come to the earth. Oil represents the Holy Spirit[33] and as Jesus was anointed with the Spirit in heaven, as our high priest, some of that oil

[29] 1 Corinthians 5:7

[30] 1 Corinthians 15:20, 23

[31] Hebrews 8:1, 2

[32] John 16:7

[33] 1 Samuel 16:13

fell on the disciples waiting on the earth.[34] The outpouring of the Holy Spirit occurred exactly fifty days from the resurrection of Jesus, on the day of Pentecost.[35]

Thus, concluded the spring festivals which pointed to the first coming of Jesus. The fall festivals pointed to the events relating to his second coming.

The first of the fall feasts, on the first day of the seventh month, was the feast of trumpets. The trumpets were to sound announcing the soon coming day of judgment, which was to occur ten days later.

The day of atonement, on the tenth day of the seventh month, was also called the day of judgment.[36] On the day of atonement (and only once a year on that day) lots would be cast for two goats, one the Lord's goat, and the other the scapegoat. Then the high priest would sacrifice the Lord's goat, taking the blood of the sacrifice into the most holy place to cleanse the sanctuary of sin. The sins were then transferred to the high priest who would take them out of the sanctuary and place them on the head of the scapegoat, then to be led by a fit man[37] into the wilderness to die. Jesus is represented as our high priest, cleansing the heavenly sanctuary of all confessed sins, and placing the responsibility, and thus the punishment, for them on the head of Satan, who has tempted God's people to commit these sins. Those whose sins have not been confessed—and thus not placed in the heavenly sanctuary to ultimately be blotted out forever—will themselves bear the penalty for their sins. This cleansing of the sanctuary demonstrates the grievous nature of our sins, even the record of which have contaminated the very throne room of the universe. This cleansing must occur before Jesus returns for his people. "For Christ is not entered into the holy places

---

[34] Acts 2:1-4 "And when the day of Pentecost was fully come, they were all with one accord in one place. And suddenly there came a sound from heaven as of a rushing mighty wind, and it filled all the house where they were sitting. And there appeared unto them cloven tongues like as of fire, and it sat upon each of them. And they were all filled with the Holy Ghost..."

[35] The giving of the law at Sinai was also fifty days from the wavesheaf offering, on the day of Pentecost.

[36] Atonement and Trumpets were solemn holy days, or ceremonial sabbaths, in which no work was to be done. The others were all joyous festivals or feasts, but not ceremonial sabbaths.

[37] The fit man who will take Satan to his final destruction also represents Jesus.

made with hands, which are the figures of the true; but into heaven itself, now to appear in the presence of God for us: Nor yet that he should offer himself often, as the high priest entereth into the holy place every year with blood of others; For then must he often have suffered since the foundation of the world: but now **once in the end of the world** hath he appeared to put away sin by the sacrifice of himself. And as it is appointed unto men once to die, but after this the judgment: So Christ was once offered to bear the sins of many; and unto them that look for him shall he appear the second time **without sin** unto salvation."[38]

This investigative judgment, in the end of the world, prior to the second coming, is necessary since every case will have been decided, for when Jesus comes, his rewards are with him: "And, behold, I come quickly; and my reward is with me, to give every man according as his work shall be."[39]

Just as God promised, "Surely the Lord GOD will do nothing, but he revealeth his secret unto his servants the prophets,"[40] he revealed to the prophet Daniel, exactly when the anti-typical day of atonement would occur: "Unto two thousand and three hundred days; then shall the sanctuary be cleansed."[41] Daniel was so overwhelmed by the scope of this time period[42] that he "fainted, and was sick certain days," and reported, "I was astonished at the vision, but none understood it."[43] This fainting spell interrupted the angel Gabriel's explanation of the vision. Gabriel returned in Daniel 9 to finish his explanation: "Yea, whiles I was speaking in prayer, even the man Gabriel, whom I had seen in the vision at the beginning, being caused to fly swiftly, touched me about the time of the evening oblation. And he informed me, and talked with me, and said, O Daniel, I am now come forth to give thee skill and understanding. At the beginning of thy supplications the commandment came forth, and

---

[38] Hebrews 9:24-28

[39] Revelation 22:12

[40] Amos 3:7

[41] Daniel 8:14

[42] Daniel 8:27

[43] Daniel 8:27

I am come to show thee; for thou art greatly beloved: therefore understand the matter, and consider the vision."[44]

The angel's explanation of the vision of Daniel 8 breaks the total time period of 2300 days into smaller pieces for easier understanding. "Seventy weeks are determined upon thy people and upon thy holy city, to finish the transgression, and to make an end of sins, and to make reconciliation for iniquity, and to bring in everlasting righteousness, and to seal up the vision and prophecy, and to anoint the most Holy."[45]

In symbolic Bible prophecy a day represents a year.[46] Seventy weeks, therefore, would represent 490 years. "The word here translated 'determined' literally signifies 'cut off.' Seventy weeks, representing 490 years, are declared by the angel to be cut off, as specially pertaining to the Jews. But from what were they cut off? As the 2300 days was the only period of time mentioned in chapter 8, it must be the period from which the seventy weeks were cut off; the seventy weeks must therefore be a part of the 2300 days, and the two periods must begin together. The seventy weeks were declared by the angel to date from the going forth of the commandment to restore and build Jerusalem. If the date of this commandment could be found, then the starting point for the great period of the 2300 days would be ascertained."[47]

"In the seventh chapter of Ezra the decree is found.[48] In its completest form it was issued by Artaxerxes, king of Persia, 457 B.C. But in Ezra 6:14 the house of the Lord at Jerusalem is said to have been built 'according to the commandment of Cyrus, and Darius, and Artaxerxes king of Persia.' These three kings, in originating, reaffirming, and completing the decree, brought it to the perfection required by the prophecy to mark the beginning of the 2300 years. Taking 457 B.C., the time when the decree was completed, as the date of the commandment, every specification of the prophecy

---

[44] Daniel 9:21-23

[45] Daniel 9:24

[46] Numbers 14:34; Ezekiel 4:6

[47] E. G. White, *The Great Controversy* (1911), p. 326.2.

[48] Ezra 7:12-26

concerning the seventy weeks was seen to have been fulfilled.

"'From the going forth of the commandment to restore and to build Jerusalem unto the Messiah the Prince shall be seven weeks, and threescore and two weeks'—namely, sixty-nine weeks, or 483 years.

"The decree of Artaxerxes went into effect in the autumn of 457 B.C. From this date, 483 years extend to the autumn of A.D. 27. At that time this prophecy was fulfilled. The word 'Messiah' signifies 'the Anointed One.' In the autumn of A.D. 27 Christ was baptized by John and received the anointing of the Spirit. The apostle Peter testifies that 'God anointed Jesus of Nazareth with the Holy Ghost and with power.'[49] And the Saviour Himself declared: 'The Spirit of the Lord is upon Me, because He hath anointed Me to preach the gospel to the poor.'[50] After His baptism He went into Galilee, 'preaching the gospel of the kingdom of God, and saying, The time is fulfilled.'[51]

"'And He shall confirm the covenant with many for one week.' The 'week' here brought to view is the last one of the seventy; it is the last seven years of the period allotted especially to the Jews. During this time, extending from A.D. 27 to A.D. 34, Christ, at first in person and afterward by His disciples, extended the gospel invitation especially to the Jews. As the apostles went forth with the good tidings of the kingdom, the Saviour's direction was: 'Go not into the way of the Gentiles, and into any city of the Samaritans enter ye not: but go rather to the lost sheep of the house of Israel.' Matthew 10:5,6.

"'In the midst of the week He shall cause the sacrifice and the oblation to cease.' In A.D. 31, three and a half years after His baptism, our Lord was crucified. With the great sacrifice offered upon Calvary, ended that system of offerings which for four thousand years had pointed forward to the Lamb of God. Type had met antitype, and all the sacrifices and oblations of the ceremonial system were there to cease.

"The seventy weeks, or 490 years, especially allotted to the Jews, ended, as we have seen, in A.D. 34. At that time, through the action of the Jewish Sanhedrin, the nation sealed its rejection of the gospel by the martyrdom of Stephen and the persecution of the followers of Christ. Then the message of salvation, no longer restricted to the chosen people, was given to the world. The disciples, forced by persecution to flee from Jerusalem, 'went everywhere preaching the

---

[49] Acts 10:38

[50] Luke 4:18

[51] Mark 1:14, 15

word.' 'Philip went down to the city of Samaria, and preached Christ unto them.' Peter, divinely guided, opened the gospel to the centurion of Caesarea, the God-fearing Cornelius; and the ardent Paul, won to the faith of Christ, was commissioned to carry the glad tidings 'far hence unto the Gentiles.' Acts 8:4, 5; 22:21.

"Thus far every specification of the prophecies is strikingly fulfilled, and the beginning of the seventy weeks is fixed beyond question at 457 B.C., and their expiration in A.D. 34. From this data there is no difficulty in finding the termination of the 2300 days. The seventy weeks—490 days—having been cut off from the 2300, there were 1810 days remaining. After the end of 490 days, the 1810 days were still to be fulfilled. From A.D. 34, 1810 years extend to 1844. Consequently the 2300 days of Daniel 8:14 terminate in 1844. At the expiration of this great prophetic period, upon the testimony of the angel of God, 'the sanctuary shall be cleansed.'"[52]

According to Scripture, Jesus began the process of cleansing the heavenly sanctuary in 1844. He wanted us to understand the reason for the seeming delay of his return, and know what he was accomplishing on our behalf that we might follow him by faith into the most holy place. "Let us therefore come boldly unto the throne of grace, that we may obtain mercy, and find grace to help in time of need."[53] The throne of grace, where we obtain mercy is the mercy seat, represented by the lid of the ark of the covenant, in the most holy place.

The final symbol on the Hebrew annual calendar is the Feast of Tabernacles. This represents the second coming of Jesus when God will once again tabernacle with men, and "will dwell with them, and they shall be his people, and God himself shall be with them, and be their God."[54]

Not only do the symbols of the sanctuary services point to Jesus, they also point to the truths of the process of salvation that are the steps to Christ, still today.

---

[52] E. G. White, *The Great Controversy* (1911), p. 326.3-328.2.

[53] Hebrews 4:16

[54] Revelation 21:3

When one of the Israelites committed a sin, they were to bring a lamb without blemish from their flock. This first step in the plan of salvation was an admission of guilt and an acknowledgment of the need of a savior, which was to be found only in the "Lamb of God which taketh away the sin of the world."[55] That lamb was brought to the door of the tabernacle, which represents Jesus. To Jesus we must come even to plead the merits of his sacrifice.

The sinner, in repentance, was then to confess his sin on the head of the lamb and with his own hand take its life. This was to impress on the mind of the sinner the terrible nature of sin, and that it was his own sin that took the life of the innocent Savior. The lamb was then burnt on the altar of burnt offering demonstrating that the sin was consumed and cleansed by the sacrifice of Christ. Yet, some of the blood of that lamb was taken by the priest (which represents Christ) into the holy place (heaven itself) and sprinkled on the veil between the holy and most holy places. This indicated that, though the sinner was justified, by the sacrifice of Christ, the record of their sin was not yet erased.

Next, came the public consecration of baptism, where the priest (Jesus) having become sin for us[56] washes the stain of sin away by baptism. Baptism, symbolized by the laver, represents death to sin, burial of the old nature, and resurrection to new life. Jesus did this on our behalf, though he had no sin of his own, and asks us to follow his example.

As we arise from the waters of baptism, a new creature, we are then to live in the very atmosphere of heaven. We enter, by faith, the holy place not made with hands. Here the spirit of Christ in the form of the Holy Spirit (the candlestick, oil, and light) guides us as we search the Scriptures (the bread of life, or showbread) and as we offer our prayers and petitions at the altar of incense where Christ's righteousness makes them acceptable before the throne of God.

---

[55] John 1:29

[56] 2 Corinthians 5:21

As we breath the atmosphere of heaven, God brings us into conformity to his character, of which his law is a transcript.[57] His power enables us to gain the victory and keep his holy law while the mercy seat shields us from its condemnation. At the second coming, we will see Jesus face to face with no veil between.[58]

In 1844, Jesus, as our high priest entered the most holy place in the heavenly sanctuary to begin the final process of eradicating even the record of sin. As each name is brought for consideration, one of two things will occur, either the record of their sins will be forever erased, or their name will be erased from the book of life.[59]

"All who have truly repented of sin, and by faith claimed the blood of Christ as their atoning sacrifice, have had pardon entered against their names in the books of heaven; as they have become partakers of the righteousness of Christ, and their characters are found to be in harmony with the law of God, their sins will be blotted out, and they themselves will be accounted worthy of eternal life."[60]

"In the prayer of Moses our minds are directed to the heavenly records in which the names of all men are inscribed, and their deeds, whether good or evil, are faithfully registered. The book of life contains the names of all who have ever entered the service of God. If any of these depart from Him, and by stubborn persistence in sin become finally hardened against the influences of His Holy Spirit, their names will in the judgment be blotted from the book of life, and they themselves will be devoted to destruction. Moses realized how dreadful would be the fate of the sinner; yet if the people of Israel were to be rejected by the Lord, he desired his name to be blotted out with theirs; he could not endure to see the judgments of God fall upon those who had been so graciously delivered. The intercession of Moses in behalf of Israel illustrates the mediation of Christ for sinful men. But the Lord did not permit Moses to bear, as did Christ,

---

[57] E. G. White, *Christ's Object Lessons* (Nampa, ID: Pacific Press, 1900), p. 305.3.

[58] 1 Corinthians 13:12

[59] Revelation 3:5 "He that overcometh, the same shall be clothed in white raiment; and I will not blot out his name out of the book of life, but I will confess his name before my Father, and before his angels."

[60] E. G. White, *The Great Controversy* (1911), p. 483.2.

the guilt of the transgressor. 'Whosoever hath sinned against Me,' He said, 'him will I blot out of My book.'"[61]

Once every name has been reviewed, the blood of Christ will permanently erase even the record of the sins of those covered with his sacrifice. This is the good news of the judgment.[62]

During the dark ages, every single truth of the sanctuary service was obscured by the traditions of the papal church. The truth of the altar of burnt offering, that our sins are forgiven by the sacrifice of Christ, was replaced with the doctrine of salvation by works and the Eucharist. The rite of baptism, represented by the laver, for those of an age who could understand its meaning, was modified into infant sprinkling—once again creating a doctrine that salvation could be achieved by our own deeds, or by the performance of a ritual, rather than placing our faith in the saving power of Jesus. The Bible, represented by the showbread, was taken from the people and in its place was substituted the traditions of men and the authority of the priest. In place of the fire of the Holy Spirit, or light of the candlestick to guide the conscience, the fires of the Inquisition determined what most could believe. Rather than going to Jesus for the forgiveness of sins, and having the smoke of his incense cover us with his righteousness, the sinner was directed for forgiveness to a fellow sinner in the form of the priest. And, just as prophesied in Scripture, this same power thought "to change times and laws,"[63] even modifying the very law of God, and substituting the commandments of men.[64]

During the protestant reformation, each of these sanctuary truths were returned, step by step, to prominence in the minds of God's people. Martin Luther recovered the truth of the altar of burnt offering—that we are saved by grace alone through faith in the death of Jesus. John Smyth rediscovered the Bible truth of baptism by immersion, following our Savior's example. Wycliffe, Tyndale,

---

[61] E. G. White, *Patriarchs and Prophets* (1890), p. 326.3.

[62] Revelation 14:6-7—gospel is good news. This text announces the good news of the hour of the judgment of Christ, which began in 1844.

[63] Daniel 7:25

[64] See Martin Klein, *Above All Thy Name*, God Knew All Along.

Erasmus, Luther, and others restored to the people the Bread of Life—the word of God. John Calvin resurrected the Bible doctrine that we can bring our prayers "boldly unto the throne of grace, that we may obtain mercy, and find grace to help in time of need,"[65] understanding that rather than going through a priest, "there is one God, and one mediator between God and men, the man Christ Jesus."[66] John Wesley rekindled interest in the work and person of the Holy Spirit.

The final sanctuary truths to be reignited were the facts of the existence of the true tabernacle in heaven, and the eternal nature of God's law as the foundation of his throne. This revealed the binding claims of the Sabbath as the signature of authorship of the lawgiver[67] and the soon return of the Judge of all the Earth. These truths were brought to view by William Miller, Ellen White, and others, in the great American reformation—the advent awakening—during the ten years leading up to 1844.

What does all this have to do with Bible versions and the preservation of Scripture? From the time of his ascension in A.D. 31 until 1844, Jesus was ministering in the first apartment, or holy place of the heavenly sanctuary. This was the location of the seven-branched candlestick, the golden altar of incense, and the table of showbread. Jesus said "I am the bread of life;"[68] "And the Word was made flesh, and dwelt among us."[69] The true Word of Life must be present, preserved, and prominent prior to 1844, for this was the time during which he was ministering at the table of showbread.

There are two thrones in heaven—the throne of Jesus represented by the table of showbread, and the throne of the Father represented

---

[65] Hebrews 4:16

[66] 1 Timothy 2:5

[67] "All who keep the seventh day signify by this act that they are worshipers of Jehovah. Thus the Sabbath is the sign of man's allegiance to God as long as there are any upon the earth to serve Him. The fourth commandment is the only one of all the ten in which are found both the name and the title of the Lawgiver. It is the only one that shows by whose authority the law is given. Thus it contains the seal of God, affixed to His law as evidence of its authenticity and binding force." E. G. White, *Patriarchs and Prophets* (1890), p. 307.2.

[68] John 6:48

[69] John 1:14

by the ark of the covenant: "To him that overcometh will I grant to sit with me in my throne, even as I also overcame, and am set down with my Father in his throne."[70]

"I saw a throne, and on it sat the Father and the Son. I gazed on Jesus' countenance and admired His lovely person. The Father's person I could not behold, for a cloud of glorious light covered Him.... Before the throne I saw the Advent people—the church and the world. I saw two companies, one bowed down before the throne, deeply interested, while the other stood uninterested and careless. Those who were bowed before the throne would offer up their prayers and look to Jesus; then He would look to His Father, and appear to be pleading with Him. A light would come from the Father to the Son and from the Son to the praying company. Then I saw an exceeding bright light come from the Father to the Son, and from the Son it waved over the people before the throne. But few would receive this great light. Many came out from under it and immediately resisted it; others were careless and did not cherish the light, and it moved off from them. Some cherished it, and went and bowed down with the little praying company. This company all received the light and rejoiced in it, and their countenances shone with its glory.

"I saw the Father rise from the throne, and in a flaming chariot go into the holy of holies within the veil, and sit down. Then Jesus rose up from the throne, and the most of those who were bowed down arose with Him. I did not see one ray of light pass from Jesus to the careless multitude after He arose, and they were left in perfect darkness. Those who arose when Jesus did, kept their eyes fixed on Him as He left the throne and led them out a little way. Then He raised His right arm, and we heard His lovely voice saying, 'Wait here; I am going to My Father to receive the kingdom; keep your garments spotless, and in a little while I will return from the wedding and receive you to Myself.' Then a cloudy chariot, with wheels like flaming fire, surrounded by angels, came to where Jesus was. He stepped into the chariot and was borne to the holiest, where the Father sat. There I beheld Jesus, a great High Priest, standing before the Father. On the hem of His garment was a bell and a pomegranate, a bell and a pomegranate. Those who rose up with Jesus would send up their faith to Him in the holiest, and pray, 'My Father, give us Thy Spirit.' Then Jesus would breathe upon them the

[70] Revelation 3:21

Holy Ghost. In that breath was light, power, and much love, joy, and peace.
"I turned to look at the company who were still bowed before the throne; they did not know that Jesus had left it. Satan appeared to be by the throne, trying to carry on the work of God. I saw them look up to the throne, and pray, 'Father, give us Thy Spirit.' Satan would then breathe upon them an unholy influence; in it there was light and much power, but no sweet love, joy, and peace. Satan's object was to keep them deceived and to draw back and deceive God's children."[71]

The truths of the sanctuary service were being reestablished, step by step, by the Protestant reformation. "It was the work of the Reformation to restore to men the word of God."[72] Through the dark ages the word of God became corrupted by error, tradition and superstition, but that very Word had predicted and promised that "The words of the LORD are pure words: as silver tried in a furnace of earth, purified seven times."[73] That prophecy, as we have seen in the chapter "The Glorious King James Version,"[74] was fulfilled exactly, in the seven purifications of the reformation Bibles. God's Word was purified seven times, and that purification process must be accomplished before 1844, while Jesus still ministered in the first apartment.

That Word was defended by the blood of millions of martyrs.[75] For more than 200 years, from 1611 to 1844,[76] that purified Word, the King James Version of the Bible was without rival. Satan was not allowed to tamper with the table of showbread while Jesus was still there. Not until after the ministration of Jesus moved into the most

---

[71] E. G. White, Early Writings (1882), p. 54.2-56.1.

[72] E. G. White, *The Great Controversy* (1911), p. 483.2.

[73] Psalms 12:6

[74] See Martin Klein, *Above All Thy Name*, p. 138-140.

[75] All the weapons of men and demons have tried without success to annihilate the King James Bible and its predecessors. They survived only by the blood of martyrs and the mighty power of God. Modern bibles have not been defended at the cost of blood. People have not been killed for their allegiance to these modern preferences. Satan does not need to fight against them, for they accomplish his designs.

[76] The Sinaitic manuscript was first discovered in 1844.

holy place in 1844, did corrupted bible versions arrive on the scene. Satan appeared to be by the throne in the holy place, or table of showbread, trying to carry out the work of God, continually copying and counterfeiting the true bread of life—the word of God. Through this work of counterfeiting the preserved word of God, Satan has breathed upon the church an unholy influence; "in it there was light and much power, but no sweet love, joy, and peace. Satan's object was to keep them deceived and to draw back and deceive God's children."[77]

"Brethren, cling to your Bible, as it reads, and stop your criticisms in regard to its validity, and obey the Word, and not one of you will be lost. The ingenuity of men has been exercised for ages to measure the Word of God by their finite minds and limited comprehension. If the Lord, the Author of the living oracles, would throw back the curtain and reveal His wisdom and His glory before them, they would shrink into nothingness and exclaim as did Isaiah, 'I am a man of unclean lips, and I dwell in the midst of people of unclean lips' (Isaiah 6:5)."[78]

"I will worship toward thy holy temple, and praise thy name for thy lovingkindness and for thy truth: for ***Thou Hast Magnified Thy Word Above All Thy Name.***"[79]

---

[77] E. G. White, *Early Writings* (1882), p. 54.2-56.1.

[78] E. G. White, *Selected Messages,* Vol. 1 (1958), p. 18.1.

[79] Psalms 138:2

Appendix: Abbreviations

ASV - American Standard Version

BBE - Bible in Basic English

CEB - Contemporary English Bible

CEV - Contemporary English Version

CJB - Complete Jewish Bible

DRB - Douay Rheims Bible

ECB - ExeGeses Companion Bible

ERV - Easy to Read Version

ESV - English Standard Version

GNB - Good News Bible

GS - Goodspeed New Testament

GW - God's Word

ICB - International Children's Bible

ISV - International Standard Version

JPS - Jewish Publication Society

LEB - Lexham English Bible

LITV - Literal Translation of the Holy Bible

Moff - Moffat

MSG - The Message

MKJV - Modern King James Version

NAB - New American Bible

NASB - New American Standard Bible (Sometimes NASV - New American Standard Version)

NEB - New English Bible

NIV - New International Version

NKJV - New King James Version

NLT - New Living Translation

NRSV - New Revised Standard Version

NWT - New World Translation

REB - Revised English Bible

RSV - Revised Standard Version

RV - Revised Version

TCW - The Clear Word

TLB - The Living Bible

TNIV - Today's New International Version

WNT - Weymouth New Testament

YLT - Young's Literal Translation

Index

Glimpses of the Open Gates of Heaven

A verse by verse study of the books of Daniel and Revelation

The books of Daniel and Revelation have fascinated theologians, archeologists, historians, monarchs, peasants and children, for millennia. Filled with fascinating symbolic imagery, of beasts rising from seething waves; a bloodthirsty dragon chasing a fair maiden; apocalyptic plagues pouring over the planet; cryptic numbers and mysterious predictions; all calling for the curious and the concerned alike to heed the warnings they contain.

"The present is a time of overwhelming interest to all living. Rulers and statesmen, men who occupy positions of trust and authority, thinking men and women of all classes, have their attention fixed upon the events taking place about us. They are watching the relations that exist among the nations. They observe the intensity that is taking possession of every earthly element and they recognize that something great and decisive is about to take place—that the world is on the verge of a stupendous crisis."The calamities by land and sea, the unsettled state of society, the alarms of war, are portentous. They forecast approaching events of the greatest magnitude.... Great changes are soon to take place in our world, and the final movements will be rapid ones." In a most dramatic way, the future is laid open in these prophetic pages. These messages will prepare a people to stand in the great day of God.

Paperback: 777 pages
Publisher: Savannah Pictures
ISBN-13: 978-0997589733 ISBN-10: 0997589736
BISAC: Religion/Christian Theology/Eschatology

Download free pdf sample of this book:
https://savannahpictures.wistia.com/projects/i25r2uifkm

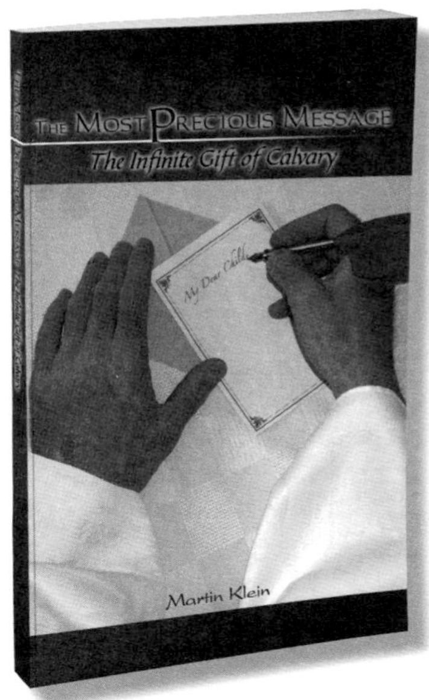

The Most Precious Message:
The Infinite Gift of Calvary

The most precious message ever given to mortals is the message that Jesus became our substitute, taking the penalty for our sins, that we might take his perfect righteousness and stand faultless in the judgement, appearing before the Father as if we had never sinned.
This is the message of righteousness by faith.

"'He was wounded for our transgressions, he was bruised for our iniquities: the chastisement of our peace was upon him; and with his stripes we are healed.' This penalty Christ bore for the sins of the transgressor; He has borne the punishment for every man and for this reason He can ransom every soul, however fallen his condition, if he will accept the law of God as his standard of righteousness."

"The same healing, life-giving message is now sounding. It points to the uplifted Saviour upon the shameful tree. Those who have been bitten by that old serpent, the devil, are bidden to look and live...
Look alone to Jesus as your righteousness and your sacrifice. As you are justified by faith, the deadly sting of the serpent will be healed."

"By pledging His own life Christ has made Himself responsible for every man and woman on the earth. He stands in the presence of God, saying, 'Father, I take upon Myself the guilt of that soul. It means death to him if he is left to bear it. If he repents he shall be forgiven. My blood shall cleanse him from all sin. I gave My life for the sins of the world.'"

"Jesus cares for each one as though there were not another individual on the face of the earth." "Come near... to Christ the Mighty Healer.... This wonderful manner of His love was evidenced at His crucifixion, and the light of His love is reflected in bright beams from the cross of Calvary. Now it remains for us to accept that love, to appropriate the promises of God to ourselves.
"Just repose in Jesus. Rest in Him as a tired child rests in the arms of its mother. The Lord pities you. He loves you. The Lord's arms are beneath you.... Wounded and bruised, just repose trust in God. A compassionate hand is stretched out to bind up your wounds. He will be more precious to your soul than the choicest friend, and all that can be desired is not comparable to Him. Only believe Him; only trust Him. Your friend in affliction—one who knows."

Paperback: 130 pages
Publisher: Savannah Pictures
ISBN: 978-0-9975897-4-0 (paperback)
BISAC: Religion/Christian Life/Inspirational